SOJOURN IN HELL

A GI's JOURNEY
FROM BOOT CAMP TO POW CAMP

BILLY CONDON WITH THOMAS KOEHL

Library of Congress Cataloguing-in-Publication Data:
Thomas F. Koehl 1948 –
Sojourn in Hell / Thomas F. Koehl

ISBN:979-8-9867737-0-4/Sojourn in Hell/Kindle Edition
ISBN:979-8-9867737-1-1/Sojourn in Hell/Paperback Edition

2022 Watermark Publishing, Melbourne, Florida

To Hazel, my beloved wife of fifty-six years,
who never gave up on an ex-POW.

-- BC

In loving memory of my mother and father,
and to Barbara.

--TFK

ABOUT THE COVER

Scottish artist Colin Duggett captures the moment when the C-47 Skytrain "Buzz Job Mike" from the 99th Troop Carrier Squadron is hit by German antiaircraft fire on September 23, 1944. The Waco CG-4A glider has been released well short of LZ "Oscar," the destined landing zone at Overasselt.

"Buzz Job Mike" crashed north of Boxtel, Holland, killing the copilot 2nd LT Cecil M. Babcanec and the crew chief T/SGT Orville B. Journey. Pilot CAPT Robert H. Kirry, navigator 1st LT George A. Bennett, and radio operator S/SGT Eldon R. Robbins successfully bailed out and were captured by German troops.

The CG-4A, flown by F/O Allen D. Story, carried heavy equipment for the 325th Glider Infantry Regiment. F/O Story landed the glider safely, but he was also captured and became a POW. All four POWs were repatriated at the end of the war.

The family of Orville B. Journey commissioned the painting. It's reproduced with the gracious permission of the family and the artist.

INRODUCTION

In 1991 I was an intelligence analyst at the Special Operations Command, MacDill AFB, during Operation Desert Storm. My uncle, Billy Condon, and his wife Hazel lived only an hour away, and after the collapse of the Iraqi army, I spent a weekend at their home. I knew Bill had been in the 82nd Airborne in WWII, but he had never spoken of it. After supper and coffee, I persuaded Bill to tell me more about his wartime experience. Hazel surprised me when she quickly excused herself and retrieved Bill's POW journal, a slim, delicate, and tattered little composition book. As I slowly read the terse daily entries I posed questions to add context. Hearing Bill's account was fascinating, and I urged him to write his memoirs. He protested, claiming to be a poor writer, so I proposed that we collaborate on the project. I never imagined it would begin a thirty-year odyssey.

In the years to come, we met frequently and gradually filled out the details of his WWII years. As the internet evolved, my research uncovered new information that Bill had long since forgotten and some that he had not known. Weaving these details into Bill's memoir took patience to create a complete, accurate, and cohesive narrative. I am proud to have authored this, but it's Bill's story. By the late 1990s, his health began to deteriorate, but he read and approved the manuscript's first draft before passing away in 2004.

To develop a complete account of Bill's WWII experience, I extensively researched the sites featured in his journal and post-war notes, the history of Operation

Market-Garden, and the ill-fated flight of his glider, number "13". As I studied other POW accounts, I discovered numerous incidents that confirmed the accuracy of Bill's narrative. Internet research led me to Dutch historians and the son of a German veteran who participated in Bill's capture. It seemed as though each new contact led to another.

I hope I have done justice to Bill's story. Any errors, historical or otherwise that may have crept into the narrative are mine alone.

Thomas Koehl

California Coast – Pacific Coast Highway

The Netherlands, Brabant

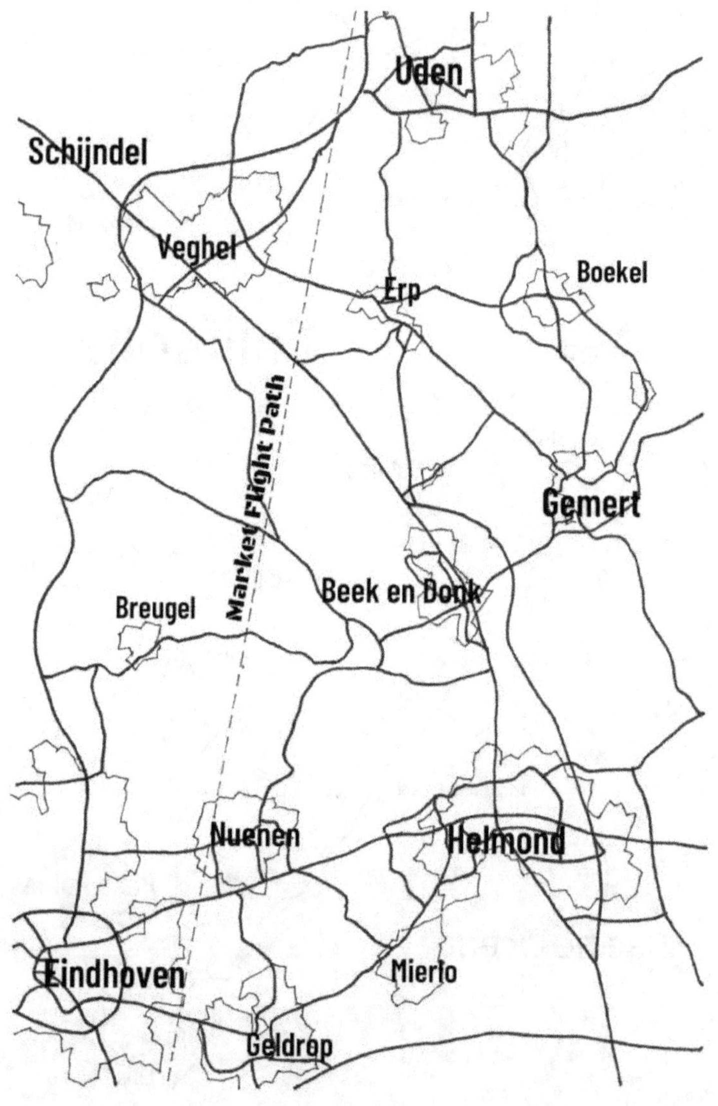

Glider 13 Landing Site

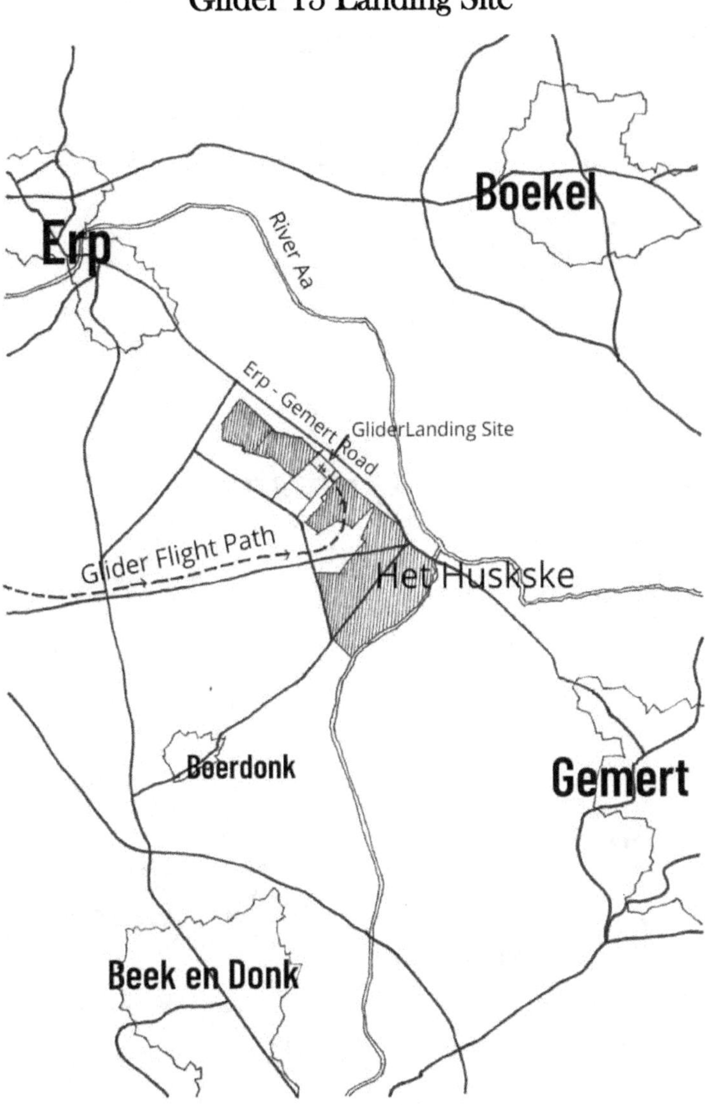

German POW Camps from SSGT Condon's Journal

LIST OF MAPS AND PHOTOGRAPHS

Maps

California Pacific Coast Highwayo

The Netherlands, Brabant

Glider 13 Landing Site, September 1944

German POW Camps from SSGT Condon's Journal

Photographs

Billy taking a break on the road delivering buses, 1940

Whitey, Billy Condon, and Smitty, Camp Livingston, LA, June 1940.

Billy staking out the first bivouac at Seligman, AZ, 1942.

Billy Condon with Harvey Girl at Seligman, AZ, bowling alley, February 1942.

Setting up the punching bag, 1943.

Getting ready for patrol, 1943.

Jack Szacon and Billy, June 1942.

Saturday morning parade at Stanford University stadium, 1943.

Billy with Rusty Sawyer on patrol, 1943.

Billy with CQ, Nello crouched in back of Billy, fiancé, and a few other buddies, Carmel, CA. 1943.

Billy Condon at home on leave from Camp Maxey, TX, March 1944.

Coffee and donuts before the first jump at RAF Ramsbury, 23rd TCS aircraft. June 1944.

C-47s and CG-4A gliders at RAF Folkingham, September 23, 1944.

American and British POWs being moved out of the Gemert monastery to waiting German trucks on the morning of September 24, 1944.

German registration photo of Billy Condon, POW Number 11071.

Billy Condon's slim and worn POW Journal.

Billy's portrait by Soviet POW.

Stalag VI-G, believed to be the Hoffmanstahl Hospital, October 1944.

War Department telegram to Billy's family reporting him MIA, 1944.

Billy Condon at home on leave, July 1945.

SOJOURN IN HELL

Chapter 1

Beginnings

When I was seventeen, I cheated death for the first time, but it wouldn't be the last.

Late in the spring of 1936, my sophomore year of high school, my best friend Jimmy Winters persuaded me to join him and two other school buddies, Gale Palmer and Eugene Robillard, to attend a dance at the Park Island amusement park on Lake Orion, west of Pontiac, Michigan. None of us had steady girlfriends, but we all felt the teenage desire to pair up with the fairer sex. Anxious but typically awkward when meeting girls, we joked about whether we could, just maybe, get lucky.

Gale, the only one of us with a driver's license, borrowed his family sedan, and we all piled in. Jimmy rode shotgun, Eugene sat behind Gale, and I sat behind Jimmy. It was a very dark night, and the roads from my home in Rochester to Lake Orion wound around the many lakes in the area. On one of the blind turns, an oncoming car crossed over the center line and struck us head-on. Gale tried to avoid the other vehicle by steering to the left, but it just placed the point of impact at the right front fender.

Police estimated the closing rate at more than a hundred miles an hour. Jimmy died instantly. Gale and Eugene, on the left side of the car, were banged up but not seriously injured. Sitting closer to the point of impact, I sustained a fractured skull that left me in a coma.

I carried no identification, and because Gale and Eugene were treated at the scene, it took some time for the hospital to learn my identity and contact my parents. By the time they arrived at the hospital, several hours had elapsed. When they finally arrived, the doctors told them that I was unlikely to recover and probably not survive the night. Either I was more resilient than the doctors gave me credit for, or the good Lord had other plans because I came out of the coma in just a couple of days. After a long recovery, I returned to school in time to start eleventh grade, but Jimmy was buried while I was in the coma. Losing him was a severe blow, and it changed my life forever.

My parents, Emmanuel and Antigone, came to America from Greece in the early twentieth century, during the tidal wave of immigration. They met in Chicago, fell in love, married, and promptly began a family. My two older brothers and I were born in Cicero, an ethnic melting pot west of Chicago. Andy was born in 1914, John in 1916, and I came along on September 16, 1919. My father's relentless pursuit of the American dream soon took us to Michigan, where we settled on a small vegetable farm in Rochester, and our family continued to grow. My sister Eleanor was born in 1921, and my younger brother, Steve, in 1930.

My father worked as a chef at several upscale restaurants in the area, but he knew we needed additional income. The vegetable farm provided some, along with fresh produce for our family, and we older boys helped with the farm chores. With the beginning of the Great Depression in 1929, we each found part-time work before beginning high school. When I turned fourteen, I followed Andy's lead and began working as a caddy at the Brookwood Golf and Country Club. My earnings were meager by today's standards—just sixty-five cents per round—but I could accumulate as much as five dollars a week, all of which I turned over to my mother, the family banker. She was frugal but gave us spending money when we needed it. Most importantly, I enjoyed golf, and caddying was infinitely better than bagging groceries.

By a stroke of luck, the caddy master chose me to caddy for the legendary golfer Walter Hagen during a club tournament at Brookwood. By then, Hagen, considered the father of professional golf and one of the best of all time, had retired from the professional tour but was still an active golfer. Walking the course with him, listening to his commentary, and watching him play was inspiring. I think any of us caddies would've carried his clubs for free.

Those who caddied during tournaments had greater prestige, so the weekend golfers often sought our advice on club selection, rules, and the lay of the course. Naturally, the novice caddies looked up to us. But the real perk for most of us was getting to play golf for free on Mondays. Neighbors who lived down the road from us had an old set of clubs they let me borrow, and the caddy master gave us free lessons and secondhand balls. I was pleased to discover that I had natural coordination and a smooth, consistent swing, and in just a few months, my handicap dropped into the single digits.

With no transportation and little money, I got to the golf club by hitching a ride on the Martin Bus Line. The bus stopped at an intersection just a quarter of a mile from our house. As it began to pull away from the curb, I dashed after it, leaped onto the rear bumper, and held on to the spare tire. Had my mother ever seen me do this, she would've had a heart attack, and I would have gotten the whipping of my life. But it worked out fine for me, and the bus was usually on schedule.

I was only an average student, but like many classmates, I regarded school as merely one of life's hoops to jump through. In those days, school athletic programs were not as dominant as today, and many kids like me held part-time jobs. Football, baseball, and basketball were the typical high school sports in the 1930s, just like they are now, but several things kept me from participating. First, I was only five-foot-seven and 145-pounds soaking wet, which made me a poor candidate for football or basketball despite my coordination and physical fitness. But more importantly, without transportation to and from school, it was difficult for me to participate in the sports programs and after-school practice was out of the question because I had to work.

In 1935, shortly after I turned sixteen, my buddy Jimmy Winters decided to take up boxing. When he told me I could get a ride to the gym with his family, I decided to take the sport up as well. The gym provided all the equipment, so it was a sport I could afford. And I could squeeze it into my work and school schedule. Golden Gloves boxing was well organized in the 1930s, and most towns had a club. We trained at the Pontiac YMCA, which had first-rate facilities. With a good meal under my belt, I just made the cutoff for the welterweight class at 147-

pounds and fought competitors of comparable size. We wore sixteen-ounce gloves and protective headgear to minimize injuries, and although our matches were limited to just three rounds, we gave it 100 percent and pounded each other mercilessly.

We trained for an entire season, then fought two or three matches to decide which boxers would go on to represent the club in the state finals. Jimmy and I both qualified, but Jimmy lost in the semi-finals, and I lost in the final round. Despite the loss, I was satisfied that I had given it my all. It was an experience that would serve me well in years to come. But the accident that killed Jimmy and nearly killed me came six months later and shattered my youthful expectations. It was the first time I had lost anyone close to me, and it hit me hard. After that, I became very depressed, and during my junior year of high school, my heart just wasn't in it. When my grades began to slip, I decided to quit at the end of the year.

I turned eighteen in September 1937 and took a job as a driver for Fleet Carrier Corporation, a contractor for General Motors that supplied dealerships in the Midwest with trucks and busses. I took newly assembled vehicles on a test run, then delivered them to dealerships as far east as upstate New York, west to Chicago, and south to Kentucky.

I loved the freedom of the open road and the responsibility that came with the job. To my surprise, I had some authority to deal with emergencies while on the road and had a small travel allowance that enabled me to eat modestly and return home by bus or train. It only took me one trip to realize that the money was mine to keep, no receipts required. I decided that I would be thrifty with what I spent on meals, hitchhike home and pocket the remaining money. I quickly accumulated a nice nest egg and was still able to contribute to the family budget.

Billy taking a break on the road delivering buses, 1940 (Author's Collection)

My parents had ingrained me with the habit of pinching pennies since childhood, but on a winter delivery to Buffalo, New York, I pushed it to the limit. Snow had started falling as soon as I crossed the border into Ohio, and by the time I delivered the truck to the dealer in Buffalo, the roads had drifted over and were nearly impassable. Most hotels and rooming houses had already filled up, and those with vacancies had upped their prices, hoping to make a windfall. I had a heavy jacket but no boots or gloves, so hiking through town looking for a room was out of the question. Plus, with hotels and rooming houses jacking up their rates for a windfall, the room rate for a single night would've exceeded my total travel allowance. With necessity being the mother of invention, or perhaps frugality leads to deviousness is more apt, I came up with a crazy scheme and headed for the nearest police station.

Shaking off the heavy snow, I walked into the bright light and warmth of the station house and approached the desk sergeant, a balding, bespectacled, middle-aged man perched behind a high oak-paneled desk.

"I'm stuck here until tomorrow," I told him. "Do you have an empty cell I could sleep in for the night?"

He looked over his wire-rimmed glasses and slowly examined me, taking in my worn but neat appearance as I stood in a puddle of melted snow. Then he leaned over his desk and glared at me. "You haven't committed a crime, have you, sonny?"

He sat back down when I shook my head, clearly dismissing me as a nuisance. "The cells are for criminals. This ain't a hotel, sonny. Unless you've broken the law, get outta here!"

As stubborn as he was about his precious regulations, I was equally determined to get my way, so I laid it out for him.

"If you won't give me a bunk to sleep on, or even a space on the floor, I'm going out that door to commit the first crime that comes to mind. Take your pick, but one way or another, I'm gonna sleep in here tonight!"

He must've thought I was nuts, but he could see I was not a derelict; I just looked desperate and broke. He probably decided that the paperwork to book me wasn't worth it, so he led me back to a jail cell, where I got a comfortable and warm night's sleep for free. When I awoke the following morning, I walked out of the cell, bid the new desk sergeant a good morning, and hitched a series of rides back to Pontiac with my travel allowance safe in my wallet.

In the aftermath of World War One and the Treaty of Versailles, the U.S. government rapidly scaled back the military. But when the Nazis marched into the Sudetenland and Czechoslovakia, and the Japanese overwhelmed Manchuria and much of Southeast Asia, President Franklin D. Roosevelt ordered the War Department to rebuild our military forces.

On September 16, 1940, my twenty-first birthday, President Roosevelt signed the Burke-Wadsworth Bill into law as the Selective Training and Service Act. It required all males born between October 17, 1904, and October 16, 1919, to register for the draft with their local board and, when ordered, to report for a physical examination. The Selective Service held the first lottery drawing in Washington D.C. on October 29, witnessed by 1,300 congressional representatives and officials. During the radio broadcast, the Secretary of War, Henry Stimson, stuck his hand in a giant glass bowl and drew the first number.

Of course, as luck would have it, having been born on September 16, 1919, I was eligible, as were my two older brothers. A few weeks later, John and I both received postcards in the mail ordering us to report to the Pontiac Courthouse for a physical exam. On the appointed day, we dutifully took the bus downtown, where a smartly uniformed sergeant met us, complete with Smoky-the-Bear campaign hat, jodhpur breeches, and leggings. After checking us off on his clipboard, he loaded us onto another bus with two dozen other candidates. After a bit more than an hour's ride, we arrived at the Detroit exam center, an abandoned mattress factory.

We joined a long line of several hundred young men, winding around two sides of the building, and when the doors opened, we surged into a large hall. I'm sure we all felt the same mixture of apprehension. Would we pass and shortly be inducted into the army for twelve months (the current term of enlistment), or would we fail and be sent home? We lined up in groups at the various stations designated alphabetically by our last names. Nurses and medics methodically checked us for height, weight, eyesight, blood pressure, hearing, and general physical condition.

When one of the fellows failed for flat feet, a heart murmur, bad teeth, curved spine, or other congenital conditions, we openly envied him his good fortune, taunting him with jibes: "Lucky stiff, get the hell out of here!" or, "Your feet are so flat you walk like a duck!" But at the same time, many of us wanted to pass. After all, being young, fit, and ready to serve the country was a source of pride. Who wanted to be a reject?

Two things happened at the exam that surprised me. First, although I had been nearly killed in the accident just over a year earlier, I was passed as medically fit for service, labeled 1-A. Ironically, Gale Palmer and Eugene Robillard, who had only sustained a few cuts and bruises in the wreck, were both classified as unfit, 4-F. As I recall, one had high blood pressure, and the other was color blind. It was a real awakening to the randomness of life.

Second, during the eye exam, after my first reading of the chart, I asked the doctor if I should put on my new eyeglasses that Martin Optical in Pontiac had recently prescribed for my occasional headaches and eye strain. The doctor scrutinized the eyeglasses, then looked at me as though I was trying to pull a fast one.

"What are you talking about, son?" he challenged me. "There's nothing wrong with your eyesight. These spectacles are nothing more than plain glass."

I was taken aback and tried to stammer a protest. The doctor just slid the glasses back into their case and handed them back to me. He thought I was trying to weasel out of the draft, and his look of disdain was humiliating. I was embarrassed and said nothing.

I met up with John shortly afterward, and we killed some time until the next scheduled bus departure, eating a quick lunch at the drugstore soda fountain down the block.

I went back to Martin Optical a few days later, demanding to know why they had prescribed glasses for me in the first place. To my surprise, without hesitation, the optician accepted the eyeglasses back with no excuse.

He showed no emotion as he said, "Well, I'm certainly not qualified to argue with a real doctor." I was stunned by his nonchalant admission that they had scammed me. When he handed over my refund, I snatched the money and stomped out of the shop. When I reflect on the experience, I never had headaches since, and my eyesight never gave me trouble until I was in my late 40s, when I finally needed reading glasses.

By the autumn of 1940, my golf game had improved to the point where my handicap dropped to zero. I loved golf, and my natural coordination gave me a smooth swing that I could control, and my putting was just as reliable. My skill got the attention of the Brookwood club professional, and apparently, he had spoken to some of the more affluent club members. One day, as I arrived at work, he approached me with a stunning offer.

"Billy, some club members asked me to speak to you. It's common knowledge among the caddies about how well you play, and of course, they talk to the members as they walk the course. Several of them are impressed and want to know if you would be interested in a sponsorship to turn pro."

I was nearly at a loss for words and replied, "Oh, my God. I never expected anything like that. I'm excited by the offer, but I can't just say yes, or no right now. It's a lot to consider. Would you please tell them that I appreciate the offer and that I'll give them an answer in the spring?"

He hesitated for a moment, then answered, "Sure, but don't wait too long. They may change their minds if they think you aren't motivated."

I was flattered by the offer and thought that making a career doing something I loved was exciting. As soon as I got home, I discussed it with my family. They were impressed and proud, but my parents quickly pointed out that a golf career was hardly enough to make ends meet—at least in those days—but perhaps it would be sufficient for a young single guy like me. With golf on hold for the winter, I kept toying with the idea, but the government had other plans.

Chapter 2

Luck of the Draw

My brother John and I each received our call-up from the draft board at the end of February 1941, ordering us to report for duty. I still recall the tidings beginning with the preamble, "Greetings from the President of the United States," and then continuing to inform me that my country required my services in uniform. At that time, neither of us was paying much attention to the world situation, let alone being concerned about the war raging in Europe. There was a significant and vocal national movement throughout the country opposed to America joining another European conflict, and neither of us was concerned because the term of enlistment was only one year, with a further ten years in a reserve status. We would be back to our old lives in twelve months. How bad could that be?

On March 7, 1941, John and I again reported to the Pontiac Courthouse as ordered, each carrying just a small gym bag with enough clothing for three days. As before, there was a seasoned army sergeant in a crisp olive drab uniform to muster the score of new draftees. After methodically checking us off on his clipboard, successfully mangling the pronunciation of several names, he ordered us to take our seats on a Greyhound bus for the two hour trip to Detroit.

I was surprised to see dozens of buses converging on the massive Central Michigan railroad station. It was the biggest train station I'd ever seen, a gigantic neo-classical structure with a cavernous hall, marble columns, decorative inlaid floors, rows of carved wood benches, and a scattering of kiosks selling newspapers, tobacco, magazines, and refreshments. I had never been in such a vast building before, and I was in awe as I craned my neck, gazing up at the glass-paned skylight more than sixty feet above me. It was breathtaking, and the constant flow of people made for a fascinating cavalcade of characters.

I amused myself for a while just people-watching, wondering why they were traveling and where they may be going. My imagination created plausible scenarios just from the appearance of people: men in suits traveling for business; women with children likely traveling to visit friends or relatives; and men in rough clothing perhaps traveling to find work. As we waited for directions from the army officers, we crowded onto the wooden benches and overflowed onto the great hall floor. Some lounged against the columns, while others just tried to get comfortable on the floor. Many were shy and sat quietly, but others were a bit more gregarious, like John and me. We soon made introductions, started conversations, smoked, and speculated about what lay in store for us. In response to our questions, one of the sergeants told us that we were bound for Camp Grant, near Chicago, which he explained was the main induction center for the Midwest region and added that we would arrive early the following day.

John had mentioned to some of the other fellows that I had been a truck driver and had regularly made the journey to Chicago. As a result, I was peppered with questions about the city. I couldn't tell them much because I had never stayed long enough to learn my way around or to sightsee. Besides, we were pretty sure we wouldn't be near the downtown area. Few of us had heard of Camp Grant, and the sergeants were indifferent to our anxious questions and ignored us.

By mid-afternoon, the NCOs began to call us out by name and formed us up into groups for boarding the train. We were escorted onto the platform and assigned to coaches for the trip. A couple of officers and a half-dozen NCOs kept a close watch on us, perhaps fearing one of us might try to slip away. John and I found a seat together and settled in for the ride. I stared out the window in fascination as the train chugged its way through Detroit and westwards across southern Michigan, northwest Indiana, and on into Illinois. We passed through rolling farmland, forests, and the dunes that skirted the south shore of Lake Michigan, then turned northwest around Chicago.

Poker games had started in several coaches, and a few flasks of whiskey made the rounds, but most of us just made small talk and stared out the windows, watching the miles roll past, lost in our thoughts about the future. What would Army life be like? Would I adjust well or be a miserable misfit? How and why had I come to be here? There were no answers. The train rolled on through the night, and I tried to make myself comfortable. I rolled my jacket up as a pillow and tried to sleep, the monotonous clicking of the rails lulling me, but each time we stopped to pick up additional draftees, I was jolted awake, and sleep became fitful. Finally, we arrived at the Camp Grant rail terminal in the early morning hours, just south of Rockville, Illinois.

As a primary induction center, the sheer size of Camp Grant was hard to take in. Situated south of the town on the Rock River, it had been established in the late 1800s. It had grown by leaps and bounds during the First World War to accommodate the rapid influx of recruits, eventually covering over 3,200 acres. By 1941 the camp had a dedicated train depot and freight yard to handle the volume of men and material that arrived daily, as well as an airfield for Army Air Corps training. Specialist schools were scattered around the post, including a school for medical orderlies that turned out combat medics as quickly as possible.

Acres of identical, two-story, white wooden barracks formed perfect columns and rows, each sporting short wooden awnings over the doors and windows to protect them from the elements while still allowing fresh air to circulate. The buildings were elevated about eighteen inches on pilings, with wooden steps leading up to small decks and doorways at each end. The barracks were designated by company "streets," a layout we all quickly became familiar with, interspersed with supply warehouses, classroom buildings, and the headquarters of the numerous training battalions, companies, and schools.

Each barracks accommodated a platoon of about forty-eight men on each floor. Rows of cots, with olive drab footlockers at the foot, flanked the central aisle while stairs, lavatories, and storerooms were located at each end. The

Guard Room was located on the ground floor at the front of the building, from which the duty non-commissioned officer, or NCO, monitored the comings and goings of the platoons, pouncing upon any poor soul who committed a transgression of army regulations, real or imagined.

The drill sergeants wasted no time giving us a rude introduction to army life. They treated us like the lowest form of existence with shouted orders, colorful profanities, and pushing and shoving us into position. Frequent push-ups were demanded of anyone who seemed too stupid to follow orders. We were prodded and marched through a succession of evolutions to get us looking and almost acting like GIs. We were all promptly given a regulation buzz-cut haircut and a new identity: I became serial number 36-104-401.

Our first issue of uniforms was just sufficient to get each new inductee to his divisional training center, where our new regiment would issue the balance of the equipment and uniforms. My first allotment consisted of one set of olive drab Class A wools (the dress uniform), one set of khakis, a pair of shoes with leggings, both wool and khaki hat, three sets of skivvies and socks, a web belt with brass buckle, brass collar insignia, brass polish, toothbrush, shaving gear, and of course a heavy duffle, or "barracks bag," in which to carry everything.

We lined up outside the supply warehouse, then paraded into the gloomy interior in single-file and squared-off, one at a time, in front of wooden counters manned by totally bored and ill-tempered quartermasters, or QMs. The first QM quickly ordered me to raise my arms, whipped a tape measure around my waist (thirty inches) and chest (thirty-six inches), and asked me my shoe size. His partner at the counter jotted the numbers down on a slip of paper and handed it to me to hold. Each QM distributed a specific article: shirts, trousers, jackets, boots, and other items as if they were perfectly confident of judging our sizes. It was a very efficient, albeit inexact, process, and as I moved down the line from one station to another, QMs pulled each required item from the shelves and piled it up on my outstretched arms. I thought they treated us as though we were just so many stupid cattle being processed for slaughter.

There was no opportunity to try on any item for size. Some things were incorrectly labeled, stacked on the wrong shelves, or grabbed randomly. By the time I reached the exit door, I was carrying a tall stack of new belongings that blocked my view and threatened to trip me as I went down the stairs. Outside again, still blinking in the glare, a drill sergeant barked at me to quickly stuff all this new paraphernalia into the issue duffle bag, form up with the others, and prepare to march back to our barracks.

We unloaded at our footlockers and promptly began checking out our new "skins." Thanks to the calculating eye of the QMs, and a military procurement system that produced all uniforms in standard sizes, the fit was seldom good. Immediately after trying on the clothing, we began swapping trousers, "blouses" (the army term for jackets), and shirts to assemble a complete kit that would suffice for the time being. It would not be until we arrived at our assigned regiments that uniforms could be altered or exchanged for a proper fit.

Over the next three days, I underwent processing which entailed taking aptitude tests, answering questionnaires, and filling out countless forms for personal history, unique skills, work experience, educational background, next of kin, etcetera. A much more thorough medical exam followed this. The few men who failed this one were reclassified 4F and sent home. Finally, we took our oath of allegiance as a group.

Meanwhile, clerks worked at the tedious process of cutting orders to assign us to the different army regiments and divisions. Camp Grant served as both an induction center and a basic training site, but in those pre-war days, with each division expanding at a brisk pace, a centralized training scheme to cope with the high volume of draftees and volunteers was still evolving. I was unaware of any opportunity to request a particular regiment or skill training, and none was offered. The instructors explained that our new regiments would conduct our basic and advanced training.

The four days I spent at Camp Grant were a whirlwind, from the haircut and uniform issue to the essentials of military drill: falling-in and falling-out of formation; learning the correct positions of attention, parade rest, at-ease, right face, left face, about face; miles of marching in formation; and lectures on personal hygiene, how to properly pack our footlocker, and how to maintain our uniforms.

In the early evening, we cleaned our barracks, "policed" the parade grounds (i.e., picked up debris and rubbish), and took KP duty (kitchen police). We learned the all-important skill of "field stripping" a cigarette butt: picking it apart into tiny pieces to prevent littering. All of this was to the shouted orders and curses of our drill sergeants. It's hard to imagine how the army packed so much into those few days. It was bewilderingly efficient, and the adage, "If it moves, salute it, and if it doesn't, paint it olive drab," was hardly a joke.

Our work history, family background, age, and aptitude testing all determined which inductees were eligible for Officer Training. I couldn't have cared less about being an officer. I expected to do my one-year stint on active duty and then return to driving for Fleet Carrier. But to my surprise, my older brother John, who had finished high school and had worked for a few years, accepted the offer of Officer Candidate School and was promptly shipped off for specialized schooling. After commissioning, he went to the West Coast for advanced training and became a Second Lieutenant in the 1st Cavalry Division. He saw action in the Pacific in the Admiralty Islands, the Leyte-Samar campaign, and the liberation of Manila. His unit would have participated in the invasion of the Japanese home islands, but by the grace of God and the atomic bomb, he survived the war.

On March 11, 1941, perhaps a hundred of us were once more loaded onto a train and shipped to Camp Livingston, Louisiana, the home of the 32nd "Red Arrow" Infantry Division. All we knew about the 32nd was that it was composed of national guardsmen from Michigan and Wisconsin.

This train ride wasn't much different from the ride to Camp Grant, except that now we were in uniform and were beginning to feel like soldiers. We spent interminable hours staring out the window at the passing landscape, chatting, napping, and playing the occasional poker and dice games. The noticeable warming as we sped south promised us better conditions than the whipping cold winds of Rockford, Illinois, in March.

Chapter 3

Camp Livingston, Louisiana

Established in 1940, in months, Camp Livingston had blossomed from a small base into a large tent city as the division's ranks swelled with new recruits and draftees. Besides the main headquarters building and a few other permanent structures, it consisted of acres of pyramid tents in neat rows. Each was about twelve feet square, pitched on top of concrete pads with rough wooden siding up to about three feet. Bug screens extended from the top of the siding to the underside of the tent awning. Anyone who has watched the "M*A*S*H" television show and remembers Trapper John and Hawkeye's "Swamp" will be familiar with these tents. The tents had extended roll-down sides for protection from the rain that reached down to the ground, but when lowered, they cut off all air circulation, and the tents became unbearably hot.

As the spring weather warmed and Louisiana's intense heat and humidity set in, we rarely unrolled the sides except for torrential rain. Lighting in the tents amounted to a single unshielded bulb, but even gloomy daylight was preferable to the added heat of the bulb, not to mention the thousands of insects that swarmed to it in the dark. We dispensed with the light almost entirely as the spring days grew longer.

The first few months at Camp Livingston comprised four weeks of basic infantry training. Afterward, we moved on to more specialized training with specific weapons and equipment, tactics, map reading, fortifications, and operating as a squad.

Our drill sergeants were generally a bit older than us, mostly in their mid-twenties, although a few may have even been an ancient thirty. Most had been Michigan or Wisconsin national guard NCOs who became regular army when the regiment was federalized on October 15, 1940. It seemed as though most of them were Poles from Hamtramck, Michigan, the sprawling ethnic Polish neighborhood near downtown Detroit.

Because all the regiments in the division were still under strength, with most companies mustering less than a hundred men out of a nominal allotment of nearly 200, the drill sergeants were kept busy, each with thirty or forty men under their tutelage. They continually trained batches of new men as they trickled in from the induction centers. By the time summer arrived, my "class" were considered full-fledged infantrymen. We were assigned to the various companies, lettered A through L, four companies to each of the regiment's three battalions.

As a newly minted army private, I joined B Company, or Baker Company, to use the army phonetic alphabet, of the First Battalion, 125th Infantry Regiment. Four men were assigned to each tent, and my first tent mates were Otto R. Smith, who quickly became "Smitty," Nello

Whitey, Billy Condon, and Smitty, Camp Livingston, LA, June 1940 (Author's Collection)

Ratliff, who went by "Whitey", and Albert "Al" Slivatz. Smitty and I bunked on the same side of the tent, and because the Army wanted everyone to pair off with a "battle buddy," we quickly became good friends. At night, listening to the buzzing of the mosquitos, we would talk for hours in the darkness, rehashing the day, relating childhood experiences, and critiquing the competence, or in some cases the ineptitude, of the NCOs and officers. Of course, some army regs' apparent stupidity and pointlessness were high on our gripe list.

After we completed our month of basic training, the four of us earned passes to allow us to explore the nearby town of Alexandria, about a dozen miles southwest of Camp Livingston. The post maintained a regular bus service to and from town, which ran hourly until about 2200 hours (10:00 P.M. for civilians). We were anxious to get the next bus, so Smitty borrowed a clean pair of my khaki trousers to save time, and twenty minutes later, we disembarked in the center of town and began to explore. I suppose Alexandria was typical of small towns that flourished near military bases, with small shops, a couple of movie theaters, bars, drug stores, and several restaurants, all within a three or four-block area. We bought some items we thought we would need, including some snacks, which the army refers to as "pogey bait." After grabbing burgers and a Coke for an early dinner, we sampled a few of the local bars. It was a relief to blow off some steam, and we got thoroughly pie-eyed.

The four of us staggered back to catch the final bus of the day. It was full of GIs, and Smitty and I took the only bench seat available, all the way in the back. The rear seats gave the roughest ride, and we hadn't even cleared the town limits before Smitty got sick and puked all over himself, then on me. It was disgusting! He had destroyed my best two pairs of trousers in seconds. After a few expletives to vent my anger, I congratulated him on his aim. "Nice going, buddy! You've trashed both my khakis at once! Thanks a lot."

By the time we walked back to our tent, we were sober enough to make a half-hearted attempt to clean the trousers, then collapsed on our cots. By morning I had cooled off, but all four of us suffered horrible hangovers. We worked together to get our uniforms moderately presentable, but the Sunday routine did not include a formation, so we escaped inspection. We attended the church service, where I sat perfectly still to keep my head from falling off and refrained from singing. I remembered my father's caution about drinking and gambling and vowed not to make a habit of getting plastered, though poker might be a different story. We were free to do whatever we wanted for the remainder of the day, so I stayed on my cot until late afternoon.

Training at Camp Livingston dragged on into summer, with morning inspections followed by close order marching and rifle drill. The daily physical activity included bayonet drill, hand-to-hand combat, crawling under knee-high wire obstacles with live gunfire whizzing overhead, calisthenics, the obstacle course, and occasionally, the exhausting twenty-five-mile route marches. Due to the Louisiana heat, afternoons usually consisted of classroom lectures or weapons training with live firing on the hand grenade, rifle, and pistol ranges. The sergeants spiced the schedule with random tent inspections, kitchen police (KP) duty, and trash pickup. Today, when I see all this on paper, it sounds awful, but much to my surprise, I began to enjoy army life. The orderly routine suited me, and there was comfort in knowing what to expect from day to day. Within a month, it all became nearly automatic. I was already physically fit and skilled with a rifle, so much of it came naturally to me and I felt like I belonged.

As a teenager, I hunted ducks, geese, and pheasants back home with a sixteen-gauge shotgun and the occasional rabbit, squirrel, and deer with a .22 caliber Remington or .30-30 Winchester rifle. With my firearms experience, I had no difficulty qualifying as an expert with each of the infantry weapons, including the Springfield M1903 bolt-action rifle and the semi-automatic Colt M1911 .45 caliber pistol, as well as the bayonet, hand grenade, and Browning Automatic Rifle, referred to as the BAR. The BAR was developed during World War I as a squad automatic weapon for clearing enemy trenches. It had a selective firing rate, either single shot or fully automatic, and chambered the same .30-06 round as the Springfield rifle. The drawback was that it weighed more than twenty pounds, a heavy weapon to carry into combat. I felt sorry for the poor guys assigned to it, but I felt better knowing we had one in my squad.

The venerable WWI-era Springfield M1903 rifle was an excellent weapon, combat-proven and accurate. It was a derivative of the German Mauser bolt-action rifle but fired a heavier .30-06 cartridge at a blistering 1,200 feet-per-second. Versions fitted with a slightly modified bolt and a Weaver 2.5 power scope were deadly long-range weapons in the hands of a trained sniper.

The M-1 Garand rifle, which fired the same .30-06 cartridge, had just been accepted as the new infantry rifle. With an eight-round clip and a semi-automatic gas-operated action, it had a much higher rate of fire, a significant improvement over the Springfield rifle. The Garand was being mass-produced and would soon be issued as the primary infantry rifle, but for now, we would carry the Springfield.

The flamethrower scared the living daylights out of me. It had a pistol grip and trigger, with a fore grip just behind the nozzle and gas tanks mounted on a backpack. The operator could lay down a blast of liquid incandescence and roll it into the target, incinerating anything in its path. I pitied anyone on the receiving end and prayed I would never have to carry one into combat. One bullet into the tanks and the carrier would be instantly incinerated.

Another weapon I quickly learned to hate was the grenade launcher attachment for the M-1 Garand. It used a blank cartridge to propel a special grenade that fitted onto the muzzle. It kicked like a mule, and the first time I fired one, the recoil knocked me ass-over-teakettle, and my shoulder was bruised for a week. I concluded that the best way to fire it was to put the butt of the rifle up against a tree trunk, wall, or the sole of my boot. To hell with trying to sight it onto a target.

After basic training, our instructor for advanced weapons training was Sergeant Frank Sieracki. Even though we hated most sergeants, he was a big ox of a guy, gruff but big-hearted. Although he worked us mercilessly, he never tolerated taunts or criticism from outsiders: we were his grunts, and he protected us like a mother hen. It created a real love-hate relationship, but we couldn't help but like him. Sieracki was not the most coordinated or intelligent soldier I had ever met, and one day on the grenade range, the sergeant and I were together in the throwing pit that gave us protection from shrapnel. Sieracki pulled the pin on a grenade to demonstrate the proper technique and promptly dropped it. The spring-loaded handle popped off, igniting the fuse and giving us seconds before it would explode. He reacted quickly, scooped up the grenade, screamed, "Hit the dirt!", pitched it away, and shoved me down into the pit just before it detonated just yards in front of the wall. It scared the hell out of me, but it was a good lesson. The Mark 2 "pineapple" grenade had about a four-and-a-half-second fuse. Trying to outrun it would be futile. The only option was to throw it as far as possible and drop to the ground.

On another occasion, when Sieracki was patiently teaching us squad tactics, Whitey struggled to visualize using hand signals under different circumstances. He asked Sieracki how signals were given at night when even the light of a full moon was often insufficient to make them discernible. Not to be at a loss for an answer, Sieracki replied, "It's simple. You just use your bayonet to signal with long and short taps on your rifle's receiver."

It took only a moment before Smitty, a quick wit, asked the obvious question. "Sarge, what's the difference between a short and a long tap?" Sieracki stared at him for a moment, then turned red, muttered something about "smart asses," and moved on to the next subject. We all nearly choked, trying not to laugh out loud.

Shortly after I finished basic training, the 32nd Infantry Division participated in the biggest war games ever held up to that time, the V Corps Maneuvers, which ran from June 16 to 27, 1941. The operation focused on squad tactics, map reading, scouting and reconnaissance, and the preparation of defensive positions. We lived in field conditions in rain and mud, cramped in two-man foxholes, and tried to avoid the occasional snake, scorpion, and spider of every size and description. As I crawled through the brush on the second day, I was stung in the leg by a scorpion. Within an hour, my calf swelled up like a balloon and became painful to the touch. Sieracki promptly sent me to a field hospital for treatment, but I developed a high fever and spent several days there. The fever was temporary, and I ate meals prepared in the field kitchen when I began to feel better. Unlike the boxed K-rations or canned C-rations, which were high-calorie but not very appealing, the field kitchen turned out rather tasty beef stews, fried chicken, fresh eggs, and steaming hot coffee. I almost felt sorry for my buddies in the field who subsisted on the field rations.

When the entire division returned to the post, we resumed the monotonous routine of drills, route marches, more specialized training, guard duty, and the occasional off-post pass. Like most of my contemporaries, I spent little time worrying about the future. It was when we had an opportunity to get to a movie theater that we saw newsreels of the fighting in China, Europe, and North Africa. By late summer, our nighttime bull sessions began to center on discussions about American neutrality. At times war seemed to be creeping closer.

On September 15, our routine was again interrupted by the Louisiana Maneuvers. This exercise was more complex, lasting two weeks, involving nineteen divisions and over a half-million troops divided into two armies, Blue versus Red, pitted against each other in a fictitious struggle for control of the lower Mississippi River. The war game would cover more than 3,400 square miles of rolling, wooded terrain in central Louisiana and east Texas. The Blue army role was assigned to the Third Army, commanded by Lieutenant General Walter Kreuger, and the Second Army, commanded by Lieutenant General Ben Lear, became the Red army.

During our briefing, we learned the objective was to test the effectiveness of fixed defensive positions against mobile armor and airborne attack. The army had not forgotten the painful and wasteful experience of trench warfare in World War One and post-war innovations in armor, artillery, and aircraft, as well as radio communication, had never been fully integrated with the infantry. The blitzkrieg tactics that the German army demonstrated in Poland, the Low Countries, and France highlighted the need for the US Army to implement such tactics immediately.

All branches of the army, infantry, artillery, armor, and air corps, were to be intensely exercised for the first time to develop tactics for future combined operations. Each side would take a turn defending, allowing ample opportunity to experiment with combined arms tactics and evaluate the officers' and NCOs' leadership ability and proficiency. The Army Chief of Staff, General George C. Marshall, anticipated our eventual involvement in the war raging in Europe and North Africa and set the tone for the event. He famously declared, "I want mistakes made down in Louisiana, not over in Europe. If it doesn't work, find out what we need to make it work."

Our most significant handicap was a shortage of proper equipment. The country's industrial base had not yet mobilized for war, and new weapons and vehicles were still trickling into the supply lines. Some reserve and national guard troops used wooden rifles, and tanks were in such short supply that trucks were stand-ins for tanks, with stovepipes mounted on sawhorses and the word "TANK" painted on the side in big white letters. Many of the tanks still lacked their main gun armament and the gun mantle opening was covered in canvas.

A hurricane swept up through Louisiana just a week before the maneuvers began, swelling the rivers, lakes, and ponds with rain, and the mud made all off-road movement a challenge. I was lucky this time and was assigned to the Third Army staff. While my buddies wallowed in the mud, slept in foxholes, and fought their way through swamps and forests, I spent most of the time riding in a command car and carried a staff flag for the Chief of Staff, a colonel named Dwight D. Eisenhower. As a full "bird" colonel, he was next to God as far as I was concerned. At first, I was in awe, not knowing my role. The driver, a newly promoted corporal, and I had little direct interaction with the colonel other than exchanging formal courtesies and taking his directions. Still, he was pleasant, good-humored, and treated us with respect. My task was pretty simple: anytime he left the vehicle, I was to follow him and plant his staff flag wherever he paused so subordinates could quickly find him.

When not maneuvering, the staff officers spent their nights' lodging with local families while we resorted to tent living. It was an exciting experience to see some of the officers who would become famous in the next few years, such as George Patton, a Brigadier General at the time. Patton was a cavalry officer and embraced the potential of armored warfare early in his career. During the Louisiana Maneuvers, he demonstrated his tactical skill by driving his armor column in rapid flanking movements that proved decisive in each war game phase. On the occasions I was near him, I noted that he was wearing high cavalry boots and holding a riding crop that he vigorously used as a pointer.

Most mornings, Colonel Eisenhower made a point to ensure that the driver and I got fresh hot coffee and a few minutes to sample the pastries that the local women made. I would have thought that the locals would be hostile to having the army swarming all over the countryside and clogging up the roads. But that was not the case. Most locals were excited to see the activity and enjoyed the temporary economic boom. Both the driver and I were pleasantly surprised. All the fuss over the staff, and us by association, made us feel we were essential cogs in a big wheel.

I shadowed Ike closely but at a respectful distance. I was often close enough to listen as he conferred with subordinate unit commanders and the exercise staff. I had no prior experience with officers above the rank of captain, and his demeanor struck me. He was generally quiet-spoken, considerate, and easy to work for. Still, he was focused and had high expectations for his staff and the conduct of the exercise itself. On more than one occasion, I overheard him critiquing subordinate officers who either failed to exercise initiative or leadership. After more than two decades of peace, it was evident that many officers, especially in the reserves and national guard, had achieved promotion due to time in grade and who they knew, not for their professionalism. I guessed that some of the inepter officers would be sacked or retired based upon body language and bits I overheard. But it impressed me that Eisenhower hardly ever raised his voice and always tried to keep the ass-chewings private. It was a lesson in leadership that I never forgot.

Our life off-post at Camp Livingston consisted of frequenting the bars and movie theaters in Alexandria or, if we wanted to slum it, we could head to nearby Pineville, a hamlet on the river's eastern bank.

One Friday evening in late November, several of us, including Sergeant Joseph "Jack" Szacon, one of Baker Company's platoon sergeants, spent our hard-earned cash in a Pineville honkey-tonk. It was a dump of a bar appropriately named the Tin Shack. Knocked together out of corrugated tin nailed to a scrap lumber frame, it featured a bandstand, a makeshift bar at the rear, about a dozen beat-up tables and chairs, and a smelly, unsanitary toilet in an attached shed. It was totally and unapologetically low-life, with a dirt floor perpetually covered with discarded peanut shells. At least it soaked up the spilled booze and tobacco juice.

A local band had played a set, and when they took a break, Jack, a good piano player who taught music before joining the army, sat down and played a ragtime tune for fun. Within minutes, an attractive woman approached Jack and started purring up to him. None of us was surprised since Jack was a bit of a ladies' man, a tall, broad-shouldered, good-looking Polish boy with unruly blond hair, blue eyes, and big biceps.

None of us had seen the woman before, so we didn't pay any particular attention to her. It turned out that she was the girlfriend of one of the musicians and he was the jealous type. Maybe she was just trying to tease or annoy her boyfriend. If so, it worked. He flew into a rage, dashed over to the piano, and took a swing at Szacon. The unexpected roundhouse punch caught Jack on the ear, tumbling him off the piano bench, and sprawling on the ground and scattering peanut shells.

Jack sprang to his feet like a cat and promptly landed a solid right to the musician's jaw that dropped him to the ground. The rest of the band instantly came to their buddy's defense, and a free-for-all erupted with fists flying, chairs breaking, beer spilling, and blood splattering from noses and split lips. It was a Hollywood western bar fight, except the punches, curses, and blood was real. As the musicians ganged up on Szacon, the recovered boyfriend pulled a knife and stuck it in Jack's ribs. I don't think that Jack even realized he had been stabbed. He went into a rage, swatted the boyfriend away like a fly, then grabbed the keyboard with both hands and dumped the upright piano over onto two of the musicians.

We all jumped to Jack's defense. I nailed the trumpet player in the cheek and he went down for the count, while Whitey kicked the living daylights out of the drummer, trying to crawl out from under the piano. The bartender started screaming, "Stop!" at the top of his voice and hollered for the MPs. Smitty shouted that it was time to leave and I grabbed Szacon by the collar, dragging him out of the fray. We followed our buddies out the shit-house window just as the MPs came in through the front door.

We beat the MPs back to the bus, boarded quickly to get out of sight, and Al stripped off his t-shirt to make a crude bandage for Jack. We huddled around him to hide his blood-stained uniform and tried our best to act as if nothing had happened. No one made a sound as the bus paused briefly at the front gate, but in the glare of the overhead floodlights, we could see that Jack was white as a sheet and had lost a good bit of blood. We disembarked in the dark, and one of the guys took Szacon to find the company medical corpsman. The rest of us quickly scattered to our tents to catch a couple of hours of sleep before reveille and morning assembly.

At morning formation, Szacon was upright but ashen-faced and obviously hurting badly. Just before dismissal, the company brass showed up with the owner of the Tin Shack. He was pissed off and blamed the army for all the damage to his fine establishment, which was an absurd exaggeration. He probably knew he couldn't get any money out of the musicians that started the fight, so he shouted at our company commander, Captain Kruczyk, about the "hundreds of dollars of damage" and who would pay for it. He claimed the soldier who started the fight had a knife wound in his side.

Captain Kruczyk ordered the entire company to pull up our shirts and T-shirts to expose our waists. As Lieutenant Audie inspected ranks, there was Sergeant Szacon with a big field dressing applied to his right side. The knife missed anything important, but the damage was apparent. Jack protested that he was attacked without provocation and was just defending himself. The captain questioned several of us about the brawl, but our testimony didn't help. Jack got company punishment: a forfeiture of pay for one month, lost his sergeant's stripes and was busted back to private. It was hardly fair, but what could he do? He eventually got his stripes back, first to corporal in April and then to sergeant by September. After the incident, we became good friends and occasionally went to town together. He was a good guy and a fine soldier.

At the end of November, Captain Kruczyk handed Baker Company over to Captain Samuel Blocker, and First Sergeant Floyd Radike took over as top NCO, but nothing much changed for us until the afternoon of

Sunday, December 7. Smitty and I went to a motion picture show in Alexandria. I think it was "The Corsican Brothers," a swashbuckler starring Douglas Fairbanks Jr. Suddenly, the show stopped in the middle of the film, and the lights went up. The theater manager walked down to the front of the auditorium and announced that all military personnel should immediately report to the post.

When we emerged from the theater, puzzled by what might be going on, we were grabbed and hugged by a couple of sobbing, semi-hysterical girls who told us that the Japanese had bombed and destroyed the Pacific fleet at Pearl Harbor, Hawaii. Between sobs, the girls repeated what they had heard on the radio: that the Japanese had launched a sneak attack and thousands of sailors had died. The news reported that President Roosevelt would immediately ask Congress for a declaration of war against Japan. We were incredulous. The girls must have misunderstood, or at least exaggerated. It was all we could talk about on the bus ride back to the post.

We soon learned the full extent of the disaster in Hawaii, and the camp was locked down. Everyone started guessing what would happen next. Most of us expected that we would be shipped to the Pacific, but one thing was sure: we were now in the army for the duration of the war.

The 32nd Division was federalized on October 15, 1940, as part of the pre-war military expansion. At that time, it was still a "square" division, meaning it had four "maneuver" regiments of infantry - the 125th, 126th, 127th, and 128th Infantry Regiments, as well as a heavy weapons brigade that consisted of three field artillery regiments and supporting medical and supply units. The day after the Pearl Harbor attack, on December 8, all infantry divisions were restructured into "triangle" divisions of just three maneuver regiments, augmented by the same supporting units. Most of the detached regiments would become the origin units of new divisions.

The essential infantry element was still a squad of twelve men: ten riflemen, a Browning Automatic (BAR) rifleman, and a sniper. Three such squads, plus a single weapons squad (armed with machine guns, mortars, and bazookas), comprised a platoon. Three platoons made a company, three companies formed a battalion, and three battalions became a regiment.

After totaling the company and battalion headquarters personnel, the strength of an infantry battalion was now 870 men of all ranks, and a division numbered about 9,400 men. Looking at the numbers, I was amazed to realize that only a little more than a quarter of the men were riflemen, another quarter were artillerymen, and the remainder were staff and support personnel. Throughout the war, a division would double in size as the army added more supporting units.

The army ordered the 125th to detach from the 32nd Division, and regimental headquarters ordered us to prepare to ship out. Of course, no one bothered to tell us GIs where we were going. On December 11, the day Germany declared war on America, we packed our duffle bags, assembled on the parade ground, and marched to the Camp Livingston railroad station. Speculation about our ultimate destination went wild: the Philippines, Hawaii, Australia, and England were all possibilities. No one seemed to know the real story; if they did, they didn't bother to pass the word down the line.

Chapter 4

Go West, Young Man

We boarded the train and began rolling out of Louisiana and across North Texas. The scenery became increasingly arid, and the land began to rise into foothills. It was apparent we were headed for the West Coast, and we thought the most likely destination would be a troop ship to the Philippines. Every day, with each new stop, more war news poured in as American forces in the Philippines came under heavy air and naval attack by the forces of the Japanese Empire. By the time we reached New Mexico, we had heard that Clark Field on Luzon was abandoned, most of the army aircraft in the Philippines were destroyed, and our naval base at Cavite Bay had been heavily bombed and evacuated. Most U.S. troops would make a stand on Corregidor, the island fortress in Manila Bay. If the Philippines were already lost, where the heck were we going?

The train ride west seemed endless, monotonous, and particularly uncomfortable for the enlisted men. We rode in simple, well-used coaches fitted with lumpy and tattered upholstered bench seats. Within hours posterior paralysis began to set in. I just had to get up and move around the car to see what was happening. The officers had appropriated the Pullman cars equipped with actual fold-down beds and sleeper cars with separate compartments for four. They ate in real dining cars, served by stewards, while our food was brought up and down the aisles on carts and mainly consisted of sandwiches, coffee, and soft drinks.

A serious poker game began in an adjacent coach and continued for days until we reached our destination. Players rotated in and out of the game as they alternately went broke, slept, or ate, all the way to California. Father had always cautioned us boys about gambling and had forbidden us to play cards, but garrison life had ensured that every GI had ample opportunity to try his hand at poker. I was no exception; by now, I was becoming a seasoned player and made some extra cash to supplement my meager pay. I got cleaned out more than once while learning, and I made it a policy to quit when I was ahead. It was amusing to watch a couple of the junior officers get cleaned out by the card sharks. Most of them had fewer opportunities to sharpen their skills.

The powerful steam locomotives of our double-headed train consumed enormous quantities of coal and water, which necessitated frequent stops to resupply. We took advantage of every stop to disembark and stretch our legs. We poured out of the coaches and swarmed the station to restock on snacks and cigarettes, buy an occasional beer or soft drink, and get a quick wash-up in the station restroom. Invariably, the men's washroom looked like a disaster area after hundreds of GIs departed.

At one watering stop, we spotted a vast orange grove, and several soldiers jumped off the train to collect fresh oranges, much to the dismay of the officers. At least we knew we were now in California and it would not be too long before we reached our destination.

We learned much later that back in Louisiana, the reorganized 32nd Infantry Division was preparing for deployment to the Pacific. The division finally shipped out of San Francisco in April 1942 for Australia, eventually seeing action in New Guinea, Leyte, and Luzon as part of MacArthur's drive up the island chain in the Western Pacific. They were involved in some of the bloodiest combat in the Pacific and took heavy casualties. The army constantly replenished the division with soldiers from every state in the union. By the summer of 1944, the division muster rolls had few of the original Michigan and Wisconsin national guard boys who departed from California.

Ironically, once the overseas movement of troops had emptied much of Camp Livingston of most of the GIs, a large portion of the camp was designated as a prisoner of war camp for Axis captives. The first Japanese POW to arrive was the sole survivor from one of the midget submarines that tried but failed to infiltrate Pearl Harbor and ended up stranded on the beach.

This same scenario was repeated at dozens of Midwest and Great Plains camps. German Africa Korps soldiers, Japanese sailors and soldiers, U-boat survivors, SS and Wehrmacht soldiers, and Luftwaffe aircrews made their way into the heartland of America. The humane conditions they encountered in America were a stark contrast to the austere and often brutal conditions our POWs would suffer in Japan and the Third Reich.

Well fed and clothed, housed in more permanent facilities, the Axis POWs worked the fields and towns, maintaining our military installations as replacements for the American boys serving overseas. They enjoyed unprecedented freedom, and many developed strong relationships with the local population. Romances flourished with American girls, and many returned as soon as possible after the war. Ironically, it did wonders for post-war Japanese-American and German-American relations. Still, I would have been furious if I had known of the Axis POWs' conditions a few years later when I languished in a German Stalag.

The army hadn't completely sorted out the logistics involved in the transfer of the 125th Infantry Regiment, so when the train arrived at the Los Angeles railroad depot, trucks took us to the Santa Anita racetrack. Our orders were to create a temporary encampment on the infield for the headquarters, officers' tents, and an assembly area while the rest of the men bivouacked in the bleachers. Two days later, Baker Company was redeployed to Arizona for special duty. We all were relieved to hear this; the bleachers were uncomfortable, the restrooms inadequate, and we had been confined to the grounds of the racetrack.

Back to the train station, we boarded an eastbound train while the remainder of the regiment made plans to move to a different campsite in Los Angeles. We would catch up with them later.

Between Flagstaff and Kingman, Arizona, parallel to Route 66, lay the mainline of the Atchison, Topeka and Santa Fe Railroad, the southern artery for war material destined for West Coast ports. The War Department was concerned that enemy saboteurs could blow the tunnels, plant bombs on the tracks, or perhaps trigger landslides that could cut the right-of-way, so our new mission was to patrol the vulnerable sections of the line. As our train chugged eastward, we frequently pulled off onto passing sidings, allowing long westbound freight and troop trains to pass. With the constant delays, it took us three days to reach our destination, Seligman, Arizona.

Roughly seventy-five miles west of Flagstaff, Seligman had critical railroad locomotive servicing facilities, including shops, a roundhouse, and a turntable. Support of the vast surrounding ranches, the railroad and Route 66 highway traffic gave the town importance. The town supported several cafes, boarding houses, and hotels as a terminal and a layover for train crews. Command decided it would serve as the ideal midpoint for our patrols, with the company HQ personnel billeted there.

Following the railroad west from Seligman, the terrain started relatively flat and followed US-66 for about forty miles. At that point, the Juniper Mountains forced the rail line to diverge and follow a riverbed through multiple passes and a tunnel before reaching the village of Valentine. Nestled in the broad bottom of a canyon on the Hualapai Indian Reservation, Valentine was merely a tiny hamlet on Route 66: a gas station, trading post, Indian affairs office, an abandoned two-story brick schoolhouse, and a few dozen houses that were little more than shacks.

When we arrived at the Seligman station, the First and Second Platoons disembarked, while Third Platoon continued to Flagstaff. The sunshine melted the last vestiges of recent snowfall, but a chilly, dusty breeze swept across our formation as I examined our surroundings.

The railroad station was a large two-story brick building with a colonnade along the platform side, impressive for a small town. In addition to the normal railroad station functions, the building also contained a Harvey House Restaurant, one of many along the Santa Fe rail line, and lodging on the upper floor. Our first order of business was food, and we wasted no time filing into the dining room of the Harvey House for a meal.

Fred Harvey, an English immigrant of the late 1800s, recognized a need to feed railroad travelers because dining cars were not yet a regular part of passenger trains. He partnered with the Santa Fe Railroad and opened a string of restaurants along the railroad mainline, quickly named "Harvey Houses." The system was cleverly organized, with orders collected on the train and wired ahead during watering stops; then, at the next station, the passengers could disembark for a hearty meal served by the Harvey Girls. These were attractive young ladies, recruited from across the country, trained, and dressed in crisp black and white uniforms. In support of the war effort, the Harvey Houses served millions of meals to troops on the move, and it became the favored hangout for the officers for obvious reasons.

After our meal, we reassembled out in the street and waited patiently while Captain Kruczyk took the officers into the station office to confer with the locals about billeting arrangements. Seligman wasn't quite ready for the army invasion, and they never knew we were coming!

The captain made up the patrol assignments: my platoon took the first duty at Valentine, which covered the tiny villages of Pica, Yampai, and Nelson to the east. The captain decided we would rotate the assignment with the second platoon since Valentine was such an isolated place. They began duty in Seligman and covered two checkpoints along the track at the small towns of Peach Springs (the model for Radiator Springs in the 2006 Pixar animated movie "Cars") and Crozier, as well as the railroad engine servicing facilities at Seligman.

Third Platoon was quartered to the east in Flagstaff, assigned to a series of additional checkpoints that spanned the distance between Seligman and Flagstaff, roughly seventy-five miles. Should our Arizona duty extend beyond February, the plan was for all the platoons to rotate assignments. While the officers lodged at the Harvey House, we enlisted men set up a temporary bivouac for a few nights on the outskirts of town until the staff could arrange more permanent housing.

We shouldered our duffle bags, marched from the station, turned left onto the dirt main street, and headed west through the commercial district. Scores of surprised and excited locals turned out to watch, crowding the boardwalks that lined the street. Women, who we hoped were single, waived and called," Hello, boys!" and, "Welcome to town!" As we made our way down the main street, several little boys joined our parade and marched beside us, much to my amusement. In less than a few hundred yards, we passed out of the commercial area and emerged onto the high ground on the west side of town, where we would pitch tents and settle in for a few days. Once our company vehicles arrived, we would relocate to more permanent quarters, either abandoned buildings or perhaps billeted with welcoming locals. For now, however, we stacked our gear on the ground. We began staking out the rough outlines of an encampment, digging shallow drainage trenches around the perimeter of each tent site, then pitching our tents in orderly rows. Within a few hours, a small tent city had sprouted, and we were ready to scout the area.

Billy staking out the first bivouac at Seligman. AZ, 1942. (Author's Collection)

The locals often walked over to watch our progress, especially the youngsters, who seemed fascinated by our organized confusion. As I worked, I started a conversation with a couple of teenage boys. Smitty joined the discussion, and as we explained what we were doing here, we learned a bit about the town and what the locals did for entertainment. There wasn't much to offer, just a few small bars and cafes, a bowling alley, a rudimentary movie theater, and the Harvey House, which had better meals complete with tablecloths and China (if we could afford it). There was also the prospect of being invited to eat a home-cooked meal with a local family. It was hardly encouraging, but we would have to make the best of it until we got settled into our patrol base in Valentine.

In late 1941 Seligman was still not much more than a one-street western town, with dirt streets, boardwalks lining the main drag, and several false-fronted buildings reminiscent of western movies. The big tourism boom would not hit this part of the country until the early 1950s, when Route 66 lured tourists to the Grand Canyon, the Four Corners (where Utah, Colorado, Arizona, and New Mexico meet), Las Vegas, Palm Springs, and the California coast.

In the 1970s, the construction of Interstate 40 would bypass the town and make it a footnote in history once more. But for now, we were the most exciting thing to happen to Seligman since the range wars of the late 1800s. As we marched through town, we took note of the pool hall and bowling alley, which became our real home-away-from-home during the coming winter months.

The Valentine detachment rotated every two weeks with the engine terminal duty in Seligman, but I spent Christmas and New Year's Eve in Valentine. We moved into the old brick two-story schoolhouse that had once been the Indian School for the Hualapai Indian Tribe. It meant to educate the Native Americans in the skills necessary to be successful in White society, but it was eventually accepted as a failure and closed in 1937. With several classrooms, resident student rooms, a lavatory, and a kitchen, it made perfect quarters for us once we took the plywood off the windows and cleaned it up. Most of the old beds and kitchen furnishings were still there. Two men shared each bedroom. We took turns cooking and were careful to keep the big iron stoves hot around the clock to ward off the Arizona winter.

A lieutenant nominally commanded each detachment. But the real supervision fell to staff or technical sergeants who made up the duty assignments, handled supply requisitioning, and hired a few local women to take care of our laundry. Valentine may have been remote, but it was reasonably comfortable. Even better, we were out from under the watchful eyes of the company staff.

As a member of the First Platoon, I began with the first rotation to Valentine. The most vulnerable spot on the AT&SF right-of-way for sabotage was a tunnel near the tiny hamlet of Nelson. The tunnel was located roughly midway between Seligman and Valentine. It was the eastern end of our patrol area and our primary responsibility. Two armed guards patrolled it, one from each end, and the routine of the four-hour shift was to walk halfway through the tunnel, meet in the middle, then return to the entrance. Boring duty, but at least there was a fellow guard to talk to occasionally.

Al Slivatz, Whitey, Smitty, and I were still together, but our little band had expanded to include Walter Barc, a new corporal. Walt came from Pontiac, Michigan, and two other recent arrivals to our squad: Nello Ratliff, a big dark-haired and a rather taciturn fellow from Detroit, and Rocci Cardaro, a curly-haired, perpetually cheery Italian boy from Chicago. We composed half of the first squad and set up the iron framed beds in one large room with a stove we could keep stoked to mitigate the bitter Arizona

*Billy with Harvey Girl at Seligman, AZ bowling alley, February 1942.
(Author's Collection)*

winter cold. Once we discovered that Rocci had been a
short-order cook in a Chicago diner, we ate well. I must
give him credit for being creative and improving upon

army chow. Sadly, the local entertainment was non-existent, and we resorted to poker, checkers, and chess.

After our first two-week stint at Valentine, we wasted no time exploring Seligman. On our first foray into town, we found our way to the bowling alley, which offered recreation, beer, and decent food at a fair price. The place featured duck-pin bowling, which I had never seen before. It seemed rather strange with little pins and a smaller ball, but I became pretty good at it after a while. It helped pass the time and brought out our competitive natures.

In their off time, the Harvey Girls would frequently join us, and I struck up an acquaintance with one of these charming ladies. For the duration of our assignment to Arizona, whenever I was in Seligman and not on duty or posted to Valentine, we spent our evenings together, bowling, dancing, and sometimes at the lone movie theater. Suffice it to say, we became close very quickly, but it was short-lived. I think her name was Agnes or Angie, but it was long ago.

The corner beer hall in Seligman, a rough-edged honky-tonk saloon, was another place to socialize but more of a hangout for the locals. The movie theater was small, with a single projector, and the reels had to be rewound each time. I never minded that because it provided a short break to get a drink or popcorn, and there was plenty of variety since the featured picture changed every few days.

The newspapers, the motion picture newsreels, and the radio kept us in touch with the rest of the world and the war's progress, which at this time was not encouraging. The Japanese were advancing steadily into Burma and had taken Rabaul and Bougainville in the Solomon Islands. The German U-boats were sinking American shipping with increasing frequency off the Atlantic coast and Caribbean, while the German Wehrmacht controlled most of continental Europe. In North Africa, Erwin Rommel's Afrika Korps counter-attacked British forces and pushed them back into Egypt. I couldn't help but feel a bit frustrated. What were we contributing by sitting here in the high desert of Arizona?

I can't say enough about the hospitality of the people of Flagstaff, Seligman, and Valentine. We were frequently invited to dine with families, especially during the holiday season. Most of us were just in our early twenties, some even younger, and we all missed our families. I usually preferred to shy away from these commitments because I felt uncomfortable socializing with strangers, so I often took extra duty so others in my platoon could be off.

I preferred the occasional company of my Harvey House friend and I wasn't alone in my choice of holiday duty. Many men requested duty over Christmas and New Year's Eve to not dwell on thoughts of home. It was also an opportunity to collect IOUs that could be put to good use later. Christmas packages and mail were consistently late getting to us, but we made the most of the situation. For some reason, turkey was in short supply this year and our Christmas and New Year's dinners consisted of ham, mashed potatoes, and gravy, with pumpkin and apple pie. Booze was plentiful, and we had our fill of it when not on duty, so things weren't too bad.

Seligman turned out to be a historic town. Located in the heart of cowboy country, it has a rich history of gunfights, Indian wars, and the infamous Pleasant Valley War that raged for almost a decade in the late 1880s. It was a classic range war, pitting the Graham cattlemen against the Tewksbury sheepherders. Eventually, the remorseless killings left only one surviving family member, Edwin Tewksbury. The infamous hired assassin, Tom Horn, played a part in the war, as did the legendary Apache County Sheriff, Commodore Perry Owens, who eventually settled in Seligman.

The third largest cattle and horse ranch in the continental United States is just north of Seligman and extends for miles, right up to the south rim of the Grand Canyon and west to Kingman. Originally the Boquillas ranch, it became the Three V's ranch when it changed ownership shortly before the war. A vast range, it spread over 775,000 acres, with over 30,000 head of cattle and 40,000 sheep. It was the last ranch to sell cavalry horses to the U.S. Army and is still the largest cattle ranch in Arizona, now known as the Cholla Cattle Company.

One of the most interesting local characters we met in Arizona may have worked at the Boquillas ranch in his younger days. He was a private security guard in Seligman working for the AT&SF railroad, responsible for the roundhouse facility. We often encountered him when we patrolled the Seligman rail yard. This fellow, whose name I have long forgotten, was a stereotypical cowboy straight off the range. He was roughly handsome but unshaven and outfitted in a beat-up Stetson hat, a long duster coat, well-worn jeans, and boots, and carried a Colt Model 1873 six-shooter in a tooled leather holster. He was a bit of a curmudgeon and claimed that he could take care of security at the railroad without the help of any snot-nosed soldier boys, but we gradually warmed up to each other.

One day, when several of us were chewing the fat with the old codger, I boldly asked if he was any good with his single-action revolver. He just stared at me for a moment, leaned over to spit some tobacco juice, and suddenly the gun was in his hand. The muzzle blast deafened us as he hammered a stray tin can with bullets, making it spin and dance with each pull of the trigger. My God, was he fast and accurate! From fifty feet, he didn't miss, and he was shooting from the hip. We'd never seen anything like it, having always assumed that such marksmanship was just Hollywood hoopla. Our respect for the old codger jumped up about ten notches in the blink of an eye. We all called him "sir" after that!

Snow came down heavy in late December, creating the whitest Christmas season I can recall. The locals claimed the winter of 1941-42 was the harshest in recent memory, but it did little to alleviate the drought that damaged the cattle business. Snowfall in the higher elevations exceeded ten feet, and some drifts were nearly twenty feet deep. We prayed we'd be gone from Arizona before it got any worse.

We brought the Baker Company vehicles to Arizona, and the Valentine detachment had two. Access to the railroad line and tunnel was challenging in some locations were little more than wagon trails led to the isolated hamlets, and the tunnel was quite a ways from the nearest wagon track. The quarter-ton truck that GIs had quickly dubbed the "jeep" was indispensable for its ability to negotiate the trails and the edges of the AT&SF right-of-way. With the trailer attached, we made regular runs back to Seligman for supplies to augment what little we could obtain in Valentine.

The drive to the tunnel near Nelson each day, while nearly an hour each way, soon became second nature, and patrolling on foot through the tunnel was not lousy duty because it sheltered us. We met in the middle, chewed the fat for a few minutes, then returned to the portal for a smoke break. So, despite the boredom, our morale was pretty high. The most arduous duty was on the open rail line, where a heavy topcoat and wool uniform was barely adequate against the cold winds. We never looked forward to those patrols, each of which covered about two miles of cuts and gullies that posed a potential for sabotage.

Whenever it was my turn to stand tunnel duty, I got into the habit of sheltering in the rocks above the tunnel entrance for a smoke before I relieved the sentry on duty. An hour-long winter ride in a jeep, open on the sides with just the canvas top, is chilling and rough. We were thrown from side to side by the rough and rutted tracks, filed with muddy puddles of melted snow, and it was impossible not to be splattered with mud and soaked on the exposed side. It was a relief just to arrive, stretch and then huddle for a few minutes among the sun-warmed rocks. At night it was just a brutal journey.

But on calm days, it was a joy to bask in the fresh air, solitude, and the spectacular view of the mountains, especially during the evening shift changes, when the ridges to the north slowly faded into purple and the desert to the west held the orange glow of the setting sun.

One day, just before relieving the sentries, Whitey and I were finishing a smoke and briefly soaking up the late afternoon sunshine above the east portal. Out of the corner of my eye, I noticed a large animal moving down the tracks below me, sniffing as it crept towards the tunnel. It took me a moment to identify it as a big mountain lion, probably hungry and looking for game. He seemed to be stalking the sentry sheltered inside the tunnel entrance waiting to be relieved. Once the big cat entered the cutting at the tunnel entrance, the sentry would be trapped, faced with two options: run the length of the tunnel, nearly a mile, with the cat in hot pursuit or shoot it if he saw the cat in time. But the cat was fast, and he would get only one shot before it was on him.

From my vantage point above, I could see the scenario evolve, and I had only a moment to react before the cat passed out of sight. Whitey hadn't noticed the animal, and without a word, I quickly shouldered my rifle, flicked off the safety, cycled the bolt to chamber a round, took careful aim, and fired. Bam! The big cat dropped to the ground.

Whitey was shocked and said, "Billy, what the hell was that about?"

"Didn't you see that mountain lion stalking the guard," I asked?

Hearing the shot, the sentry ran out of the tunnel to investigate. As he watched me lead the scramble down the rocky slope, he shouted, "Hey, Billy, was that you shooting? What happened?"

He hadn't seen the animal, so I pointed to the big cat lying on the edge of the roadbed ballast about a hundred feet in front of him.

"Yeah, that was me. Look over on the side of the track. It was a mountain lion. I think he wanted you for dinner and nearly cornered you in the tunnel!"

We cautiously approached the cat, but it was dead from the headshot. We dragged the cat's body off the tracks and dropped it down the embankment where it was out of sight. I cautioned Whitey and the sentry to keep quiet about the shooting because I feared I might get in trouble for discharging my rifle. Looking back on the incident, I wish I had skinned it as a trophy. None of us mentioned it for weeks, and there was no repercussion for my unauthorized hunting or the discharge of my firearm.

Chapter 5

California Dreamin'

By late February 1942, Baker Company was finally relieved of duty in Arizona and ordered back to California to rejoin the regiment in Los Angeles. Not long after we left in mid-December, the 125th Infantry departed from their temporary residence at the Santa Anita racetrack. With wartime mobilization in full swing, there was no horse racing, especially not with nearly two thousand men crowded into the bleachers. Using the infield as a parade ground and headquarters' campsite had pretty well destroyed the once-pristine grass. On January 7, 1942, Western Defense Command ordered the regiment to relocate to the heart of Griffith Park, a green oasis of 4,000 acres of nature nestled between Glendale on the east and the Hollywood Hills on the west, where its famous "Hollywood" sign bordered the park.

For those who have never been to L.A., Griffith Park is the largest municipal park and urban wilderness area in the United States. It's a natural sanctuary covering a five square mile portion of the Santa Monica Mountains, which range in elevation from 384 to 1,625 feet above sea level and include sparsely covered ridges and densely wooded valleys and canyons. The facilities included an observatory, planetarium, swimming pool, museum, hiking trails, a Greek amphitheater, and a large sports field complex.

When Baker Company returned, we found our regiment next to the Municipal Plunge, the Griffith Park swimming pool, a large, butterscotch-colored, 1920's two-story Spanish-revival building located near the eastern border of the park. The spacious pool building, outfitted with showers, toilets, and changing rooms, made an excellent support building for us. Meanwhile, the regiment spent more than three months there, idly passing the time until the army decided on a mission for us.

When we detached from the 32nd Infantry Division on December 8, 1941, we were reassigned to the General Headquarters Reserve, Army Ground Forces, Western Defense Command. The army reorganized defense units as quickly as possible, believing in an imminent threat of Japanese attacks on our west coast. Of course, we couldn't have cared less what mission we were assigned. Most of us would have been delighted to spend the entire war in Los Angeles, even if it meant permanent tent living.

California was heaven after the heat, humidity, and bugs of Louisiana and the freezing mountains of Arizona. Duty in LA was easy. We had no route marches, and formal assemblies were rare. If truth be told, I think the brass were as interested in seeing the sights as we were, knowing it wouldn't last forever. We received frequent off-camp passes, but after taps and lights-out, it was simple to huddle under a blanket in your Class A uniform, wait until after bed-check, then pull on your boots and slip out of camp for a night on the town. You were safe as long as you made it back before first light and didn't cause trouble or get picked up by the police or the MPs.

Less than a half-mile hike through a lightly wooded area brought us to the broad concrete flood control channel for the Los Angeles River, a veritable Yellow Brick Road to Oz. We carefully side-stepped down the concrete slope to the bottom, which gave us cover from the camp sentries, and after a short walk, we climbed up from the channel to emerge near Los Feliz Boulevard. From there, we caught a ride on a Pacific & Electric streetcar to the Hollywood nightlife, all in about thirty minutes. It was so easy that I suspected some of the camp sentries were sympathetic and just turned away as we hurried out of the park.

The nightlife was an irresistible lure for us, and we soon discovered Victor McLaglen's nightclub, managed by his brother Cyril. A colorful character, Victor was born in Tunbridge Wells, England, but ran away from home at just fourteen. Because he was a big kid, he successfully lied about his age and joined the famous Lifeguards Regiment. In the First World War, he served in the trenches with the Royal Irish Fusiliers, then gained a battlefield commission in the Middlesex Regiment. After his discharge, Victor went to Hollywood to pursue an acting career.

GIs were always welcomed at Victor's place, and I felt at home because, among all the celebrity photos, there were dozens from Victor's many boxing matches. At one time, he held the title of heavyweight champion of the British Army. After two or three visits per week, the bartenders quickly got to know me on a first-name basis. I knocked back a few drinks with Cesar Romero and Victor himself, among others.

West Hollywood sported several up-scale nightclubs, such as the Cafe Trocadero and Ciro's, and my buddies and I tried them all at least once. The Mocambo, a newer club, was located over on Sunset Strip. It became famous in the 1950s as the club of Ricky Ricardo in the "I Love Lucy" television show. All these clubs were more expensive than most of us GIs could afford, but if I saved up for a few days and rationed myself to only a few drinks, I could see the celebrities. Dorothy Lamour, Errol Flynn, Betty Grable, Humphrey Bogart, Esther Williams, Cary Grant, and a score of others I cannot recall all made an appearance. Occasionally, if we were lucky, a celebrity would stop by our table to chat and buy a round of drinks. It was fun, and I think the stars enjoyed it as much as we did. We made the most of it while it lasted.

When we wanted to be frugal and still cut a rug, we went to the Hollywood USO, where we could be assured of dancing with beautiful movie stars, not just gazing at them from across the room. We quickly began to take the high life for granted. Mary Martin was a terrific dancer and made me feel like a pro, but one of my highlights was dancing to a slow, romantic tune with Lana Turner. And yes, she was a knock-out, even more so in person than on the big screen, with long silky platinum hair and all the right curves.

That night I made the USO run with Smitty, Al, and Walter. After maneuvering ourselves to a table close to the dance floor, we methodically began checking out the female patrons. Suddenly Al grabbed my arm and whispered, "Holy cow, Billy, isn't that Lana Turner over at that corner table?"

The room wasn't that bright, and a haze of cigarette smoke further obscured the patrons, so it took a moment for me to make out to whom he was referring. He was right: there she was, one of the most stunningly beautiful women I'd ever seen. "Looks like she needs a dance partner," I said.

Smitty laughed at that. "C'mon, Billy, you don't have the nerve to ask her."

I never hesitated in the face of a challenge, and I was anxious to see Miss Turner up close. I slapped the tabletop and quickly stood up. "Just watch me, boys!" I announced.

I worked my way between the tables, oblivious to the other patrons, with my eyes locked on my platinum blond target. As I approached, I smiled and asked, "Miss Turner, may I have a dance with you?"

I'd be lying if I said I wasn't nervous, but I nearly melted as she looked up at me and smiled.

"Of course, soldier," she replied. As I escorted her onto the dance floor, I couldn't resist glancing over at my buddies and saw looks of envy on their faces. She asked me my name, and as we swayed to the music, not quite cheek-to-cheek, she casually commented, "My, but you are a firm young man."

I couldn't resist a comeback and replied, "Yeah, I'm hard all over!" She seemed amused and just smiled at me teasingly. Oh, to think that a lowly GI could have a chance with such a stunning beauty! At that moment, my life was good. But, just to keep things even, she danced with each of us that evening.

During this period, we turned in our WWI-style doughboy helmets and venerable Springfield rifles and were issued the new M-1 steel helmet and liner and the M-

1 Garand rifle. Personally, I liked the Springfield M1903 better because it was a bit lighter than the M-1 and had a very smooth bolt action like the Remington I hunted with back home. I qualified as a sniper with the '03 at Camp Livingston. Still, after the first trip to the firing range with the Garand, the greater firepower of the new semi-automatic rifle was undeniable.

The M-1 helmet was an improvement, too, giving better protection from falling debris, but more importantly, the steel pot was a practical tool. When you pulled out the lining shell, the helmet pot made a fair seat on cold, damp ground; it doubled as a digging tool or bucket; made a serviceable wash basin; and a convenient carry-all for your toiletries. It also made a fair rain hat, as long as you remembered to turn up your collar so the water wouldn't drain down your neck. As a negative, being longer at the back, it tended to tip forward over your eyes when you were in the prone firing position.

The army brass were concerned that we were quickly becoming soft, so after about a month in Griffith Park, they scheduled us for a week of maneuvers in the wilderness. We couldn't conduct live firing and tactical maneuvers in the park, so we were loaded up and trucked 250 miles east into the Mojave Desert. After a day's truck ride on wooden bench seats, crowded railroad coaches seemed positively luxurious.

Our destination was Camp Coxcomb, one of eleven new tent camps in the vast Desert Training Center, recently created in the heat and dust of the Mojave. The Army Chief of Staff tasked General George Patton to develop a desert training facility to prepare troops for combat in North Africa, and the DTC was his creation. It covered more than 3,000 acres of the Mojave and Sonoran Deserts and boasted separate camps for small arms, artillery, tactical training, and several supporting airfields.

For a short spell, our lives resumed a strict training regimen of PT, mortar, pistol, and rifle live-firing, with machine gun and mortar firing for the weapons platoons. We spent hours sweating and maneuvering in the desert, sharpening our squad tactics and unit coordination.

We suffered mightily in the heat of the high desert, but it was so blast-furnace dry that the sweat barely stained our clothing. The steady, hot wind blew dust everywhere: in our hair, in our ears, in our coffee, in our chow, in our cots, in our rifles, and in our boots. Thank heaven, it only lasted for a week, and we were soon back in Los Angeles. It took days to get rid of the lingering dust, and I concluded that desert warfare would be miserable even without facing an enemy. Griffith Park looked better than ever.

It was no secret that I was a Golden Gloves boxer in high school, and with a reputation to uphold, it seemed natural that I would box for the regiment. After sweating off several pounds in the desert, I was still a welterweight, and for the few months we were in the Los Angeles area, I regularly boxed on Thursday nights at Jim Jeffries' barn in Burbank.

Jim, "The Boilermaker" Jeffries, was the heavyweight world champion from 1899 to 1905. After retirement, he opened his barn as a gym and boxing venue for aspiring Southern California fighters. The Jeffries barn was a spacious, low-roofed pole barn located at Victory Boulevard and Buena Vista Avenue, across the street from Jim's house.

With all due respect to Muhammad Ali, many boxing authorities consider Jeffries the greatest champion of all time. He earned his title in the days when matches often went to 40 rounds of brutal, bloody sledgehammer action. Although now an old man, Jeffries was always in attendance and often refereed the amateur matches. I was in awe when the legendary boxer spoke to me before my first match. Seeing my buddies with me, all of us in uniform, he approached us. Because I was carrying a gym bag, he looked me in the eyes and asked, "Are you fighting for your unit, son?"

"Yessir," I replied, "For the one-twenty-fifth infantry. We're posted just north of here, in Griffith Park."

He looked me over carefully, and I suppose I seemed pretty small. In his prime, Jeffries had been six-foot-two and 225 pounds of muscle, sculpted by years of twelve-hour shifts as a boilermaker. He was still an impressive man, and although he topped out now at over 300 pounds, it was easy to see the former champ in that scarred face. "Do you have any experience?" he asked.

"Yessir, two years Golden Gloves back home in Michigan," I responded proudly. Jeffries was a legend in the boxing world, and for a twenty-two-year-old kid, this was an experience to be savored.

He looked me over carefully, taking note of my modest stature, but my physique was muscular, with a narrow waist and broad shoulders. "Okay, I'll put you on the card, but you'll be up against a pretty good amateur from Glendale. He's boxed here before. I hope you're up to it tonight. Good luck."

Mine was the third fight on the night's schedule. I changed in the locker room and then walked down the aisle to the ring. It was a heady experience with shouting fans and clouds of heavy cigar smoke mixed with the scent of wintergreen from the boxers' liniment. I got my first look at my opponent when I climbed into the ring. He was a bit older and slenderer but taller and proportionally broader in the shoulders. With his longer reach, he could really hammer me unless I could get inside and rely on my quickness to compensate. At the bell, we came out to ring center, listened as Jeffries recited the rules, touched gloves, and stepped back.

I wasted no time and moved in close, ducked a right haymaker, then feinted with my right and slammed him in the face with a stiff left jab. I drew blood, and he backed away with a surprised look. We circled, then he came at me, jabbing with his right again, then he landed a hard left to my ribs that took my breath away. I moved in, we clutched, and then Jeffries pulled us apart. We circled again, and I thought this guy could hurt me with body blows. I needed to find his weak spot.

In the second round, I noticed that every time he tried to land that right, he moved his left foot forward a bit, shifted all his weight to his right foot, and turned his body ever so slightly to the right, cocking his body and momentarily leaving himself open. As we circled again, I quickly moved in, jabbed with my left, and then blocked his right. His right arm was outstretched for a split second, and his left was drawn back. I stepped forward and put all my weight behind my right, giving him the hardest uppercut I've ever thrown. It caught him square on the jaw, and he just sagged to his knees, then fell forward onto his face. He took the full count, and when Jeffries raised my arm in victory, all I could think was that I wished Jimmy Winters could have seen this moment.

After the backslapping and congratulations, we drove back to camp. I said very little, lost in my memories of those days of boxing with Jimmy, the state championship in Lansing, then the night of the fatal crash. I missed him terribly and struggled to hold back a tear.

I boxed several more times at the Jeffries barn, winning all but one of my matches, and that one was a draw. But none was ever as memorable or challenging as that first one.

Chapter 6

Coast Patrol

Shortly after Pearl Harbor, the Imperial Japanese Navy ordered five of their largest submarines to attack shipping off the coast of California. Thirteen ships were attacked: six were sunk, four were damaged, and three successfully evaded the torpedoes. On February 23, 1942, one of the submarines surfaced close in-shore and shelled the Ellwood Oil Field and Refinery on the Santa Barbara Channel. That ratcheted up the army defense posture, and on at least two occasions in 1943, a submarine lobbed shells at fortifications near San Francisco. The Fourth Army was organized for the express purpose of Pacific coastal defense, and we became one of several units attached to fulfill the mission.

On April 21, 1942, the regiment moved again, this time north to Gilroy, California, a town roughly midway between San Jose and Monterey on State Route 101, where we assumed dual missions: patrolling the Pacific Coast from Morro Bay State Park in the south, to

Pescadero in the north, approximately a 200 mile stretch of coast; and training recruits at Camp San Luis Obispo, the California Army National Guard training center. First Battalion, which included Baker Company, was assigned the coast patrol mission, while the other two battalions became the training cadre for newly inducted troops.

Within weeks, a civilian contractor, the Del Webb Company (which now builds over-55 communities across America), prefabricated the single-story wood frame buildings for our camp off-site. The pre-finished sections arrived at the camp site ready for assembly, and buildings were completed at the rate of one per hour!

Our Gilroy camp comprised the regimental, battalion, and company headquarters, a motor pool, multiple quartermasters' storehouses, a barber shop, mess hall, armory, ammunition bunkers, woodworking and vehicle workshops, and dozens of single-story wooden barracks complete with washrooms and NCO offices at the ends, similar in layout to the two-story barracks back at Camp Grant.

Leaving the Los Angeles nightlife behind was a huge disappointment, but this new encampment got us out of tents and felt more permanent. We would still have opportunities for overnight passes to San Jose and San Francisco, possibly as far as Malibu, or even back to Los Angeles. But that would be pushing the limit and required a forty-eight-hour pass. Our recreational facilities were limited, so a couple of us who boxed rigged up a punching bag behind our barrack so we could continue training. When time allowed, we did group beach runs on the hard sand between the surf line and the high tide limit.

With several hundred miles of coast to patrol, the battalion staff established rotating patrol duties with

Setting up the punching bag. (Author's Collection)

separate company detachments posted along the coast at Morro Bay State Park, Monterey, and Pescadero. The Morro Bay Park unit was anchored by a small support detachment, while San Luis Obispo, just thirteen miles inland, offered administrative and logistical support and vehicle maintenance.

In the north, the regimental and battalion HQ stayed at Gilroy, a bit inland but well positioned to support the two northern patrol legs. The Pescadero patrol detachment drove to Monterey and back. The Morro Bay and Carmel-by-the-Sea patrols drove north and south towards each other, meeting roughly midway at Sand Dollar Beach, then returning.

Patrol units rotated bases each month to keep us from getting stale, watching the same stretch of coastline every week, gradually moving further and further north along the Pacific Coast Highway. Morro Bay was my first posting, then the northern leg from Monterey, and finally the patrol from Pescadero.

The patrol routes were spectacular drives along some of the most scenic parts of the Carrillo Highway, California's Pacific Coast Highway, referred to as Route One. From Morro Bay, it wound north past William Randolph Hearst's famous San Simeon estate, the lighthouse at Big Sur, and the fishing port of Monterey, with the Los Padres Forest to the east, then it followed Monterey Bay to Pescadero.

From my experience, the best billet was the one near Monterey, once again in an abandoned school. This one was at Carmel-by-the-Sea, which made for comfortable, scenic, and almost luxurious surroundings when not on the road. In retrospect, patrolling the considerable expanse of the central California coast by road seems to me to have been a relatively futile gesture. Because of the way the terrain forced the highway inland at spots, large stretches of the coast were left unobserved, but I suppose, in principle, it was not without merit. In any case, it was cushy duty.

Getting ready for patrol, 1943. (Author's Collection)

Our typical patrol was composed of three or four men in a Dodge command car, a soft-topped truck with tandem bench seats. A sergeant was in charge, armed with a Thompson submachine gun and a .45 caliber Colt pistol sidearm. The other three men had rifles or carbines but taking any weapon out of the vehicle racks was rare.

We took the patrols seriously, carefully observing the shoreline out to the horizon. We covered the roughly sixty-mile leg in two to three hours, depending upon the number of stops, before meeting the opposing patrol. We exchanged news, shared a smoke, and ate a boxed meal; then, we would head back. The whole round trip from each patrol base took between six and eight hours, sometimes longer if we had to stop to investigate something. We ran the patrols day and night, and with four patrol teams at each base, each team took six runs to complete a "string" of patrols in just over a week.

After completing a patrol string, we had two full days off, and a third day was devoted to drill, inspection, and physical training. Occasionally our company commander threw in a ten-mile route march so that we wouldn't get too out of shape from constantly riding in vehicles. During our breaks, we had ample time for passes that allowed us to get back to Los Angeles from Morro Bay or San Jose and San Francisco from Pescadero or Monterey. Although the routine got monotonous, the scenery was beautiful, the weather was generally delightful, and we had plenty of time to swim in the surf, sunbathe, hunt up in the hills, or just hang out with a few cold beers.

I explored during my off-time, and after I made sergeant, I often got permission to check out a jeep. I always took one of the other guys with me on what I called a "wild goose chase" into the mountains along the coast. Sometimes we just followed a road to see where it led. Driving through the coastal redwood forests was a beautiful excursion, and a few of the California national parks were within reach, such as Yosemite and Sequoia.

Chapter 7

Movin' On Up

While at Camp Livingston, Louisiana, I volunteered to help build the wooden duckboard walkways that lined the rows of company tents. I was pretty handy with tools, and just sort of took over ramrodding the project. Sergeant Scott appointed me company artificer, and I drew tools from supply and requisitioned the lumber. I made up a simple jig, and it was a simple matter to cut the boards to length for the walkways. Within a few weeks, we had nice boardwalks to keep us out of the mud of the Louisiana summer. My efforts drew praise from the regimental and company commander and now paid a dividend in California.

At one time or another, most of the NCOs in the regiment were temporarily transferred to Camp San Luis Obispo to become instructors for recruits. Shortly after morning formation on June 1, 1942, I was ordered to report to regimental HQ. Since I was only a private first class, a PFC, I had no idea what to expect. I couldn't imagine what I might have done to deserve a reprimand, but when I reported, I was stunned to learn that I had been promoted to sergeant. A soldier usually had to be promoted to corporal first; then, after showing leadership and proving yourself worthy of greater responsibility, you might be considered for sergeant. But to my surprise, Sergeant Scott had recommended me for immediate promotion to sergeant, and apparently, the company and regimental commander supported his choice.

I was delighted, not just because the rank gave me more responsibility and privileges, but the pay was substantially more. Even better, they had backdated my promotions: to corporal on May 2, then to sergeant four days later. I felt at home in the army and enjoyed the structure, but this was a surprise. I admit to feeling a bit guilty and self-conscious about my new rank. I had no time to adjust to corporal, and suddenly I had become one of the creatures we all hated. I was determined not to conform to the sergeant stereotype. I knew what I didn't like about sergeants, and I vowed to be firm but fair in all my decisions. Following Eisenhower's example, I decided to be respectful of my men, but I would expect nothing less than proper performance.

Shortly after my promotion, we heard a rumor that someone in divisional public affairs thought it would be a good idea to have Hollywood movie stars volunteer to serve in units stationed between Los Angeles and San Francisco. It would garner publicity for the celebrities seen doing their patriotic duty, and undoubtedly newsreel camera operators and photographers would feature them and get good newsreel footage and newspaper coverage. As luck would have it, shortly after arriving at San Luis Obispo, I got called to regimental headquarters one morning to meet a new addition to my recruit class. I squared off in front of the regimental adjutant's desk, saluted, and reported.

"Sergeant Condon," he announced, "we have assigned Private Renaldo to your squad for brief basic training. You'll need to get him checked in, draw the necessary uniforms and equipment. Please try to ignore his celebrity status and treat him as you would any one of your men."

Needless to say, I knew very well who Duncan Renaldo was. The Romanian-born actor's trial and conviction for passport fraud had made headlines back in the mid-1930s. When cast to film "Trader Horn," shooting on location in Africa, he had applied for his U.S. passport and claimed he was born in Camden, New Jersey. But the deception caught up with him, and he was arrested, tried, and convicted of falsifying his birth record. Despite his excuse of patriotism, he was fined $2,000 and sentenced to two years in prison. The backlash from the entertainment media prompted President Roosevelt to pardon him in 1936.

I was sure that the studio's public relations people decided that having Renaldo seen and photographed in uniform would help to rehabilitate his image. I was skeptical and had a somewhat cynical opinion of Hollywood celebrities. But I also reasoned that having him riding patrol with us might make for some interesting conversation. As a bonus, he might be able to wrangle invitations for us to hobnob with other celebrities.

"Yessir," I replied, saluted, did an about-face, and went back out to the anteroom, where the clerk introduced me to a GI sitting patiently in the corner. I had ignored him on my way in, but now I recognized Duncan Renaldo. He stood, smiled, and gave me a firm handshake. He made an elegant impression, impeccably dressed in a tailored Class A dress uniform. It was as though he had just stepped out of central casting and was waiting for a cue call to go on-camera. But his long, slicked-back hair covered his collar and was flagrantly unmilitary. I couldn't imagine how he thought he would get away with it. As firmly but tactfully as possible, I informed him that he would have to get his hair cut. After all, I explained, he was a high-profile example and needed to reflect the highest standards.

"Of course, Sergeant, I understand completely," he replied.

"Okay," I said, "Go to the post barbershop. It's just a few doors down the street and get a fresh haircut. Report back to me here at company headquarters. I'll make the arrangements to draw your gear and weapon. Then I'll get you settled in and set up a training schedule." He saluted, and I held up a hand to stop him.

"I'm a sergeant, not an officer, and I don't rate a salute," I said. "But if in doubt, render a salute. You'll quickly get used to the ranks and protocol. Oh, and I'm not a "sir," just sergeant."

He nodded, then turned and marched off while I made a few phone calls for visits to supply and the armory.

About thirty minutes later, my new charge strolled back into the regimental office, a big, white, toothy smile on his face, and reported that he was ready to get to work. I looked him over carefully. Other than having the hair on the back of his neck cleaned up, I couldn't see any difference. The black, wavy hair was off his collar but still just as full and luxurious as before, bushing out from beneath his cap.

"Did you get a haircut as I ordered?"

"Yes, Sergeant," answered the smiling star. I knew exactly what had happened. The silly starstruck barber was so excited to be cutting a movie star's hair that he was only too happy to oblige and just give him the slight trim he wanted, not a regulation haircut. He wasn't about to tarnish his matinee idol image. But celebrity or not, he wasn't going to get away with that crap in my squad!

"Come with me!" I ordered and led him right back to the barbershop. His smile quickly disappeared when I ordered him to sit in the chair. I gave the barber my most threatening glare and snapped out, "GI this man, just like everyone else in this regiment!" I just stood there and watched.

If looks could have killed me, I would have been dead on the spot, but to Renaldo's credit, he sat there and took it without a word. As the barber swiveled Renaldo's chair so he could examine the results in the mirror, he glared at my reflection over his shoulder.

"Don't worry, it'll grow out," I told him without sympathy.

The barber whisked the sheet off his victim, and Renaldo followed me out. I held the door for my recruit and glanced back at the barber. He was just standing there, looking down at the gobs of hair on the floor. I suppose he wondered how much money he could get for clumps of a movie star's hair! I marched our new GI back to headquarters and turned him over to my corporal with instructions to escort him to the quartermaster's, draw his equipment, and take him to the billeting sergeant to get him settled into a barracks.

Not unexpectedly, the following day, Renaldo was missing at formation. Suspicious, I went to headquarters, where a lieutenant informed me that Private Renaldo had been reassigned. For weeks afterward, there were smiles in the company whenever his name was mentioned. I was just as happy to be rid of him.

Jack Szacon still had not earned his sergeant stripes back since the bar fight in Louisiana, He was still in Baker Company, so I occasionally picked him to ride with me on patrol. He was a pleasant fellow, just a year younger, and like me, he had quit high school after only three years. He supported himself as a piano teacher for a time but knew it would never be a career, so he joined the Michigan National Guard in 1939 for some extra money. When the regiment became federalized in October 1940, it suddenly became full-time.

Jack was conscientious and liked the army life as much as I did. By the time I had joined the unit in April of 1941, he had made sergeant. At six-foot-one and 195 pounds, anyone would think twice about messing with Jack. I always felt comfortable when he was with me. I knew it wouldn't last though because Jack was too good a soldier. In April 1942, he got a set of corporal stripes, and in early September, he was finally promoted back to sergeant and moved to a different patrol base.

On our patrols, it was not unusual for us to stop and soak up the spectacular scenery. It was intoxicatingly beautiful, with the surf crashing on the rocky cliffs, the salty scent of the sea, and the piney odor of the forests. It

Jack Szacon and Billy, June 1943. (Author's Collection)

was a perfect time to relax, smoke, and walk down to the edge of the cliffs overlooking the azure Pacific.

One day we stopped for lunch at a scenic spot. As we sat and unpacked our food, watching and listening to the seals barking as they basked on the rocks, I got it into my head to take a shot at one of the animals. I walked back to the vehicle and took a rifle from the scabbard.

"Billy, what are you doing?" asked Al, giving me a quizzical look.

"I just thought I'd see if I could hit one of those seals making so damned much noise," I replied. "How far do you think it is?"

One of the other guys responded, "I'd guess it's at least a hundred yards to the rocks down there. I'll say you can't hit it for ten bucks."

"You're on," I said and adjusted the sights, picked out a large animal, took a breath, exhaled partially, and squeezed the trigger.

I killed it with one shot to the head, lowered the rifle, and smiled at Al. I felt smugly satisfied with myself. But moments later, the other seals took up a mournful cry, shuffling over to the body, nudging it, and creating a horrible din. I was stunned!

"Oh, my God," I said. "What the hell are they doing?" It had never occurred to me that wild animals might have emotional attachments. I was suddenly ashamed of myself. "I've never shot an animal in a pack before. Just deer and game birds that take off at the sound of the shot."

I'll never forget the looks the others gave me, making me feel like a murderer. I guess I was. I never thought of the seals as legitimate game, and there was no point in the shooting. The episode haunted me for quite some time. I left the seals alone in the future and vowed never again to shoot anything I didn't intend to eat.

The Pearl Harbor attack on December 7, 1941, had triggered intense lobbying by anti-Asian groups, predominantly in the western states. Finally, on February 19, 1942, President Franklin D. Roosevelt caved in to pressure from the Toland Committee, a congressional committee chaired by representative John Toland of California, an intensely anti-Japanese politician. FDR signed Executive Order 9066, which ordered the forced evacuation and internment of all Japanese nationals in the United States, especially the Japanese-Americans living in the western states.

Of the 127,000 people in the U.S. with Japanese heritage, almost 80,000 were American citizens, and roughly 3,000 lived on the West Coast. The Japanese culture and distinctive facial features made them stand out, and those living in militarily sensitive areas became immediately suspect. Several low-level local politicians had made a name for themselves by denouncing the Japanese-American populace and whipping up racial hatred. The near hysterical paranoia of the Jap-haters was becoming infectious.

The War Relocation Authority was formed on the recommendation of the Toland Committee and charged the army with overseeing the evacuation and resettlement of the Japanese-Americans to fifteen temporary relocation sites. At the same time, ten more permanent camps were built. These relocation centers were little more than concentration camps, albeit without the physical abuse and starvation conditions usually associated with such camps.

The conditions were bleak, with quarters comprised of simple tarpaper-covered shacks, and the barracks and workshops were surrounded by barbed wire and located miles from the nearest town. The camps were located on Federal land, but most were in some of the country's most remote and inhospitable portions. The shock to the internees, most of whom came from the temperate regions of California, was acute and inflicted emotional scars that have only healed with the passing generations.

Our patrols were directed to assist in the roundup of the Japanese immigrants living on the coast and bringing them into headquarters for questioning by army intelligence. One day we stopped at the seaside cottage of an elderly Japanese gentleman and his granddaughter. The old man was working in his vegetable patch, weeding and tending his plants. The granddaughter answered our knock on the door.

I politely explained that as the homeowner, her grandfather needed to come with us for questioning at the post. The old gentleman, who acted more concerned about his garden, was impassive. Perhaps he didn't speak or understand English, but our uniforms and sidearms didn't seem to faze him. The granddaughter, however, was outraged and made a fuss despite my assurances that we were just taking him in for questioning. Finally, in frustration, I told her to come along if it would make her feel better.

To fulfill our duty, we carefully examined the contents of his house. I didn't know what to tell my men to look for except to instruct them to collect and bag anything that they thought our intelligence people might want to look at, particularly the contents of the desk, such as letters, bills, receipts, ration books, and photographs. We loaded the couple into our vehicle and took them back to camp, where the intelligence staff, G-2, took over. How the pair got back home was someone else's problem.

A couple of days later, one of the intelligence officers called us in and showed us a collection of penny postcards we had bagged. Although innocuous when shuffled and in no particular order, the cards formed a relatively complete mosaic illustration of a large section of the coast when laid in the correct sequence, end to end. I was impressed by the cunning and thought it was a pretty neat trick.

I never knew the fate of the two Japanese-Americans, and frankly, I didn't give it too much thought. While they would undoubtedly be transported to an internment camp, I doubted they would be prosecuted for espionage, even though the anti-Japanese feeling was intense.

One memorable Friday night in early 1943, I learned that Frank Sinatra was playing at the Mocambo nightclub in Los Angeles. He had recently broken his contract with the Tommy Dorsey Orchestra and was performing there for a couple of weeks in his solo debut. Al Slivatz, Rocci, Whitey, and I scraped our cash together, put on our Class A uniforms, and hopped a bus from Gilroy back to Hollywood. The club was packed, mostly with girls swooning over 'ole Blue Eyes. I thought we looked pretty handsome and desirable, but every female in the club had eyes only for Sinatra. I thought their adoration was pathetic, but it was a night to remember, and Frank put on a hell of a show. I would meet him again years later in Palm Springs, but that's a story for later.

Around late January 1943, while heading home on patrol well after nightfall, we spotted the glow of lights coming from the ridge of the coastal hills. We were tired, chilly, and still had a way to go until the patrol ended, but we had to check it out. Investigating the light source, we arrived at the front gate of San Simeon, William Randolph Hearst's fabulous 250,000-acre estate overlooking the Pacific Ocean. It's a complex of structures surrounding a massive, ornate, Spanish-style principal residence, with several more modest but sizable guest houses, surrounded by swimming pools, gardens, a croquet lawn, tennis courts, a skeet range, golf links, and riding stables.

In pre-war days this legendary estate became famous for hosting scores of wealthy and influential personalities, politicians, and Hollywood celebrities. I was a bit excited about what we would be able to see.

The private security guards confronted us at the gate and refused to allow us onto the property. It had all the appearance of a standoff as we demanded access to the property, and they emphatically told us that it was private land and we would need a warrant.

What the hell, I thought. We were on official army business, and I would not be intimidated. I had my fingers crossed behind my back when I informed the guards that we had seen unauthorized lights on Hearst land violating the blackout. They were in no position to give us any crap, let alone deny access to an official U.S. Army patrol. But they still resisted.

Aggravated by their attitude, I pulled the Thompson submachine gun out of the vehicle's scabbard and ordered the guards to open the gate, or we would drive right through the damn thing and arrest all of them. Thankfully, army authority and a dose of common sense prevailed.

The guards made a quick phone call to the main house and opened the gates. I was astonished when we drove through and up the long, twisting driveway to the main house. It was like nothing I had ever seen before. Even in the dark, the size and intricate architecture of the house impressed me. The lights flanking the entryway came on, and household security people came out to greet us. When I explained the situation, they provided an escort to help us find our way, and we drove off together in the direction of the lights. Much to our surprise, it was campfires from cowboys up on the Hearst cattle range.

We pulled up near the campfire, dismounted, and I introduced myself and my men. They were polite and welcomed us, so we sat alongside the ranch hands and warmed ourselves. I shared a smoke with the ranch foreman, a tough-looking but pleasant character.

"So, how big is the Hearst estate," I asked, trying to break the ice before telling him that the campfire had to go.

"Oh, it's somewhere around a quarter of a million acres," he replied, as though it was not an unusual size for a ranch, but I was impressed. "It's not just the cattle ranges. There's horse breeding stables, riding trails, and private airstrip, just for those VIPs who can afford to fly in."

Our security escort added some details. "The Hearst home is just a small part," he said. "Several large guest houses surround the main house, with pools and gardens. Mr. Hearst and Miss Davies often host large guest parties. It's important to him to offer them a variety of entertainments and sporting activities."

The cowboy took a long drag on his cigarette and poked the fire a bit. "Mr. Hearst and Miss Davies left shortly after Pearl Harbor and returned to the East Coast. We're permanent here, looking after beef, dairy cattle, and other livestock. Some gardeners take care of the fruit orchards. The personal servants went East with the family, but the security people and household staff will take care of everything until they return, . . . whenever that might be.

"I hate to break it to you," I said, "but your campfire is visible from the coast road and probably from miles out to sea. It's breaking the blackout regulations. I have to ask you to put it out. In the future, you'll need to find better campsites where the fires are hidden."

He understood our mission and was very cooperative. After finishing our cigarettes, we shook hands, the cowhands doused the fire, and we parted company. As we slowly drove away, we watched the cowboys saddle up and ride off into the night. I'm not sure if anyone back at post believed our description of the Hearst estate and the vast range, but I was impressed. I wished I could have seen it in the daylight.

In February of 1943, I was promoted to staff sergeant, which meant that I would now lead a platoon and was responsible for making up the duty assignments for the forty-odd men of First Platoon, Baker Company. Most of us had been together for nearly two years, and I had to be careful not to play favorites with patrol scheduling and personnel assignments. Coast patrol duty was not particularly taxing, with only about six patrols every eight days. Even without counting a few duty days off after each patrol string, the men not patrolling had plenty of time to goof off.

I frequently gave out passes to my men so they could go into town, and invitations to dine with locals were commonplace. But just as I did in Arizona, I seldom took advantage of such social activities myself, preferring to give the invitations to the men who I felt deserved some special perks. On two occasions, however, I couldn't resist the opportunity to visit the home of the Hollywood star Jeannette MacDonald for cookouts.

Scrubbed and dressed in my Class A's, I checked out a jeep from the motor pool and drove down the coast to the estate. The steaks were thick, the women were beautiful, and the liquor was first-rate and free. You never knew which Hollywood stars would show up. On my first visit, while we enjoyed cocktails around the swimming pool, Whitey and I spent several hours chatting with Nelson Eddy.

Originally trained as an opera tenor, Eddy had transitioned into motion pictures in the early 1930s at the MGM Studio. His most recent film was "Phantom of the Opera," with Claude Rains in the title role. He had just returned from a two-month USO tour of South America and North Africa, where he had entertained the troops. He was an okay guy, as I gradually discovered most of the movie stars were in those days. He was very relaxed and treated us like we were old friends as he regaled us with stories of Hollywood. I suppose that in the days of the studio contract system, the stars didn't get so self-possessed with their fame since the studio PR men were mainly responsible for creating their public images.

It was rumored at the time that Eddy and Jeanette MacDonald, with whom he had made several pictures, were lovers, although each was married to someone else. From the way the two entertained us, it was obvious that they were more than just good friends. They acted as though they were happy to have us around, and we couldn't have cared less about their marital relationships. It was just a great party with interesting people.

Chapter 8

Fort Ord & Monterey

On September 14, 1943, the regiment was alerted and transferred to Fort Ord, about 80 miles down the coast from San Francisco. A fear that Japanese submarines were lurking again in the vicinity of San Francisco Bay brought the army and navy to a high state of readiness.

The entire regiment was billeted at Fort Ord in the two-story platoon barracks, common throughout the army. It was a disappointing change from our more independent patrol duties. Suddenly back in the real army, our routine now included a Saturday morning formation and parade at the Stanford University stadium at Palo Alto, northwest of San Jose, on the western side of San Francisco Bay. It wasn't as bad as it seemed. By this time, we were old hands at spit and polish and formation drill, and once the parade was over, we usually got weekend passes to San Francisco. We wasted no time getting into the city, partied like madmen, then late on Sunday afternoon, we caught a bus back to the post.

Sadly, Smitty was transferred to a different company in early 1943, and other than at the Saturday parade, we only saw each other occasionally. But with the hunting

Saturday morning parade at Stanford University stadium, 1943. (Author's Collection)

that I was doing in the rolling hills and wooded valleys of the fort, my closest friend soon became Rocci Cardaro, who had taken it upon himself to be our mess cook ever since Valentine.

Rocci was good with a knife and skillfully dressed down the deer I shot. We all enjoyed the excellent venison steak dinners when we returned from patrol. We drank together (or rather, I drank, and Rocci sipped soda pop), went out on the town together, chased women together, and often wrestled or boxed together when we were too broke to do anything else. Within a few weeks, Rocci became as close a friend as Smitty.

With the move to Fort Ord, our standard of living changed dramatically. The fort had an excellent officers club, an NCO Club, and Soldiers Club for the lower ranks.

The weekend regimental sports competition usually pitted one battalion against another for top honors in boxing, baseball, volleyball, and cross country running. I always enjoyed baseball and played pretty well as shortstop in pick-up games back home, so I naturally joined in when not on weekend duty. One weekend in late November, while playing right field I took a line drive to the tip of my glove. The pain of the impact was intense and by the time the game ended the left index finger was swollen to twice its normal size. My company commander sent me to the Treasure Island Naval Hospital, located at the northern end of the Golden Gate Bridge, to have the finger x-rayed. Sure enough, it was broken. It was six weeks until the splint came off. I nearly went stir-crazy waiting, but at least it wasn't my right hand.

From Pescadero, it was an easy drive to San Francisco, and from regimental headquarters at Gilroy, San Jose was even closer. Both towns offered plenty of hot spots to unwind after our patrols or training days. On one occasion, while we were at one of our favorite local watering holes in San Jose, my platoon leader, Lieutenant Bartel, a shave-tail wonder from ROTC, joined our group, totally contrary to regulations. Fraternization between officers and enlisted men is strictly forbidden, but Bartel had other ideas. Maybe he was having trouble fitting in with the other officers, or perhaps he thought we had more fun.

After several drinks, the lieutenant got into an argument with Rocci for some stupid reason. I cannot recall the details of the altercation, but Bartel was drunk. Rocci, who was not a drinker, was stone-cold sober and was in the uncomfortable position of not knowing how to defend himself against the escalating verbal threats of the intoxicated lieutenant. As the noisy row moved out into the street, Bartel got louder and louder and began to ram his fingers into Rocci's chest.

I was worried we would draw the attention of patrolling MPs or even the police. I was buzzed myself and rashly decided to take matters into my own hands and punched the lieutenant's lights out! With one quick right to the jaw, he did a back flip over the fender of a parked car and landed in a heap. We helped him up and brushed him off, and he seemed none the worse for wear, albeit now dazed and subdued. We found a taxi and gave the cabbie directions to take the lieutenant back to the post.

When I sobered up the following morning, the implication of my action began to sink in. I decided that my sergeant's stripes were probably a thing of the past. At the least, I would be in company punishment and possibly a court martial for striking an officer. The lieutenant was a good guy. He knew he had been out of line and would probably have a hard time explaining why he was drinking with soldiers of his platoon. To my relief, the following day, he acted as though nothing had happened and no one filed charges against me. I concluded that Bartel had only a blurry memory in a hangover haze and didn't know who had hit him or even if he had been hit.

When posted to Fort Ord, there was seldom a Sunday night when my name wasn't on the boxing card, except, of course, for the six weeks my finger was in a splint. I admit that with my high school experience, I was a cocky character, ready to take on all comers. I had generally been successful at defeating challengers, although with only three three-minute rounds for each fight, like in Golden Gloves competition, most matches were decisions. On one occasion, however, I met up with an unexpected opponent.

Early one Saturday morning, on duty as Sergeant of the Guard, I was approached by another NCO, a stranger to me. "G'morning, sergeant, what can I do for you?" I asked.

"I'm looking for Sergeant Condon," he replied.

"You found him."

"Great. I just wanted to let you know that your scheduled opponent for tonight's fight is in the stockade."

"Oh, well," I replied, smiling at the turn of events. "I could probably use a night off."

"Oh, no," said the sergeant. "They brought in another fighter to fill out the card. We just wanted to let you know it would be someone new."

There weren't that many boxers at Fort Ord, and I had fought most of them at least once. At the time, I didn't give it much thought, but after being relieved later in the day, I made some inquiries. Nobody seemed to know anything about the other fighter. When I climbed into the ring that evening, I was surprised to see that my opponent was a little guy, shorter and stockier. I was confident that my reach was longer, and I would have no problems handling him. His smaller stature fooled me. From the moment of the bell, he swarmed all over me, stepping inside, peppering me with jabs, and winning the fight handily by a clear decision in just three rounds. I had rarely lost a match, just once at the Jeffries' barn, and I was humiliated.

After showering and leaving the gym, I spotted my former opponent on the sidewalk outside, so I walked over and struck up a conversation with him. To my chagrin, he divulged that he was a former pro boxer who had given up the game, enlisted, and began to box as an amateur in the army! As I walked away, all I could think was, don't judge a book by its cover.

Our coast defense assignment continued for over a year until the summer of 1943, when we were alerted by rumors of enemy submarines reconnoitering San Francisco Bay. The repeated false alarms convinced the Western Defense Command that security in the bay area was too lax. Several units not stationed at the San Francisco Presidio accepted the challenge to infiltrate the defenses there if they could. Sensing a fun break in our routine, First Battalion jumped at the challenge.

After careful tactical planning, two selected platoons, including mine, blackened our faces with charcoal and linseed oil and slipped through the base perimeter after dark. One group armed with flour bags attacked the coastal battery of heavy artillery, successfully "spiking" seven of the twelve guns with flour bags smashed onto the breeches.

The lieutenant in command of my group, whom I had never met, recognized a unique opportunity and led us to seize the officer's dining hall. The doors were chained shut, but it took just seconds with a bolt-cutter to gain access. We posted our guards, then proceeded to make ourselves a lavish late-night steak dinner topped with giant ice cream sundaes. The lieutenant was our day's hero, although the senior staff took a dim view of his resourcefulness. I couldn't help but wonder what his subsequent evaluation would do to his prospects for promotion. Hopefully, he didn't get court-martialed. We all thought what he did was more than fair because, after all, to the victors go the spoils!

Other units had attacked targets of opportunity, and several local police officers found themselves under lock and key in their own cells. As a result of the mock raid, the defenses were bolstered significantly. But within a couple of weeks, the scare died out, and we returned to our old patrol routine.

By now, we were all feeling like seasoned GIs and anticipated orders that would send us out to relieve a front-line unit in Europe or the Pacific. While waiting, my buddies and I had plenty of freedom to see the sights. Drinks were cheap, and people were happy to see GIs around them.

Hollywood celebrities frequently watered at a unique private resort called Brookdale Lodge. I recall it as somewhere near La Honda, southwest of San Jose, and near Pescadero. Officers and NCOs were a common sight, but it was a little pricey for the privates. Because he was a teetotaler, Rocci always had more cash. So despite him being only a private and earning less, he and I made the lodge a frequent pilgrimage.

The main building was a sprawling, woodsy, log cabin-style structure. The dining room, appropriately called the Brook Room, was the size of a gymnasium, with a vast stained-glass skylight overhead and a natural creek flowing through the center of it. The stream, at least six feet wide, was edged with boulders and ferns. It poured over a succession of little waterfalls and was cleverly dammed in several places to create pools where fresh trout congregated. The prime dining tables were positioned right at the water's edge, with more mezzanines overlooking from above.

If you were lucky enough to get a brook-side table, your waiter would supply a rod and reel, bait the hook, and when you reeled in a fish, he would net it and hustle it off to the kitchen. It would be grilled to perfection within twenty minutes, garnished with potatoes, vegetables, and a salad. The meals were delicious, and it was a unique venue. Rubbing elbows with the occasional movie star was a bonus to write home about.

We frequented several local bars near Fort Ord, and the women who made the bars their second home became well known. One such lady, and I use the term loosely (no pun intended), established a reputation as a real "cock teaser" who delighted in enticing an inebriated GI into expectations of a sex-filled night, providing he stood for round after round of drinks for her and her friends. Invariably, she would dump the poor sap just about the time the bar closed, quickly disappearing to powder her nose and exiting through the back door. The poor soldier was left to wonder where his date and money had gone. After hearing about this from several of my broke and emotionally frustrated men, I resolved to try to turn the tables on her if I could.

With a few crisp banknotes in my Class A's pocket, I arrived at the bar just as things began to heat up. A couple of my guys pointed out the girl in question, an attractive and petite brunette. From her demeanor, it was obvious that she considered herself to be something special; honestly, she was a "looker." I took the initiative as she surveyed the room, apparently looking for a new target. I strode to her table, introduced myself, and took her out onto the dance floor. As we swayed to the music, I deliberately emphasized physical contact, and after several dances and a few soft, suggestive whispers in her ear, we took a break. We sat and sipped several drinks as I played it out as carefully and deliberately as possible, coming on to her until finally, she suggested we leave and go to her place.

I finished the setup and told her I would meet her at the door after going to the men's room, but in reality, I just split through the back door, leaving her waiting in vain, stuck with the tab. It was a bit cruel, but she had it coming to her. I didn't lose any sleep over it, and the guys all thought it was fair payback, and they enjoyed the show.

I always worked out regularly, jogging and using the outdoor punching bag we had mounted on the back wall of the barrack. One day while working out, I noticed a large owl perched on the top of a nearby fence post. It piqued my hunting instincts, and I had never tasted owl, so I called for Rocci Cardaro to get one of the .22 rifles that the regiment kept for target practice. I didn't make any sudden moves so as not to scare the owl, and when Rocci returned and handed me the gun, I chambered a round, squeezed off one shot, and the owl toppled over dead. Rocci took a photo that shows the bird's wingspan to be over five feet! I caught hell for shooting the owl on post and nearly lost a stripe. I suppose it served me right.

About once every two weeks, a group of us would check out the half-dozen rifles, the .22 caliber ones and the .30-06 Springfield '03 sniper rifle that the regiment kept for target practice. We'd pile into a couple of jeeps and head out to a remote area of the post. Sometimes we would hunt deer, which Rocci would take back to the mess to be dressed down and roasted. Quite a few of us acquired a taste for venison steaks, but most often, we would just go target shooting at the post range for fun.

Over a few weeks, I had personally sighted each rifle and was confident in my ability to hit small targets at 100 yards consistently. The first time we all went out as a group, I had Rocci talk up his shooting skills while I kept my mouth shut for a while, then I challenged him to a match, best man wins. The others bought into it and placed their bets on Rocci; of course, I bet on myself.

After a few tentative shots, I cleaned them out of their cash. It only worked a couple of times before the whole company caught on to the con. The first time I kept the money, having a good laugh at my cleverness, but the next time I decided that if I wanted to keep my hide intact, it would be a good idea to stand beers for the guys at our favorite watering hole in town. At a dime a beer, we had a pretty good time.

While at Pescadero, one of the corporals assigned to my platoon was a big, dumb guy named Rusty Sawyer. He was an incorrigible troublemaker, always flaunting rules and army regulations, but always seemed to know when he had pushed the limit. Finally, fed up with what he perceived to be stupid regulations designed just to make his life difficult, he "went over the hill" after taps. I reported him absent without leave (AWOL) the following morning, and the word went out state-wide for the MPs to be on the lookout for him.

Not particularly clever, Sawyer attempted to hitchhike back home to Texas, but the Military Police picked him up within a day as he was trying to hitchhike near Fresno. As his platoon sergeant, it was my job to pick him up, so I checked out a jeep and headed east. The 160-mile trip out to Fresno did nothing to improve my feelings towards Sawyer, particularly since it was my first day off patrol that week, and I would prefer to be at the beach with my buddies.

With a warrant for him in hand, I pulled up in front of the Fresno police station, where my prodigal soldier was locked up for safekeeping. The officer on duty retrieved Sawyer from the holding cell and turned him over to me in handcuffs which I swapped for my own.

Billy with Rusty Sawyer on patrol, 1943. (Author's Collection)

I was anxious to get back on the road and make it back in time for a shower and good dinner, so I quickly signed the paperwork and shoved Rusty into the jeep's passenger seat, handcuffing his left wrist to the right side of the passenger seat frame. It would be extremely awkward for him to give me any trouble. After a couple of miles, Sawyer began to fidget in his seat and turned to me with a pleading look.

"Come on, Sarge," he said. "These cuffs are really uncomfortable. I can't sit like this for hours. Can't you take them off? I won't try anything funny."

I pulled over, unlocked the cuffs, and stared disgustedly at him, trying to get across to him just how frustrated I was with his shenanigans.

"If you try to make a run for it, I'll shoot you, and I don't care if it's in the back." To punctuate the statement, I drew my .45 pistol, flicked off the safety with my thumb, and chambered a round. I glared at him for a moment, then shoved it into the holster I was wearing on my left so it wouldn't interfere with the gear shift lever and would be well out of his reach.

He looked at me like I was nuts. "C'mon, Sarge, you've always been square with me. I wouldn't do that to you."

I just stared at him for a minute while I considered the options.

"Yeah, maybe," I replied. "But I'd shoot you, you know. I've had enough of your nonsense. You're nothing but trouble, and you've screwed up my first day off. I don't appreciate it, so don't give me any crap."

He sheepishly handed me back the cuffs, and the trip back to the regimental lockup at Gilroy was uneventful and quiet.

I couldn't figure Rusty out. He was a guy with personality and a rough charm, albeit not the highest IQ in the platoon, but seemingly without scruples or a sense of responsibility. He had consistently shown total disinterest in any attempt to give him leadership opportunities, although some hopeful officers had made him a corporal. Luckily, he still had his stripes, but he would definitely lose them this time. As I handed him over to the provost marshal at Gilroy, I asked him why he continued to pull such crap that only made his life in the army more difficult.

"Hell, Sarge," he responded, "I never volunteered, and I ain't ever again going to do anything I don't want to do. I'll guarantee you that I'll never leave the States!"

"Maybe so," I said, "but I don't see how you can just shrug off a bad conduct discharge, or even worse."

As I turned and walked back to the jeep, I thought, goodbye and good riddance! But Rusty was the proverbial bad penny, and I would see him again. But he would be someone else's problem, not mine.

Nello Ratliffe, who had earned the nickname Whitey back in basic training, found the time to fall in love with a girl while we were at Carmel. Although a few of the guys had pretty steady girlfriends by this time, I think we all thought he was nuts to get hitched, knowing full well that we could get orders to ship out at any time. But he was in love and determined to tie the knot. Perhaps he thought it would be his last chance at love and wanted to have something permanent in his life to come home to. I couldn't understand it. Rocci, Walter, Earl, and I were among the guys who attended the wedding and small reception. It was a small affair, and the reception dinner was at one of the local restaurants. I gave a toast, and we all danced with the bride and bridesmaids, but I made a point not to catch the garter. I had no intention of getting into a permanent relationship until after the war.

Billy with CQ, Nello crouched in back of Billy, fiancé, and a few buddies, Carmel, 1943. (Author's Collection)

My boxing training regimen kept me busy when I wasn't patrolling or pulling other duties on the post, but I tried to include a good long jog on the Pacific beach near Carmel as often as possible. A small black dog with a white patch on his chest, just a mutt, began following me each day along the beach. Each time he would show up at about the same spot and run alongside me. I found it amusing and took to feeding him tidbits I kept in my pockets. It was only a matter of time before the pup followed me home to our abandoned schoolhouse at Carmel-by-the-Sea. It seemed only natural for me to adopt him, and I named him "CQ," army slang for "Charge-of-Quarters," the guard duty that sergeants and privates were required to take in shifts while in barracks. The NCO is formally in charge of quarters, and a pair of privates act as "runners," doing the odd chores and keeping watch. Only the CQ is allowed to open the barracks doors.

CQ became the unofficial mascot of our patrol and went everywhere with me in my off-duty hours. He even did a few night patrols with me. Nobody objected to CQ when he moved in with us, and he shows up in several of the group photographs. Inquisitive like all dogs, CQ explored the beach as I jogged, and on more than one occasion, a sunbathing lady was startled by a cold, wet nose poking into forbidden places! It's incredible what conversation starters dogs can be!

I became very fond of CQ, but when the unit moved onto Fort Ord in September of 1943, I could not take him with me. I had no idea how long we would be on the post, and the army took a dim view of pets in barracks, so I went looking for a good home for him. In an inspired moment, I approached a K-9 training unit. "He's just a lovable dumb mutt," I told the trainers. They didn't seem discouraged and reassured me that they would see that he got adopted if he didn't make the grade. After asking them to keep me posted on CQ's progress, I said a tearful goodbye to the pooch.

Almost a year later, while in England, a letter from the K-9 trainers that my parents forwarded caught up with me. They told me that CQ had completed his training and had already seen action in Italy, where he earned a decoration for courage under fire! How's that for a happy ending for a dumb mutt? I just hope he made it home and to a good family.

Our patrol bases shifted several times during the year as the units rotated their patrol routes: Morro Bay State Park, Monterey, and Pescadero. Christmas of 1943 found us still near Pescadero, which was at least a livelier town than Seligman or Valentine, Arizona. The city had three beer taverns and a high school that hosted a New Year's dance in the GIs' honor. This time we had turkey with all the trimmings, plus a tree in the barracks that we decorated with popcorn strings, foil tinsel, and photos of loved ones.

Many local families, with members serving in the armed forces, opened their homes to us for the holidays. Only a lucky five percent of the regiment could spend Christmas at home, chosen by lottery. Those who had duty on Christmas or New Year's Eve were on the receiving end of pies, cakes, cookies, and other Christmas treats. Despite the lack of snow, we Midwestern GIs did our best to celebrate. Many of the boys ended up being carried back to camp on New Year's Day, and all the barracks had handwritten signs that cautioned, "Walk Lightly, Men Sick."

Chapter 9

On the Road Again

On February 4, 1944, the 125th Infantry Regiment finally received orders to leave California. The next day we loaded up, boarded a train, and took a three-day trip to Camp Maxey, near Paris, Texas. Maxey was a relatively new camp constructed in early 1942 as the wartime home of the 102nd Infantry Division of the Missouri and Kansas National Guard. Throughout 1942 and 1943, army contractors had built new encampments at a feverish pace, with prefabricated structures put up at the astonishing rate of one every thirty-eight minutes! At Maxey, the standard army two-story, white frame buildings with green-shingled roofs seemed to spread for miles.

Situated on a lake, the camp recreational facilities were excellent, but we had little time to use them. As usual, we were in the dark about what was in store for us, and rumors circulated like the West Texas dust. The regiment immediately pushed us through an intensive three-week training program to prepare us for combat. To confirm our suspicions, within a few days of our arrival, our captain announced that anyone who wanted to see their families or to take care of personal business should put in for leave. I had not seen my family for three years, so I put in a request chit, and on February 27, I headed home for an all-too-brief visit.

Once again, I boarded a train with dozens of other GIs and watched the sights of wartime America unfold. Since that first train ride to Camp Grant, gas rationing had noticeably reduced road traffic. Service uniforms of all branches were standard on every train station platform, and we passed dozens of long freight trains loaded with troops and military equipment. But for the most part, life appeared to carry on much as it had before the war.

I arrived home on short notice, having just had time to make a quick phone call before I boarded the train. The reception was warm, and it felt good to be home again. My parents, sister, and younger brother, Steve, were there. But my two older brothers, John and Andy, were now in the Pacific. John had become an officer with the 1st Cavalry Division in the Pacific, and Andy was an MP in the motorcycle corps on the West Coast. Andy and I had corresponded and even spoke on the phone on a few occasions, but unfortunately, we were never able to get together in California. I would not see either of them until late 1945.

The familiar surroundings were comforting, and the home cooking was terrific. Of course, my mother fixed all my favorite foods. I spent hours just walking as Steve tagged along, remembering how things used to be: the hunting we used to do as kids, hours spent on the golf course, boxing with Jimmy, and wondering what the future held for me. It was hard to relax completely, with thoughts of the war always lurking in the back of my mind. Would we be shipped out to the Pacific? The remaining 32nd Division was already making headlines in New Guinea, and we were still a detached regiment. Were we destined always to be a security force? A photo of me at home seems to show the subtle apprehension on my face.

Billy at home on leave from Camp Maxey, TX, March 1944. (Author's Collection)

Eugene Robillard and Gayle Palmer, my two old classmates who had been classified 4-F by the draft board, were still around. But now, we had little in common except the past. After an hour or two of swapping stories of the past three years over a burger and Coke, we drifted apart. I did go to a Saturday night dance and found that the uniform and sergeant's stripes attracted female attention, but mostly I just stayed around the house, doing odd chores and spending time with Mom and Dad. The week ended all too soon, and this time the whole family drove me back to the train station.

That farewell has stayed with me for a long time, and I replayed it in my mind countless times in the year to come. The Soviet Union had been pushing Churchill and Roosevelt to open a Western Front to draw German forces from Russia and the Baltic states. The newspapers were full of speculation about how soon it might happen. We all knew I was going to England and likely going into combat soon, but no one wanted to raise the subject. I was infantry and could be on the front lines in months. We didn't speak of it, just hugged and said a tearful goodbye. After boarding the train, I found a spot at an open window and stuck my head out to watch the familiar figures on the platform until they faded out of sight.

I returned to Camp Maxey on April 4, and just five days later, the 125th Infantry Regiment was reassigned to the XXIII Corps, destined to deploy to the European Theater of Operations (ETO). This move was a huge incentive to get serious about training because we all expected to be shipped overseas within a few months to relieve an exhausted front-line regiment. But there was a twist of fate that I never saw coming.

While I was on leave, the War Department had placed an urgent requisition for replacements, anticipating heavy losses in the Normandy invasion. The army was stripping stateside units of personnel to bolster the divisions overseas, and the 125th was required to supply 800 volunteers, assignment unspecified. As I saw it, my First Sergeant, a disagreeable, arrogant, brown-nosing lout named Bremer, saw a chance to get rid of me and generously added my name to the list.

Bremer was a long-time National Guard type, neither exceptionally bright nor educated and considered any subordinate NCO to be a threat to his authority. His strong suit was pushing paper, and there was no love lost between us. He made a big deal out of telling me that his choices were impersonal, that he had to choose at least one platoon sergeant and at least a dozen other men from my platoon. I didn't know any details about the War Department's demand, and if I had, I might not have been so angry, but I got right into Bremer's face and told him what I thought.

"You son-of-a-bitch," I said. "We both know you're just trying to get rid of me! This company has three other platoon sergeants; you didn't have to pick me. You chose me because I won't kiss your fat, red ass! I don't know where you'll end up in this war, but I intend to come back, and when I do, I'm going to look you up, and your ass is grass, and I'll be the lawn mower!"

I soon discovered that nearly a third Baker Company's men were getting shipped out with me, including Rocci Cardaro, Earl Robovitski, Al Slivatz, Nello Ratliff, Walter Barc, and another buddy named Charlie Schwaenk. I seldom saw them aboard our troop ship, and we were only reunited briefly at the Replacement Depot in England. Only Walter and I got assigned to the same regiment, destined to be together until the war's end. But the die was cast, and there was nothing I could do to change it, so I tried to be philosophical, reminding myself that at least I wouldn't have to put up with Bremer anymore.

I learned more than 60 years later that after the landings in North Africa, Operation Torch, the headquarters of the Army Ground Forces (AGF), complained bitterly to the War Department that a high proportion of the replacements were unsuited and unqualified for combat. Stateside regiments had seized the opportunity to eliminate the dregs of their units: disciplinary problems, those physically in poor condition, or those poorly or incompletely trained. This time they demanded better soldiers, ready for combat.

As planning for the invasion of France, Operation Overlord, moved forward in the early months of 1944, the situation became even more complex. The War Department issued an order that no inductee younger than eighteen years and six months of age could be assigned to an infantry or armored replacement depot, which we called a "repple-depple." Because the quota for those two branches was 22,000 men, any stateside regiments not attached to a division, such as the 125th Infantry, were stripped of their most experienced men. The young, ineligible inductees replaced them until they reached at least eighteen years and nine months. That would ensure that by the time they finished training, they would have turned nineteen.

Following the directive, the 125th gave up 800 men, nearly the equivalent of an entire battalion, who would be shipped to the European Theater as replacements for the divisions and regiments expected to sustain heavy losses in Normandy.

I had no idea at the time what fate had in store for the rest of the 125th Infantry Regiment, and we fully expected it to be shipped together to the European Theater. I would have been astonished to know that the regiment would never deploy overseas. Instead of the proposed transfer to the XXIII Corps, the regiment was assigned to the XXXVI

Corps, a dedicated training unit and the only corps not to go overseas in World War Two. I noted wryly in my journal, "Everything happens to Dick Tracy and me!"

My pre-overseas movement (POM) training continued at Camp Maxey through March and April, and finally, on May 5, 1944, the 800 of us boarded another train. For once, we knew our destination: Camp Myles Standish, outside Boston, which would be our Port of Embarkation. There was no doubt that we were on our way to the European Theater instead of the Pacific, but our unit assignments were still unknown. As we boarded the train, we were cautioned to keep our destination secret since there was always the danger of word filtering back to the Nazis. As the saying went, "Loose lips sink ships!"

Our journey turned out not to be direct to Boston but rather by way of Fort Meade, Maryland. We spent a day getting issued new uniforms, field gear, and other equipment to bring our kit up to the standard for overseas movement. Everything we had lugged with us for three years got replaced: blankets, web gear, haversacks, holsters, bayonets, first aid kits, canteens, trenching tools, shelter halves, etcetera. I didn't think anything was wrong with the old gear, but I believe it was to ensure that everyone started with a full allotment of new combat-ready equipment. It was easier to do it in the States than in Great Britain.

Camp Myles Standish was roughly 30 miles south of Boston near Taunton, Massachusetts. After New York, it was the second major port of embarkation on the East Coast. Myles Standish was a vast staging camp for troops preparing to ship out and a prison camp for several thousand Italian and German prisoners of war. The camp population varied weekly, but it topped out near 50,000 men by the time we arrived. Trainloads of GIs arrived daily at the camp railroad station, with multiple tracks serving both arrivals and departures for the Boston docks. The camp staff had become so efficient that they could process an entire division in a single day.

Our stay was very short, just three days. The camp personnel ran us through a final round of physical and dental exams, vaccinations, lectures, and a mock abandon-ship drill at the reservoir located at the north edge of the camp. To me, this evolution seemed like a bit of wishful thinking. I never for a moment thought that we would be able to get off a torpedoed ship in any semblance of order. The deck of a rapidly sinking ship hardly lends itself to formations and orderly evacuation, even without heavy seas, darkness, and high winds. I was pretty cynical about this and expected that it would inevitably be every man for himself unless the conditions were ideal.

We had lectures on how to handle lifeboats and the equipment stowed in them, but the water temperature of the North Atlantic was in everyone's mind. I recall one smart aleck remark about the Titanic, which brought a few snickers. Remembering how many had gone into the frozen water and drowned put a bit of fear into my heart. Mortally afraid of being trapped below decks, I resolved to spend as little time there as possible.

Everyone was restricted to camp, and we quenched our thirst with watered-down beer at the post canteen. We just had to wait for the army bureaucracy to work its magic. On the second morning, while exiting the canteen, I glanced at a group of men in prisoners' stripes cutting the grass. Lo and behold, there was my old California nemesis, Rusty

Sawyer. What a small world it was! He worked in the prison detachment and was unashamed to see someone he knew. I assumed his belligerence and defiance of army regulations landed him in hot water again! We recognized each other simultaneously, and he waved and flashed me a big grin. He reminded me of our last conversation at Fort Ord as I walked over to him.

"Hi, Sarge, I told you I'd never ship out, didn't I?"

"What did you do to get in trouble this time," I asked him.

"Oh, nothing much, just went over the hill again, but this time it took the MPs a month to catch me."

"I guess you were right, Rusty," I responded, "but it doesn't look like you're going anywhere else very soon either. I don't know how you can live with what you're doing, but good luck." As I shook my head, turned, and walked back to the transient barracks, I kept wondering which one of us was the stupid one?

Chapter 10

The Convoy

On May 11, we received word that we were to pack our barrack bags. We deposited them at the depot, and at dawn the following morning, we boarded a New Haven Railroad troop train for the short trip to the Boston docks. When the train stopped at the foot of the pier, pretty, smiling Red Cross girls served us coffee and donuts.

As we began to sort through the piles of duffle bags on the pier, I looked up at the ship, towering more than fifty feet above me, with four rows of portholes and huge double-wide cargo doors on her side. She looked enormous. The SS *John J. Ericsson* was a 609-foot long, 21,532-ton passenger liner, first launched in 1928 in Sweden as the *Kungsholm* and pressed into service for the U.S. Government as a troopship. She sported a depressing gray and blue "dazzle" camouflage paint scheme, adorned with life rafts and double-tiered lifeboats. Despite her size and twin stacks, she failed to give me any safety assurance.

We formed up by units, and the officers took a careful muster. I was surprised to learn that several men had gone AWOL to avoid sailing. It was a relief to know that none of my friends were on the list. Hoisting my bag over my shoulder, I marched up the gangway and stepped through the double doors onto the linoleum deck as an army captain shouted out our berthing assignments. A sailor was assigned to lead the way, and he showed us down a maze of ladders into a stifling, white-painted compartment on the lower deck. I didn't expect anything cushy, but the army packed us like sardines in a can, with the enlisted men bunked in the refitted crew quarters and the officers in the staterooms on the upper decks.

The portholes, which let in very little light, were permanently dogged shut. We squeezed into row-upon-row of four-tiered bunks, the lowest one just clearing the deck below and so closely spaced that occupants barely had room to roll over. A First World War sergeant who had shipped over to France in 1917, with whom I had struck up a conversation at the Standish canteen, had advised me about which bunk to take. Following his guidance and pulling rank, I grabbed the top bunk so I wouldn't risk some seasick slob vomiting onto me. Plus, I would be closer to the ventilation ducts and wouldn't have other GIs climbing over my bunk. I was glad I listened to him. It took a few tries to figure out how to get into my bunk. The easiest way to manage it gracefully was to step on the first and second bunks, grab an overhead pipe, then swing my body onto the canvas. I'm sure it drove the guys in the lower bunks crazy until I found another place to sleep.

Fresh water was at a premium on the ship, and saltwater showers were virtually impossible. The first time

I tried it, I learned that no matter how hard you tried to scrub, the salt water wouldn't allow the soap to lather up. The resulting mess was disgusting, like rubbing cottage cheese over your body. Within days the body odor on the lower deck was incredible, not to mention the added pungent aroma of vomit since more than two-thirds of the troops became seasick. Locker space was sparse, and equipment hung from every hook, angle iron, bracket, and overhead pipe, making the compartment look like an olive drab jungle.

Living in such squalor for two weeks was more than many of us wanted to tolerate, and I desperately wanted to escape from below deck. Anything was preferable to staying in the funky, stuffy berthing compartment. Some of us began to seek a better place to bed down, and by the second day at sea, I learned that if I volunteered for guard detail, I could sleep up on deck, under tarps spread between the lifeboats. The chill wind off the North Atlantic was infinitely better than sweating in the steam bath below decks. More important to me, as a staff sergeant who had to interact with the officers above decks, I could sneak in a freshwater shower every few days!

The *John J. Ericsson* sailed with the tide early on May 13, loaded with 5,452 soldiers, and proceeded slowly to the convoy assembly point off Halifax, Nova Scotia. We had no sooner cleared Boston harbor than the ship began pitching into the swells rolling in from the open Atlantic, throwing spray over the bow and rolling from side to side. The corkscrew motion grew more and more pronounced as we headed into the open seas. Soldiers by the score began to get sick, and it never ceased. It almost seemed contagious, and those of us who could keep control of our stomachs tried our best to stay away from those who couldn't.

Convoy CU-24 was a "fast convoy" capable of a sustained fourteen knots (convoys were limited to the speed of the slowest ship, usually about eight knots for merchant ships), finally assembled at the rendezvous point east of Halifax on the third day. When we joined the troop ships from New York and the tankers from the Caribbean, the convoy consisted of forty-four transports, cargo ships, and tankers formed up in three columns. Our escort consisted of fourteen warships, of which twelve were nimble little anti-submarine destroyer escorts who took up stations around the convoy, always with several positioned well ahead of the convoy to screen for U-boats.

The USS *Marblehead*, a light cruiser, provided our anti-aircraft defenses, and a navy fleet oiler was attached to resupply the escorts. We were the third ship back in the left, or northern column. When not on the guard patrols, I spent hours staring at the dark, slate-gray sea, and I wasn't the only one. We carefully studied the foam-topped waves, alert and afraid we might see a periscope or torpedo wake.

I was astonished at the number of ships: there were so many that I could not make out the tail end of the convoy stretching several miles behind. Watching the escorts weaving around the columns and taking up their flanking stations, I counted nine other troopships: the *Blenville*, *Borinquin*, *Brazil*, *Colombia*, *E.B. Alexander*, *Excelsior*, *G.S. Simonds*, *Highland Chieftain*, and *Uruguay*. A major with whom I struck up a conversation at the rail one day told me that the troop total was well over 28,000 men. The remainder of the convoy was a mixture of freighters and tankers, loaded with millions of gallons of gasoline. I felt a mix of pity and admiration for the crews of the tankers. If they were torpedoed, their chance of survival was nil: if the fire didn't get them, the freezing Atlantic would. Two types of hell.

The army has always had class distinctions between officers, NCOs, and enlisted men, but the differences were dramatic aboard troop ships. The commissioned officers lived a life of comparative luxury compared to the NCOs and ordinary soldiers. Billeted in the ship's staterooms, two, three, or four to a room, they ate in the dining room, off linen and fine China, ordered from menus, and enjoyed a level of cuisine unavailable to the men below decks.

Our GI fare consisted of boiled eggs and bread, or bread and boiled eggs. Occasionally we had chipped beef on toast (the ubiquitous "shit on a shingle"); greasy chicken-a'-la-king (greasy food and sea sickness don't mix well); mystery stew (God only knew what was in it!); boiled potatoes; and of course, the GI staple, Spam. Those who weren't too seasick to eat could indulge to their heart's content, assuming that they liked the repetitive menu.

About four days out, in the early hours before dawn, I was patrolling down a passageway when I heard moaning off to the right or starboard side. Concerned that someone was seriously ill, I turned a corner, looked in through an open hatch, and discovered a gagged GI, strapped over a barrel, wrists tied to ankles, trousers down below his knees, with his backside exposed and bleeding. Two of the ship's sailors, apparently a couple of what we called "queers," were using his rectum for target practice. Their attention was focused on their victim, and they didn't hear me approach. Momentarily shocked but furious, I pulled my service pistol, stepped into the compartment, and worked the slide loudly to chamber a round.

"Freeze!" I ordered, getting their full attention as I leveled the pistol at the nearest sailor. Their eyes were as big as cow pies as they stared down the barrel of the Colt pistol.

"Oh, God, don't shoot, sergeant!" cried the sailor.

"You're disgusting, both of you," I shouted. "Don't tempt me! Move out into the passageway, one at a time, and don't try any funny business."

There was nothing I could immediately do for the sobbing soldier, so I stepped out of the compartment, told the poor guy I'd send a medic, and pulled the door behind me. I motioned the two sailors to head down the passageway and up the nearest ladder to the guard office. It would have been a pleasure to put a slug into those two scumbags!

As soon as I explained the situation to the Duty Officer, the ship's master-at-arms took the sailors to the ship's brig, and a hospital corpsman went to tend to the GI. I gave a detailed written statement, but I don't know what the affair's outcome was. I heard second-hand that the sailors were charged and would face a court-martial and possibly a long stretch in Portsmouth Naval Prison. I think they should have turned them over to us GIs instead. It would have been swift justice, although a bit short on mercy with a cold, wet ending.

At sea, the ship went to battle stations, or General Quarters as the navy called it, every other day or so. As the ship's company ran to their stations, we troops had to muster on the upper deck or in our assigned compartments. We donned our life jackets and got lectured on how to find our life raft and how to abandon ship. The first time it made us nervous, but after the second or third GQ drill, we paid little attention. Many fellows were so seasick that they would have preferred to drown.

On the seventh day out, as we were approaching the north coast of Ireland, General Quarters sounded for real. A German U-boat was reported to have torpedoed a lone ship, but I never knew if it was a rumor, an actual sighting, a sinking, or just a bogus periscope sighting.

As I stood at the rail, staring out at sea with the next ship just 1000 yards abeam, I realized that the North Atlantic was black and white, almost devoid of color. By daytime, the sky was a constant swirling mix of light and medium grays that met the dark, cold gray of the ocean at the misty horizon. The ships were camouflaged in shades of gray and gray-blue, only accented by the bright white of the curling bow waves and the churning propeller wakes. Primary colors had ceased to exist out here. The scene made me shiver involuntarily.

I watched, fascinated but nervous, as one of our escorting destroyers, only half the size of the Ericsson, peeled gracefully out of formation to investigate the contact. Her propellers thrashed as she accelerated, and her crew rushed to their battle stations, stripping protective canvas covers off their guns. The men in the gun tubs and at the stern depth charge racks wore puffy, gray life preservers. The oversized light-blue helmets, worn over sound-powered communication headsets, looked like giant upside-down salad bowls. It struck me as odd looking, but I was glad they were there.

The lookouts, and of course the soldiers that crowded the rails, searched the sea endlessly for a tell-tail periscope wake, or "feather." A couple of the escorting destroyers crisscrossed the convoy formation in their sonar search patterns, frequently signaling to the senior escort with flashing lights. But nothing materialized except a pod of whales. It was a relief to all of us. Our briefings informed us that survival time in the frigid North Atlantic was about fifteen minutes, and few of us would be lucky to make it into one of the ship's boats.

I suffered from seasickness but stayed out of the closed compartments and on deck as much as possible. Keeping busy with guard detail helped, especially when the weather worsened as we entered the Western Approaches, the region around Northern Ireland. Winds and swells from the Irish Sea met the Gulf Stream, and the ship pitched and rolled worse than ever.

I watched the escorts, the "small boys," pitch heavily, burying their bows into the advancing swells, then shuddering upright as the foaming water cascaded down their decks. I was glad to live on a larger ship and continued to huddle on the upper decks, under the tarps between the boats, and swathed in two woolen blankets. I thought the risk of pneumonia was a better alternative to suffocating in the stink below decks. The goal was to keep something in our stomachs, as it would be better to vomit up something than retching our guts out with dry heaves. Early in the voyage, I had begun eating cans of olives and bread that I carried around and chewed slowly. It helped, but not much.

Chapter 11

Camp March Hare, England

On May 23, 1944, during a slow, steady, all-day rain, the *John J. Ericsson* moored at Liverpool, England. The voyage took twelve days, following the roundabout track north of Ireland to avoid the dreaded U-boat wolfpacks. With little fanfare but plenty of confusion, we collected our gear and marched down the gangway onto the dock, where we were sorted out by name, then loaded onto waiting trucks. I was pleased to see the familiar faces of my buddies from Baker Company, and I hoped we had the same destination.

Located on England's west coast, Liverpool is the gateway to the Midlands of England. We were promptly loaded onto deuce-and-a-half trucks and taken to the 12th Replacement Depot at Tidworth, in the south of England and not far from Southampton. From there, we would be assigned piecemeal to the various regiments needing replacement men to bring them up to full strength.

With tarps drawn down over the back of the deuce-and-a-half truck to ward off the rain, I could see very little of Liverpool as we lurched and bumped our way through the city. It was probably just as well not to have much of a view since driving on the left side of the road would have been a bit unsettling. The rain slacked off as we climbed away from the coast, and we rolled the rear tarp up and tied it off so we could get our first look at the English countryside.

The scenery was beautiful and left no doubt that we were in a strangely different country. The gentle mist softened the rich green of the hedges and woods. Aging manors, like crouching giants, were barely visible beyond the bordering trees and the low, gray stone walls and cottages flanked the road for miles laced by tendrils of ivy and moss clung to the edges. The villages were filled with half-timbered shops, some with thatched roofs. Leaded glass windows with small diamond panes reflected the soft light with uneven flashes of color. Although we passed very few private vehicles, bicycles seemed to be parked everywhere, waiting patiently for their owners. The smells were different too, and I recall the fragrance of baking bread as we passed through one village and fresh manure and freshly cut grass at the farms.

We rolled into Tidworth late in the day and unloaded, made our way to our temporary billet, dropped our duffle bags, and headed to the chow hall for a quick supper. Several of us huddled together after chow and speculated about the army's plans for us, but none of us had a clue. After a few minutes, I gave up and hit the rack. The Replacement Depots, or "repple-depples," were a depressing experience. The army policy was not to keep men together by unit but to parcel us out as needed. It certainly harmed our morale, but it had been army policy since World War One, and I guess it served the purpose of moving thousands of men into understrength units.

I worried about where I would end up, but after eleven days of boredom, I finally received orders to the 82nd Airborne Division, 325th Glider Infantry Regiment. Happily, Walter Barc received the same assignment, so at least I would know someone in my new regiment. But we were both surprised because it was common knowledge that the airborne divisions were all-volunteer outfits.

I can hardly express how disturbing it was to be assigned to an airborne unit. I had never even been in an airplane, let alone a glider, and I had always heard that the Airborne was an exclusive volunteer unit. Obviously, things had changed. If First Sergeant Bremer had known where I would be posted, he would have been pleased with himself. Perhaps he knew when he "volunteered" me that it was for the airborne, but I doubted it. I always tried to make the best of any situation, so I vowed to do my best to adapt.

Regimental camps had been set up throughout England to accommodate the massive build-up of troops preparing for the pending invasion of Europe. The standing joke was that there was so much military equipment and so many GIs in England that the island was liable to sink! Our new home was located outside the small town of Scraptoft, near Leicester, over 120 miles north of London.

Our 6x6 truck with several dozen replacements onboard pulled into our new regimental camp late on June 4. Camp March Hare, home to the 325th Glider Infantry Regiment (GIR), was just one of the regiments that made up the 82nd Airborne Division. The camp was bordered on the north by a golf course, of all things, and as we dismounted from the truck, I looked wistfully at it. How I would have loved to play even nine holes, but I learned that it was closed to golfers and reserved for our tactical exercises. Hamilton Lane bordered the camp on the west, and a one-lane road marked the eastern edge, running from Scraptoft to Beebe, the next town to the south. As I looked around the camp, I was surprised to see very few men, almost as if it was deserted. Walt asked me what I thought was going on, and all I could think was that the entire regiment was on field maneuvers. We dismounted in front of an administrative building, and a master sergeant and captain formed us up and took a muster.

A second lieutenant in our group, Andersen, asked the obvious question on everyone's mind.

"Sir," he asked, "Is the regiment on maneuvers now?"

The captain took a moment to look us over, then addressed all of us. "The 325th Glider Infantry departed five days ago. Their destination is top secret now, but you can guess where that might be." He smiled, acknowledging the surprised looks on our faces, then continued.

"For the time being, the camp is on lockdown. You will not discuss the unit's movement with anyone. As new to the glider infantry, you have new skills to learn and will be assigned temporarily to training platoons. Once the regiment returns, you will be assigned to replace losses. In the meantime, you will maintain the camp, participate in logistical support, and begin a training regimen."

We were dismissed and told what our company assignments were, and because army camps are all organized according to a uniform plan, it was a simple matter to identify our tents. We retrieved our duffels from the truck, and I looked closely at my surroundings. What I saw was depressing.

Camp March Hare was a sea of mud. The frequent intermittent rains of England and the constant foot and vehicle traffic through the camp ensured that the soil, once tilled farmland, was churned into a sticky, slippery mess. It had rained shortly before our arrival, and the mud was ankle deep. Everything and everyone was splattered with mud and damp. We had the cleanest uniforms and stood out like sore thumbs. I stepped aside as a jeep passed and splashed mud everywhere as it hit a pothole, including onto the occupants. Our tent city had the familiar twelve-by-twelve-foot tents laid out in rows on company streets that seemed more like muddy rivers. A clerical sergeant who walked with us summarized the layout, pointing out the parade ground, motor pools, mess halls, and field hospital. We passed a Red Cross canteen, catching a whiff of fresh donuts, and made a mental note to return soon. A few corrugated metal Nissen huts served as headquarters and the individual battalion mess halls. As if the mud wasn't bad enough, our companion explained that there was no hot water, little heat or electric lighting in the GI tents, and no floors either!

With new men arriving almost daily, it was organized confusion, with training taking priority over everything. Life in the tent camps was not much different than it had been in Louisiana, except now we had six men in a tent instead of four back at Camp Livingston. But at least the chow was infinitely better than it had been aboard the ship, and it didn't take long for newcomers to get an appetite back now that we were on dry land.

The camp was blessed with a well-run canteen operated by the American Red Cross. Although the original ARC lady that set it up, Edith Steiger, had been recently transferred, her successor continued the operation, and I wish I could recall her name. The canteen consisted of four larger tents. One served as a kitchen, another for food service, and one for reading, writing letters, and simple recreation that consisted of chess, checkers, and cards. The fourth tent was the office of the Red Cross. The ARC canteen offered fresh coffee and donuts from early morning until evening, and it was the bright spot in the camp. It's hard to describe the pleasure of a fresh, hot donut and coffee after an all-night field maneuver. Everyone came to appreciate the ARC lady, but Edith had left big shoes to fill, and the old-timers all spoke of her as an angel. The only entertainment in camp was in a circus-sized tent designated for movies and church services.

The following day, June 5, dawned to overcast skies, with clouds scudding east under a brisk wind as rain soaked the camp. No training took place, and the word spread rapidly that the invasion was in motion. The airborne drops would occur in the pre-dawn hours the next morning, followed by glider assaults after daybreak. The heavy equipment and engineers would go by sea on subsequent days once the Allies established a beachhead. But the new replacement troopers would not be going in with them. We airborne neophytes would help with the load-out, but we were not yet sufficiently trained or integrated with the airborne to function effectively. I felt a mixture of disappointment and relief, but this meant that the war in Europe was shifting into high gear, and our time would come soon.

As the armada began to move, we loaded trucks at Scraptoft and C-47s at the scattered airfields with tons of gear. We kept it up for the next six days, working shifts and keeping trucks and supplies moving around the clock. As a staff sergeant, I acted more like a loadmaster, lugging around a clipboard with pages of inventory, storage locations, airfield destinations, truck assignments, and aircraft loads. I worked myself ragged, catching a few hours of sleep at a time. Finally, the logistics effort began to assume a steadier pace after a few weeks. Worn out, I got a weekend pass. I had a plan in mind.

As an avid golfer, I had always dreamed of making the pilgrimage to the home of "The Game," the Royal and Ancient St. Andrews Golf Club, near Edinburgh, Scotland. Corporal Charlie Baumgartner, a fellow replacement and a fellow golf enthusiast, decided to join me. We had carefully studied the train schedule and, weather permitting, we would be able to make the trip to Edinburgh, play eighteen holes, and be back well before muster on Monday. We packed a bag late on Friday and hitched a truck ride from Scraptoft to the Great Central Railway Station, where we bought tickets on the Great Northern Railway.

The train ride was an eye-opener. Until then, all I had seen of England was out the open back of a six-by-six truck or hiking into town for a pint in the evening. In summer, the countryside was lush and green, with orderly fields and pastures interspersed with quaint villages of brick and half-timbered homes and shops. As the rails climbed slowly through Yorkshire and Northumbria into the Scottish Highlands, the weather became cooler, and the countryside thinned out to high, heather-covered hills and lush, deep valleys. It was spectacular, and so different from the sights I'd seen in the States.

Arriving at the Edinburgh station, we hitched a ride on a farm truck to St. Andrews, the high temple of golf since 1754. The kindly farmer deposited us right at the front gates. Stepping onto the gravel drive, we paused to admire the towering, many-gabled clubhouse. Set on the shore of the North Sea, the surrounding countryside struck me as remarkable for its lack of trees. The cold and often fierce sea winds scoured the land so that the clubhouse stood out like a sentinel, guarding the sacred links, seeming more like a cathedral than a warm haven.

We climbed the stone steps to be met by a liveried concierge who escorted us to the office of the club captain, an elderly gentleman with a bushy mustache and tweed coat, straight out of a movie. We didn't know if we would be allowed to play, but he assured us we were welcomed as soldiers. A lot of GIs used their passes to head into Scotland to avoid the more frequent air raids over England, not to mention the V-1 "Buzz Bomb" attacks on the Midlands and London, which had begun on June 13, just one week after the Normandy landings. But I suspected that we might be a rare sight, with most GIs preferring to seek out the nightlife of the cities. The club captain probably wondered why we hadn't sought a friendly, cozy pub with a few pints.

After introducing and telling him about our golf experience, he escorted us to the caddy shack. The club graciously rented us each a set of clubs and a ball for approximately $1.25, and each of us bought two extra balls for about thirty-five cents each. An elderly Scottish fellow, preparing to tee off, graciously invited us to join him. As we shed our caps, neckties, and jackets, we must have made a strange sight: one dapper man in tweed knickers, knit vest, and wool cap, and two American soldiers in greens and boots!

That round of golf was the experience of a lifetime. Never before had I played such rough and narrow fairways. The massive sand bunkers and grassy mounds rippled the perimeter of the fairways and greens. Compared with Brookwood Country Club back home, the course layout seemed designed more for the pleasure of mountain goats and was quite intimidating.

After warming up a bit on the first two holes, I played relatively well, although nowhere near the par golf I played back home. I avoided embarrassing myself and finished the round with a dozen balls in my bag, which tells you how much time I spent digging through the rough for my ball! Baumgartner lost several balls but found others and played like a typical weekend golfer. We both had a great time. Our companion failed to break a hundred, but he was kind, bought us each a pint of ale after the round, then graciously drove us back to the train station. We made it back to Scraptoft before taps on Sunday.

Looking back on the experience, struggling with the Scottish gentleman's accent was nearly as challenging as the golf course, and it took me a moment to realize that "laddie" was me. It was the best weekend I spent in the United Kingdom, and I would daydream of it often in the coming months.

As I learned more about how the airborne operated, I felt that I would need to put myself forward to be accepted.

I was a platoon sergeant but felt uncomfortable as an airborne "newbie." I gave a lot of thought to it and recalled that one of the officers mentioned the Pathfinders. The airborne divisions knew they would take heavy casualties in Normandy, so they were looking for eager candidates to undergo Pathfinder training. They were volunteers from each airborne battalion, with the mission to parachute onto the drop and landing zones several hours before the main force to set up marker beacons for the airlift bringing in the paratroopers and gliders. Using a combination of luminous panels, Aldis lamps, and Krypton lights, which were reportedly visible for 25 miles, the Pathfinders would mark the multiple paratroop Drop Zones (DZs) and glider Landing Zones (LZs).

Specially trained two-man teams would deploy the radio beacon system, named "Eureka," which broadcast a signal that the aircraft receivers, called "Rebecca," could home in on and ultimately be guided the last few miles by the visual markers. The system was used for the 82nd Airborne jump into Volturno, Italy, and the landings in France.

I suppose I was a bit arrogant and cocky, but I always considered myself self-confident, a cut above the average GI, and able to take care of myself in a scrap. I convinced myself that becoming a Pathfinder, the elite of the elite would be an excellent way to assert myself and gain the acceptance of the airborne veterans. Most of them had been together since basic training in the States and had become a tight-knit group. Walter Barc thought I was crazy to consider the Pathfinders, but I put in my request to volunteer.

By July 2, I had orders to the Parachute Jumping School at Chilton Foliat, Berkshire, perhaps fifty miles west of London. Several of us volunteers were trucked down to RAF Ramsbury, the airfield where the school was organized to train men who had not been through formal jump training in the States. Skirting London to the north took almost the entire day, and it was late afternoon when I arrived. After check-in, the school issued a few new pieces of equipment, including the coveted high, lace-up jump boots that give ankles better stability. I discarded the infantry ankle-high rough-out boots and laced leggings, bloused my trouser legs under condoms that I tied at the boot-top, and admired myself with the proper airborne look. This affectation made all of us stand a bit taller and straighter and began to make me feel like part of an elite unit, even though I hadn't done a darn thing yet.

Besides 2nd Lieutenant Irvin "Andy" Anderson, our replacement platoon leader, with whom I trained at Scraptoft and flew into Holland, I have little recollection of most of the other airborne officers, with a few exceptions. The most glaring one happened to be the company commander at the parachute training school. Captain Herbert Sobel had been recently replaced as the company commander of Easy Company, 506th Parachute Infantry Regiment, and made the school commander. He was rumored to be almost universally despised and distrusted by his men. (If you have seen the HBO series "Band of Brothers," the name will be familiar.)

The word in the street was that, despite his abilities as a training officer, Sobel's arrogance was exceeded only by his incompetence in fieldwork and tactics. Fortunately for the men of Easy Company, he had been reassigned to the parachute school before D-Day. As we began the course, we quickly realized that if we had someone like him leading us into combat, he would get most of us killed. His type was rare in the airborne, which was led by some of the finest officers in the army. They prided themselves on their reputation, led from the front, and were as tough as any of their men. I heard one of my classmates say in disgust that if Sobel went into combat, he would probably get a .45 caliber bullet to the back of the head or perhaps a hand grenade in his foxhole. He wore a wedding ring, so he had a wife who probably loved him. I hope Sobel made it home for her sake, but thankfully, I never saw him after parachute school. I never knew what became of him. I just hope he didn't get any men killed.

I moved into a tent on the edge of the airfield with five other guys, and with about two dozen other men, I began the compressed jump school. Not all of us were infantry. We had a couple of chaplains and a doctor learning to jump too.

It took five jumps to qualify, and then we would learn how to lay out the DZ marker lights, which consisted of a sequence of seven lights strung out downwind, one red, five amber, and a green, at the center of the DZ. Then we would be introduced to the operation of the Eureka radio beacons, which sent signals to the Rebecca receivers in the planes.

We were in the classroom within hours of our arrival, where we learned what was expected of us. From the classroom, we moved back to the Ramsbury airfield hangars to learn the intricacies of the parachute and harness. Riggers taught us how to pack our chute, laying it out full length on long tables and then carefully folding it into the backpack. After mastering that, we were taught how to execute a proper parachute landing fall, or PLF, first from a low platform, then from a tower where we wore the harness and were released about eight feet above the ground.

While the PLF may look odd to the uninitiated, learning how to land and roll to the side in a smooth three-point maneuver was essential to avoid leg injuries. The T-5 parachutes of the period got the trooper onto the ground in the shortest amount of time while not killing or crippling him. General Matthew Ridgeway, the commander of the 101st Airborne, once described the parachute landing impact, with nearly eighty pounds of extra equipment strapped to your body, as "sort of like jumping from the roof of a moving railroad car onto a paved road!" Even if done correctly, the landing would hurt unless you were lucky enough to land on soft ground. Awkward landings, especially common in the dark of night, often resulted in twisted or broken ankles.

We wore a small reserve chute on the chest, and if you were unlucky enough to need it, it might keep you from being driven into the ground like a tent stake. The T-5 was much less controllable than later post-war parachutes, so troopers learned to prepare for landings in trees, shrubbery, or rooftops. Just in case, we each carried a coiled thirty-foot length of three-eights-inch diameter rope to let ourselves down if we got stuck and a switchblade knife. The knife was zipped into a small vertical pocket just below the collar of our jump jacket, where we could reach it and cut ourselves free from the parachute shroud lines. From the tower, the next step was a big one as we boarded the C-53 and C-47 jump planes that would carry us into combat. The difference between the two aircraft is slight: the C-47, designed as an airborne truck, has an enlarged double cargo door in the aft fuselage and a reinforced cargo floor. The C-53 only has a personnel door, a military version of a commercial DC-3 airliner. Allied airborne operations employed both variants. The pathfinder school flight ops at RAF Ramsbury had no aircraft of their own, so it borrowed a couple of aircraft from the 23rd Troop Carrier Squadron, based at RAF Barkston Heath. We had only a few days to get accustomed to the equipment and procedures before they trucked us out to the planes in the early morning.

I was nervous as hell as we clustered around the Red Cross canteen truck, sipping coffee and munching fresh donuts. I'm sure we all were, and as the flight crew did the pre-flight checks, we helped each other with the harnesses, double and triple checking the straps, buckles, and releases. The jump master, an older, tough-looking technical sergeant (probably just a couple of years older than me) with a square jaw, close-cropped hair, and perpetual scowl, personally checked each of us out. Satisfied, he climbed up the few steps into the aircraft and proceeded to haul each of us aboard. Just walking in the harness, with main and reserve parachutes and no combat equipment, was difficult. Getting into the plane was cumbersome, almost impossible without help, so I loosened my crotch straps.

Coffee and donuts before the first jump at RAF Ramsbury, 23ᵈ TCS aircraft, June 1944. (Author's Collection)

On board, we filed up the center aisle and took a seat on the aluminum benches that ran down each side of the fuselage. The long bench seats were dished at intervals of about 18 inches to create a butt-pan, each with its lap belt, but there was no padding to sit on. Maybe, I thought, it would provide added incentive to get out of the aircraft. By the time the engines started and we began the takeoff roll, I was scared to death. What the hell was I thinking of when I volunteered for this? I had never been in an airplane, let alone considered jumping out of one. Combat was dangerous enough without the risk of getting myself splattered across half of Europe! But it was too late now, and none of us would dare to show fear to the other guys.

After climbing to altitude and circling the DZ, the red warning light finally came on. I swallowed nervously, and at the shouted order, "Stand up and hook up!" we all stood and snapped the static line hook onto the overhead wire. At the order, "Check equipment!" I checked the harness and chute of the guy in front of me, just as the guy behind me checked mine. Now we sounded off, "One, ready; two, ready; three, ready; four, ready . . ." and so forth, down the stick of jumpers. Finally came the order, "Stand in the door!" As I shuffled into position alongside the jumpmaster at the door, staring into space, the howling slipstream and engine noise almost deafened me. I'll swear I could hear my heart beating over the ungodly din! Then, "GO!"

The jump master's role was to get us out the door as fast as possible; any hesitation would get you a boot in the ass. The timing was critical since if we exited too quickly, we could foul our chute on the one in front, and if too slow, we would be scattered all over the drop zone, making assembly on the ground that much more complex and time-consuming. I could only imagine the added confusion and urgency when taking incoming enemy gunfire.

I shuffled towards the door, then the man in front of me suddenly disappeared. I stepped forward and must have hesitated for a split second, then I felt a boot smack into my backside, pitching me forward into space. I felt the wind blast and the opening shock of the parachute, then I nearly passed out in pain! I had forgotten to retighten the harness crotch straps, and they had jerked tight over my testicles. I thought they would pop out of my throat! As I swung beneath the canopy, I struggled to catch my breath, in too much pain to notice the view and the ground coming up fast, almost before I realized it. When I got my breath back, I swung like a pendulum a few times beneath the green camouflaged canopy, then I touched the ground and automatically performed the PLF and roll. The ground impact was worse than the tower jumps, and my feet stung sharply from the impact. As I struggled to my feet and wound up the shroud lines, I was amazed to find that I hadn't broken anything. But I was in agony, still barely able to breathe, as I walked gingerly and bowlegged back to the deuce-and-a-half truck. I knew the others had instantly detected my problem from the laughter as they pulled me onto the truck. All I could say was, "My God, but that hurt!"

On July 14, just a day after the first jump, the jumpmaster informed several of us that we were to report to the school headquarters. Had we done something wrong? Was I being washed out? I wasted no time reporting as ordered.

About twenty of us assembled in the classroom, and when the school adjutant entered, we stood to attention. The lieutenant took a seat, referred to several sheets of paper on his desk, then leaned back.

"At ease, gentlemen," he said. "I'm sorry to inform you, but your pathfinder training is suspended. You have all done fine, but the airborne divisions decided they do not require additional pathfinders. Collect your gear and leave this afternoon. Good luck to each of you. The clerk will hand out your travel orders."

My heart sank. From the adjutant's phrasing of our dismissal, it seemed that we would all be going to non-airborne units. I had just sewn the AA "All-American" divisional patch of the 82nd Airborne on my jacket a few weeks earlier, and I was finally beginning to feel at home in the airborne. I was looking forward to doing what I was trained to do, as strange as that may sound. Was it over now, almost before it had begun?

The more I thought about it, the more I began to fear being sent back to a "repple-depple" for reassignment, just to be plugged into a "leg" infantry unit. The prospect was unappealing after a taste of the elite airborne.

The clerk handed us each a set of orders and dismissed us without further explanation. Once out in the corridor, I immediately read the orders. To my relief, my fears were in vain. My orders were to return to Scraptoft and report within twenty-four hours. I guessed that I was in the airborne permanently.

I packed my duffel and hitched a truck ride into London, where I spent the better part of the afternoon wandering about until the scheduled train departure for Leicester. I saw a city subjected to German air bombardment for four years. Entire blocks of scarred townhouses and shops were broken at random intervals by piles of rubble where walls had collapsed, barricaded, and roped off to protect pedestrians and keep out the curious. Many shattered homes with no remaining facade exposed their inner rooms, furnishings still visible, plumbing hanging in mid-air, and walls scorched by fire.

Entrances to public buildings were sandbagged to give some protection from bomb damage, and of course, the blackout made travel through London at night a challenge, especially for foreigners. The constant activity of clean-up crews removing the debris from the previous night's attack forced pedestrians like me to make endless detours to avoid the shattered buildings and piles of rubble. I saw the highlights from the street: London Bridge, Westminster, Big Ben, and Piccadilly Circus. One visit was enough for me, and I gratefully caught the train back to Leicester, arriving late in the evening.

Chapter 12

Glider Training

SHAEF, the Supreme Headquarters Allied Expeditionary Force, expected to take heavy losses during the airborne portion of the invasion of France, with estimates running as high as ninety percent. They decided to increase the strength of the 325th and 327th Glider Infantry Regiments to keep them "combat effective" during the first weeks of fighting. Each regiment expanded to three battalions instead of their original two. To accomplish this quickly, on March 10, 1944, the 401st Glider Infantry Regiment was split. The First Battalion remained with the 101st as the third battalion of the 327th GIR, and the Second Battalion of the 401st was moved to the 82nd Airborne Division to be the third battalion of the 325th GIR.

Upon return to Camp March Hare, I became platoon sergeant of the First Platoon of Company G, or George Company, in the Third. Walt was now a sergeant and in charge of my first squad. I had already made a few friends at Camp March Hare and was relieved that I would stay in the regiment. I must admit to a mixture of pride and apprehension to be in the 82nd Airborne; they had already completed airborne operations in North Africa, Sicily, and Italy and had made history in Normandy. But the airborne loss rates were a sobering statistic.

A total of 1,072 ragged and weary 325th glidermen had returned to Scraptoft in the early morning hours of July 9. They flew into Normandy on D plus 1, June 7, and after thirty-three days of continuous combat in France, the regiment had suffered 1,322 casualties out of the 2,394 who took off on D-Day. That works out to 55% losses, and of those, 270 were killed in action. Airborne officers, who trained and prided themselves on leading from the front, suffered even higher casualty rates, with 71 out of 113 not coming back for a sobering casualty rate of 62%. Often, they were even more exposed to enemy fire than their troops. It was a proud record, but the regiment had much rebuilding to do in a short time. The veterans were exhausted, and most of the companies were below one-third strength. Company G was down to just twenty men out of nearly two hundred. I was shocked.

Despite careful planning and rigorous training for D-Day, very few of the "sticks" of paratroopers or gliders had landed on their assigned DZs or LZs. Cloud cover over Normandy prevented all but one of the Pathfinder units from accurately marking their drop zone (this was the 505th PIR). In addition, many of the C-47 pilots, appalled by the heavy anti-aircraft fire, maneuvered to avoid it and failed to slow before the drop, resulting in paratroopers scattered across the Normandy peninsula. Ad hoc units formed in the hours of darkness, with officers of each division collecting whatever paratroopers they could find, regardless of their regiments.

The glider landings, which came in the early morning light of the following day, suffered about as many casualties on landing. The difference was that paratroopers usually died individually. In contrast, the glidermen died in squads as their ships were torn apart in hard landings, smashed into hedgerows, suffered mid-air and landing collisions, or struck German obstacles. Some gliders were shredded, torn to pieces, and crumpled by striking Rommel's "asparagus." These were poles about ten feet tall, and six to nine inches in diameter stuck into the most likely landing fields just to impale gliders. Then, as the gliders attempted to land in the few clear areas, the airspace became jammed with aircraft, each with only one attempt at landing. Some collided in the air, but more collided or clipped each other on the ground, and others overshot the fields in their attempts to avoid collisions and plowed into trees and hedgerows.

The light construction of the gliders, combined with the heavy payloads of jeeps, trailers, anti-tank guns, and small howitzers, made for some gruesome wrecks. The first American general officer killed in the invasion of Europe was Brigadier General Donald Pratt, the deputy division commander of the 101st Airborne. He died when the glider he was in made a hard landing, and the jeep cargo broke loose and crushed him.

In the days to come, the Allied infantry pushed German troops back from critical crossroads as the beachhead expanded inland. At the same time, the paratroopers and glidermen breached barriers such as the causeways at Carentan and the Merderet Rivers. The lightly equipped airborne soldiers fought with whatever was at hand, seizing and holding key junctions and river crossings, battling Germans at every turn, including battle-hardened SS infantry and armor, Panzer grenadiers (mechanized infantry), and Fallschirmjaeger (paratroop) regiments. They fought tenaciously to clear villages and bottle up German forces until the units that landed on the beach could force their way inland to relieve them. After more than a month in combat, the airborne divisions were finally withdrawn for a much-needed rest to reorganize, reequip and replace losses.

Airborne warfare was something relatively new to the U.S. Army. The 82nd Airborne had seen action in North Africa, Sicily, and Italy, but Normandy was the baptism by fire for the 101st Airborne. After returning to England, the two divisions had to absorb and train more than 3,000 replacements to make up for the casualties in France.

Over the following days, I learned more details of the combat in Normandy: it was humbling, frightening, and awe-inspiring all at the same time. George Company had taken significant casualties, with 60% of the men killed or wounded, and the injured included Captain John B. Sauls, the company commander.

Taking the Merderet River causeway had been the worst for them. The causeway was a 500-yard single-lane road bridge with scant cover once the troops emerged from the low stone walls on the east bank. George Company had spearheaded the assault across the causeway against entrenched German positions on the west bank. Captain Sauls, a typical airborne officer who led from the front, successfully crossed in a heroic advance, but the men following him came under withering fire. The piled bodies of glidermen and a disabled Sherman tank quickly impeded progress. Only the courageous leadership of the glidermen, supported by a handful of paratroopers from the 507th Parachute Infantry Regiment, forced the Germans to withdraw, leaving scores of enemy troops to be captured.

Captain Sauls survived the action with multiple wounds but did not return to the company for several weeks. George Company had few of the original men, and the rapidly assigned replacements, including me, needed additional training to integrate us into the company, to mesh together as combat teams.

As the new staff sergeant of the first platoon, my work was challenging. With the benefit of the experience of the Normandy veterans, my fellow troopers and I began a rigorous but accelerated training program. My squad leaders, SGT Gordon R. Fisher, SGT Gordon W. Gasser, SSGT Burton L. Harris, and my old friend SGT Walter J. Barc, worked with a vengeance, setting an exhausting pace of reorganization and training.

Effective July 1, 1944, glidermen became qualified to receive an extra $50 per month, giving us equal pay as the paratroopers. It was welcome news, as much for recognizing the dangers we faced in glider operations as for the extra cash.

The encampments of the airborne division regiments were scattered all over southeast England. Two of the 82nd Airborne Division's parachute infantry regiments had camps in Nottinghamshire: the 507th at Tollerton Hall and 508th at Wollaton Park. But most of the division's regimental camps were located in and around Leicester: division headquarters was at Braunstone Park in Leicester, once the home of Lady Jane Grey; the 505th PIR was at

Quorndon; the 80th Parachute Artillery Battalion at Oadby; the 319th Glider Field Artillery (GFA) at Market Harborough; the 320th GFA Battalion in Leicester; Batteries C and D of the 456th Parachute Field Artillery Battalion at Husbands Bosworth; and our base at Scraptoft.

The commanding officer of the 325th was Colonel Harry L. Lewis, a veteran of the First World War who had taken command at its inception in June of 1942. He was a short, slender, and bespectacled man with graying hair. He looked more like an accountant or shopkeeper but was tough and demanding. He molded the regiment into an effective airborne unit, and under his leadership, it had fought through the Italian campaign and Normandy. But sadly, after returning to England, Colonel Lewis began to exhibit signs of serious illness. He became too ill to join the regiment in Normandy and was soon diagnosed with cancer. He was ordered back to the States for surgery but died shortly afterward.

The change of command took place on August 21. Our new commander, Colonel Charles Billingslea, came to the regiment from the executive officer job with the 504th Parachute Infantry Regiment. At six-foot-four, Billingslea was an impressively tall paratrooper who had parachuted into Normandy. He was a quiet, competent, and relentlessly professional West Pointer with a reputation for running a tight unit. He made it clear that he would tolerate nothing less than a maximum effort from the entire regiment.

Our schedule allowed us little time off, except for brief trips into Leicester. Reveille was at 0430, muster and calisthenics at 0500, breakfast at 0600, a full day of training, dinner at 1700, and finally lights out at 2100, unless we had a night tactical exercise. We spent at least three days each week out in the field: physical training; tactical drills; bayonet training; navigation by compass and map; loading and unloading the CG-4A gliders; practicing squad and platoon maneuvers; hand-to-hand combat; and grenade practice and the firing range, where we learned to field strip and fire German firearms, as well as re-qualifying with our weapons.

At times we were subjected to inspections and fifteen-, twenty-one-, and twenty-five-mile marches with full equipment to keep us physically conditioned. Then there was CQ, guard duty, and routine equipment maintenance. We replaced all the gear lost in Normandy, which necessitated uncrating, cleaning, and lubricating each piece, then testing it for proper operation: everything from M-1 rifles to jeeps, radios, and 75mm Pac howitzers, many still packed in cosmoline, a thick, waxy preservative which had to be scraped off before cleaning and lubricating to be prepared for action. Each platoon had its work cut out, and we were seldom idle. On the upside, we were fortunate to always eat out of field kitchens, even on maneuvers. I'm proud to say that I never ate K-rations, the individually boxed meals, during my entire time in the army.

As a coffee-lover, I never liked the taste of coffee out of a tin mess cup, no matter which field kitchen prepared it. In the field, our water usually came from tank wagons, referred to as "water buffaloes." We were always cautioned to use our halizone water purification tablets to ensure the water was potable. The taste was disgusting, and I suspected that even the water for the coffee had halizone in it. Thankfully, the coffee at the Red Cross canteen was better, and I bought a mug in Leicester instead of using the metal mess cups.

We handled and field-stripped captured German weapons, and most of us had an opportunity to fire small arms, such as the MP40 submachine gun, Mauser rifle, and the Luger and P-38 pistol. Our new training syllabus also included lectures on enemy units, their uniforms, and the various rank insignia. Proper recognition would be necessary for intelligence reports. Per army doctrine, enemy officers and NCOs were prime targets.

The days passed in a blur, but one afternoon's tactical exercise stands out in my memory. Because nitrates, an ingredient in agricultural fertilizer, were necessary to produce explosives, the British farmers used animal and human waste as fertilizer. After a complex map reading exercise with full packs, we took a short break and sat strung out along the road, our backs to the low stone wall. Along came a couple of our "honey wagons," tank trucks filled with the contents from our latrines, with clouds of flies swarming around them like smoke from a fire. They turned off the roadway and sprayed their contents over the fields around us. The stink made us gag, and I don't think we ate vegetables in the mess again after that experience.

The veterans who returned from France all had an opportunity for a brief furlough to recuperate, leaving platoons still below normal strength for weeks. When we did have a pass, it was customary for us to spend an evening in Leicester, the nearest large town.

I was always amazed at the shorter distances in England. Towns were much closer to each other than back home, and they were more compact, with narrow winding streets, small shops, and central village greens. The frequent rainfall and fog made the countryside greener than I remembered back home, and the fields were smaller, crisscrossed by low stone walls. Near Scraptoft, the smell of fresh manure seemed to predominate. As the pace of our training settled down, I felt that I was adjusting to life in rural England, and when we had an evening to ourselves, we wasted no time getting into Scraptoft or Leicester for a pint of ale.

With few exceptions, the English were kind and hospitable folks. We quickly learned to appreciate the snug little pubs, which seemed to be on every street corner. I'm sure I tried every one of them, but I quickly realized that some were hangouts that appeared to be reserved by the locals. Most of us GIs gravitated to just a few select pubs.

The British liked their "bitters," but I couldn't acquire the taste. I preferred the "mild," a pale ale piped up from the cellars below the bar, so it was served cooler than room temperature. After only one or two pints, I quickly acquired a taste for the higher alcohol content of the English brews, and if it wasn't quite as chilled as Americans liked it, I didn't take much notice after the first pint. I tried the dark, foamy stout, but it was too heavy for my taste, nor did I care for scotch or gin.

The English considered the American GIs to be overpaid and oversexed. I couldn't do much about the oversexed part. Still, in the interest of maintaining good relations, whenever I had a rare occasion to visit one of the shops in town, I tried to ensure that the locals came out on the winning end of every transaction. I found the British monetary system bewildering, with such odd names as farthings, "thrupence," shillings, florins, and pounds. I never really understood it all, so I just pulled out a pocketful of bills and coins and let the proprietor pick out the correct amount, then I gave a little bit more. I thought it only fair since we were guests and the folks of Leicester had been enduring the war since 1939.

Leicester was a center for textile manufacturing and turned out thousands of uniforms each month. Machine shops that in peacetime supported textile manufacturing were now manufacturing weapon components as quickly as possible. The city had suffered one severe Luftwaffe bombing eight months earlier, on November 19, 1944, when over a hundred civilians had perished in a devastatingly long eight-hour raid. Thankfully, the German bombing was not particularly accurate. Most industrial targets had survived, and the Luftwaffe had not returned in force.

I never seemed to have trouble making friends with the opposite sex, and Leicester was no exception. I met an attractive young lady named Hilda Wright, who introduced me to her family. She was blond, petite, and charming, with big blue eyes, and I fell in love with her soft English accent. Her mother, a trim and very proper woman, was very welcoming, and nearly every week I could count on a home-cooked meal. To reciprocate, I made it a point to collect fresh oranges and whatever else I could scrounge from our battalion mess and take them to the Wright's. The English rarely saw such delicacies during the war, and on a couple of occasions, I scored points with Mrs. Wright by bringing a side of bacon. They were a gracious family, and I will always have a soft spot in my heart for them.

I rarely mixed with the British soldiers, but on three occasions, I climbed into the boxing ring again to defend the regiment's honor. They were not much more than sparring matches, and we wore the same protective headgear and sixteen-ounce gloves. One memorable opponent was a rather tough-looking British trooper who, despite appearances, did not demonstrate much expertise in the ring. I gave him a hard right to the face during the first round, and he dropped to the mat and didn't get up. It just proves that looks aren't everything.

In early August, a fellow sergeant on the regimental staff tried to get me to return to London for a weekend pass, but I declined. I thought Captain Sauls would deny the request since London was a three-hour train ride away, but my memory of London was the damage caused by years of constant Luftwaffe bombing. I also had no desire to expose myself to the risk of death or injury from Hitler's new V-weapons. Apparently, the army staff shared my feelings, and he learned that London was now off limits because of the ongoing bombing.

The new Nazi V-1 "buzz bombs," or "doodle-bugs," had begun raining down on the British at all hours of the day and night since June 13, 1944, just one week after D-Day. Slightly smaller than a fighter plane, the V-1s were launched from a ramp at sites in Holland and Belgium and flew a straight line to their targets. Reportedly, the eerie engine sound was a distinctive muttering, which cut off just before it pitched over into its dive onto the target. British anti-air defenses could shoot some down, and the Royal Air Force mounted a vigorous defense against the buzz bombs, doing their best to intercept them with the few fighters fast enough to catch them.

The newest versions of the twin-engine Mosquitos and the new Hawker Tempests were fast enough, but only a few Spitfires, P-51 Mustangs, and P-47 Thunderbolts with engine modifications could catch the V-1s. The RAF and Air Corps fighter squadrons could spare very few for that role. The interceptors either shot them down with gunfire, where an exploding V-1 warhead could potentially destroy the attacking fighter, or, in a more daring maneuver, used a wingtip to cautiously flip up the V-1's wing, tumbling the buzz bomb's gyros and causing the missile to fall out of control.

RAF Bomber Command and the USAAF launched air attacks against the V-1 launch sites on the French coast until Allied forces overran them. During such an experimental attack, using a remote-controlled B-24 as a flying bomb packed with high explosives, Lieutenant Joe Kennedy, elder brother of JFK, was killed when the bomber prematurely exploded in mid-air before the pilots could bail out.

The V-2 ballistic missiles, launched from much greater ranges from both fixed and mobile launch sites, did not begin to fall on England until September 8, 1944, and the last one impacted on March 27, 1945. During the first week of the V-2 attacks, more than a dozen had fallen on Greater London. As a terror weapon, the V-2 was a more frightening weapon. As it fell from its apogee, the top of its ballistic trajectory, about 50 miles high, it reached speeds over four times the speed of sound and gave no warning of impact, the faint wail heard only after the impact blast. The high-explosive warhead could level an entire city block.

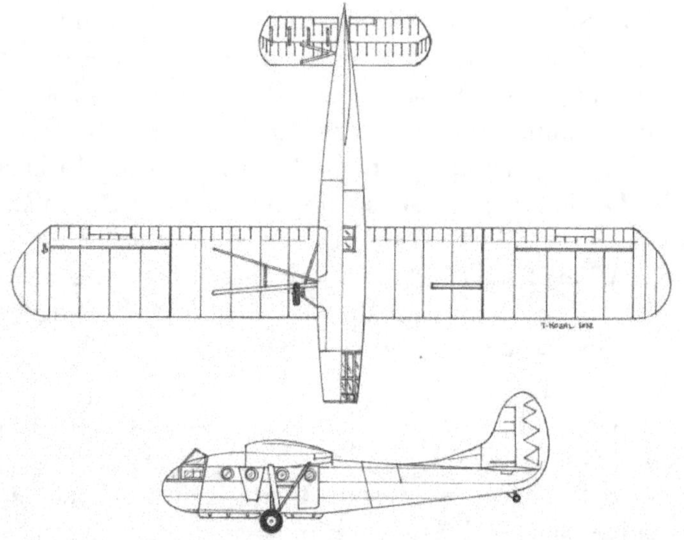

Waco CG-4A Combat Glider

Back at Scraptoft, we trained with the Waco CG-4A glider, a frail-looking contraption with a forty-eight-foot fuselage of steel tubing and aluminum fittings, all covered in doped fabric. The wings and tail surfaces were fabric-covered wood. With a strut-braced, high-wing monoplane configuration, it had an eighty-three-foot wingspan, giving the glider a load-bearing capacity of over 4,000 pounds. The cargo compartment was thirteen-feet two-inches long, and the glider could accommodate either fourteen soldiers, a jeep, a 75mm Pac howitzer or 37mm anti-tank gun, a jeep trailer, a field kitchen, or a miniature bulldozer and the operator.

The glider pilot and copilot sat side-by-side in bucket seats behind a rounded plexiglass nose, all supported by a web-work of tubular framing that dipped to a shallow "V" between the seats for easy access to the cargo section.

Forward visibility was excellent, with the clear nose and side windows, each fitted with small sliding panels and small dome-shaped air scoops for ventilation. The simple instrument panel was a horizontal piece of plywood mounting an altimeter, magnetic compass, airspeed indicator, turn-and-bank indicator, and a vertical speed indicator.

The glider controls consisted of a jeep steering wheel for each pilot and two sets of rudder pedals. The entire nose section of the glider was hinged behind the pilots' seats, allowing it to open upwards, giving a seventy by sixty-six-inch opening for loading and unloading vehicles. There were small access doors on each side of the fuselage, just beneath the wings, and larger rectangular doors to the rear of the landing gear.

The Waco glider used a conventional, or "tail dragger" landing gear arrangement, with two main wheels and spring-loaded nose and tail skids. The main landing gear, which lacked brakes, could be jettisoned for landings on soft ground. Braking was accomplished by either deploying a small drag parachute, tipping the glider onto the spring-loaded nose skid, or both methods. The landing was always precarious, and since we expected to land on rough fields or meadows, one of the last commands before touchdown was, "Raise feet!" It sounded silly but was serious because it was not unknown for the plywood honeycomb floorboards to be torn to pieces.

During the war, sixteen companies in the U.S. produced nearly 14,000 Waco CG-4As, with the Ford Motor Company alone producing 4,190 of the contraptions, more than double the output of any other manufacturer. Only Ford, Cessna, Waco, and the Timm

Aircraft Company had any experience building complete aircraft. Four companies had no prior experience: Ward Furniture of Fort Smith, AR; Ridgefield Manufacturing of Ridgefield, NJ; National Aircraft of Elwood, IN; and Robertson Aircraft of St. Louis, MO. One manufacturer was a casket maker, which didn't inspire much confidence in the soldiers who would ride the aircraft into battle! Since the airborne assault on Sicily, the gliders had earned the nickname of "flying coffins," perhaps a reference to the manufacturers. The Air Corps warrant officers who flew them wore special wings with a bold "G" emblazoned on the center shield: they proudly claimed it stood for guts.

Usually, the gliders would fly in a three or four-ship echelon formation, with the lead aircraft high on the left and each of the others about fifty feet lower and to the right. Gliders were either towed one per tug or in pairs separated horizontally and vertically, one high and one low. The two-glider pairing was crucial for cargoes of a jeep matched up to a towed gun (usually a 75mm Pac howitzer) or a jeep and a towed trailer. One glider carried the jeep, and the second one the towed equipment. Most gliders in the first wave of any air assault would bring infantry troops.

As a staff sergeant, I was the NCO responsible for a platoon commanded by a second lieutenant. I had four squads of mostly new replacements. The three rifle squads were each led by a sergeant, and the weapons squad had a more senior staff sergeant. Under the watchful eyes of the Normandy veterans, we learned how to properly load the gliders, tie down equipment, and then rapid unloading. With the nose section raised, the men would pull out the wheel ramps stored under the floorboards, then roll the howitzers and jeeps on board, tie them down securely, and load the ammunition and remaining equipment. Loading was critical, both in sequence and weight. The proper balance of the load was essential to maintain flight control, and it was imperative to unload in the least amount of time since we could expect the landing zones to be under enemy fire. We repeated the procedures repeatedly until we could finish the job in a few minutes, in darkness and daylight.

One clever design feature of the CG-4A was how the hinged nose section could open after landing. A cable attached to the rear of a jeep was run to a sheave at the back of the cargo compartment, then up and forward through an overhead pulley system. As the jeep drove forward, it would automatically raise the entire nose section. It was as though the glider disgorged the vehicle in one smooth motion. With only troops on board, the nose was kept closed since it was so heavy that it took at least four men to lift it. After several weeks of experimentation and repetition, we were confident that we were proficient, but we had to wait for an actual flight and landing.

The U.S. Army continually evolved, introducing new vehicles, weaponry, field equipment, and uniforms. The T-handled trenching shovel gave way to one with a folding head, khaki web field gear began to be replaced by olive drab, and the compact M-3 "grease gun" submachine gun was issued to armor crews. We were given new field uniforms sometime around the latter part of August. During the Normandy campaign, the paratroopers had worn the familiar M-42 jump jacket, hip length, with four large pockets, and baggy pants with huge, pleated pockets added to each leg. The glider men had worn the standard infantry uniform of wool pants and shirt with the waist-length cotton M-41 field jacket.

In the interest of uniformity and streamlining of manufacturing and supply, the army brass decided that all troops would wear the same field uniform, and the three-quarter length M-43 field jacket and pants were introduced. It was similar to the paratrooper's khaki jacket, but olive drab, hip-length, with four large, pleated pockets. The pants had to be modified by the parachute riggers to add the big paratrooper leg pockets. Because we didn't have access to the parachute riggers, the glider men seldom had the pockets added.

Paratroopers, unlike their "leg" infantry counterparts, go into combat carrying everything they are likely to need for sustained operation for weeks, or even months, until relieved by the regular infantry divisions and armor. The pants pockets, if you had them added (I did not), were perfect for carrying two K-ration boxes, blocks of C-4 explosives, and ammunition clips. Like most soldiers, I stuffed my jacket pockets with more ammunition clips, candy bars, a few personal items, cigarettes, maps, and whatever else needed to be close at hand.

Spare clothing, like underwear, socks, more rations, toiletries, and even more ammunition, went into my musette bag issued at the Chilton Foliat jump school. Glidermen carried the infantry haversack, but I liked how the musette bag clipped onto my combat suspenders. It was easy-on, easy-off.

Veteran paratroopers continued to wear the distinctive laced-up Corcoran jump boots in defiance of the new army regulations. We glidermen had turned in the old infantry leggings and ankle boots for the new calf-high two-buckle combat boots. As an affectation to set us apart from the infantry "legs," I bloused mine above the boots, paratrooper-style, but some fellows just tucked the cuffs into the boots. I thought we looked splendid, as long as you didn't look at our feet; the mud at camp was a persistent problem.

On August 11, the 82nd Airborne Division assembled at Leicester for the division's change of command. Major General Matthew Ridgeway, who commanded in Normandy, was promoted to command the newly organized XVIII Airborne Corps. Colonel James "Slim Jim" Gavin, commander of the 505th Parachute Infantry Regiment, was promoted to Brigadier General and given command of the division. We paraded for the commanders and General Eisenhower, now Supreme Commander.

From the Stars & Stripes newspaper, we all knew of Eisenhower's elevation to command of all Allied Forces, promoted over a score of more senior officers. After the Louisiana Maneuvers in 1941, I never expected to see him again, much less face-to-face. As the lead platoon sergeant of the Third Battalion, I was in the front rank, and as Ike passed down the assembled formation, he caught my eye, and my heart skipped a beat as he stopped and approached me. He looked me square in the eyes and smiled.

"Hello, Sergeant," said General Eisenhower. "It's nice to see you again. It seems like a long time since Louisiana."

"Yessir," I replied nervously, not knowing what else to say and knowing that everyone nearby was listening closely. I was sure they were wondering what the heck Ike was talking about. I remained stiffly at attention, not knowing if I could, or should, say more.

"I'm pleased you remember me, sir," I added after a moment.

Eisenhower smiled and nodded. "We were together for several weeks. How could I forget?" He tapped my stripes and added, "Looks like you've made a lot of progress since Louisiana. You're in a hell of a good unit now. Good luck to you."

I couldn't help but think that he'd come one hell of a lot further! He had gone from a new colonel in September of 1941 to Supreme Commander of the Allied Forces with four stars in three years. I saluted, he returned my salute, and then he continued down the formation. I felt flushed, excited, and proud that he remembered me, just a lowly flag bearer. Later, several of us retired to a Leicester pub, where they peppered me with questions. I'm sure some of the fellows found my story hard to believe, but Walt had been with me at Camp Livingston and confirmed everything I said. I was delighted to tell the story of driving all over Louisiana with Ike, and I felt like a celebrity, basking in my fifteen minutes of fame.

On August 29, the regiment underwent a full assault exercise, including glider loading, a brief flight, then a tactical problem to practice assembly and movement to an objective. Formed up by 0400, the individual platoons were trucked to the assigned airfields, where we were given a hot breakfast as we waited for the sun to begin to burn off the morning fog. Take-off was at about 0700. We were airborne for less than 30 minutes, never climbing above a thousand feet, and I estimated that we flew less than a hundred miles before the gliders were released. We circled the LZ, then touched down in some semblance of order.

Twelve of us were loaded into the glider's cargo bay, seated on opposing benches, with very little visibility out the small round portholes in the glider's sides. Forward visibility, through the plexiglass nose and over the shoulders of the pilots, gave a good view of the C-47 tug and the tow cable, but I couldn't see our LZ until the last minute. We were supposed to evacuate the aircraft quickly through the side doors, but with full packs and weapons, it took well over a minute for fourteen men to exit. That wouldn't be a problem if we were landing unopposed, but if under enemy artillery or small arms fire, just one casualty in the doorway would create a jam and leave those inside vulnerable. The more I thought about it, the more cynical I became. As it was, the exercise went relatively smooth, with very few gliders sustaining even minor damage, and the unit assembly and movement to the objective area were apparently executed satisfactorily. I couldn't help but wonder how long it would be until we would be doing it for real.

Chapter 13

Operation Market Garden

Not surprisingly, we never knew about command decisions until the last moment, the strategy being a tightly held secret. We followed the ground campaign in France through the newspapers with keen interest. We knew it could be weeks, if not days until we went into action. Shortly after General Gavin took over the 82nd Airborne Division, the Allied armies broke out of the Normandy hedgerow country, the "bocage," and began a rapid advance across northern France. General George Patton, pushing his armored units like a tidal wave, overran German defenses, including a succession of proposed airborne objectives. Only the overwhelming demand for gasoline and ammunition finally slowed Patton.

Meanwhile, the Allied command, particularly British General Bernard Montgomery and "Boy" Browning, who commanded the British 1ˢᵗ Airborne Corps for Monty, kept pushing hard for an airborne operation that would cut off Germans attempting to withdraw from the Low

Countries. On Friday, September 1, the 325th loaded onto trucks and dispersed to four Royal Air Force airfields northeast of Scraptoft: RAF Langar and RAF Fulbeck in Nottinghamshire, and RAF Folkingham and RAF Barkston Heath, both in Lincolnshire.

RAF Folkingham, home to the 313th Troop Carrier Group, was the assigned departure point for Third Battalion, which included George Company. Situated twenty-nine miles south of Lincoln and 110 miles north of London, RAF Folkingham was roughly a three-hour drive for us by truck. We arrived late in the day, unloaded and assembled in the hangar. We learned that we would be going into France on Sunday, September 3, landing at about 0830 hours. Our mission was to take and hold the bridges over the Escaut Canal, which formed the Belgian-Dutch border. Our objective was to cut off the German retreat into Holland.

The next day we were soaked with rain, making any flight operations impossible. But it was just as well that the weather failed to cooperate because Allied armor units overran our intended LZ by early Sunday morning. We didn't know it then, but between June 6, D-Day, and September 8, no less than eighteen airborne operations were planned, then scrapped. Either bad weather, overly strong German defenses, and anti-air artillery (referred to as "triple-A"), or objectives already overrun by Allied forces forced cancellation.

Trucked back to Scraptoft, we dried ourselves and our gear, cleaned and oiled our weapons, and waited. But Generals Montgomery and Browning were determined not to be denied the glory of a successful airborne operation, and they scrambled for viable missions for the

First Allied Airborne Army. We were sure it would only be a matter of days until we saw action. While I was apprehensive and afraid at times, I was eager to just get on with it. All I could do was try to keep myself focused and busy.

On September 11, we were confined to camp, which told us something new was afoot. We cooled our heels for several days, speculating about what the target could be. Then, on September 15, the regiment was again loaded up for the trip to RAF Folkingham and the other fields. This time our destination was Holland, with the assault set for September 17. Sunday, September 17, was my 25th birthday, not one I would ever forget.

The airborne force was so massive that it would require three days to airlift it all into Holland. The 325th would fly into combat on the third day, September 19, to reinforce the paratroopers. They were to capture a series of bridges on the main roadway from the north Belgian border to the Lower Rhine River at Arnhem.

The intermittent rains came back on September 18, and our departure date began to slip daily. As the Allied commanders nervously waited for news from Holland, where the weather was even worse, we endured the lousy English weather at Folkingham. For shelter, we glidermen moved into the hangars and slept on the concrete, laying our folded shelter halves under our blankets for whatever insulation we could conjure up. A handful of men opted to bed under the gliders' wings with groundsheets pulled over them. I suppose the turf was marginally softer than concrete. At least we were out of the mud.

As soon as we arrived at the airfield, we loaded up with whatever extra gear we thought we would need. The quartermasters handed out whatever we asked for, and we could help ourselves to whatever we could carry. As I made my way down the row of tables and stacks of equipment, I picked up a handful of chocolate bars, a couple of K rations, four hand grenades, a tin of morphine syrettes, an extra first aid kit, and a packet of

C-47s and CG-4A gliders at RAF Folkingham, September 23, 1944. (Copyright, Imperial War Museum)

toilet paper. I finally made my way over to a supply sergeant in charge of issuing ammunition and side-arms.

Our 82nd Airborne Division commander, General James "Jumping Jim" Gavin, was an early advocate for the development of airborne divisions and wrote the army field manual for paratroopers and airborne operations and tactics. He had explicitly dictated that squad and platoon NCOs should be armed with a submachine gun to bring as much firepower as possible to the fight.

Officers usually carried the M-1 carbine, but Gavin was known for always taking an M-1 Garand, just like his riflemen. I brought the Thompson on our California coast patrols and was comfortable with the weapon, but I had only fired it on the range. It was a heavy weapon loaded with a full magazine and a bit awkward to carry, but I was happy to have the firepower.

I also selected a .45-caliber pistol, shoulder holster, and a handful of loaded pistol magazines that I stuffed in my jacket pockets. I picked up six loaded stick magazines for the Thompson, one for the gun, and the others went into a five-pocket magazine pouch. On my way out of the hangar, I picked up a silk escape map that covered Holland, Belgium, and the German border. I strolled back to the glider, taking a mental inventory, and tried to think if I had forgotten anything.

Would we go, or would the operation be called off once again? Rumors abounded, and all we could do was sweat it out. Each day we watched the rain, waited in chow lines at the field kitchens, and drank coffee we had to gulp down quickly before it became chilled. Anxiety played see-saw with boredom, and we all went through the motions of signing up for our GI insurance and filing our wills.

Along with the officers and other NCOs, I spent a considerable time in the hangers studying the large-scale maps of the landing zones and the tactical situation so I could brief my platoon. My squad leaders ensured that our men had drawn the rations, ammunition, and equipment we needed from the quartermasters. We waited, killing time, impatient to get the flight over with and on with the mission. Only the veterans knew what to expect, and for the most part, they were quiet.

The days dragged by, but on September 23, the weather in Holland began to clear, although it was still overcast with patchy ground fog at RAF Folkingham. The westerly winds had blown the storm system far to the east, and we would take off and follow in its wake across the English Channel. The 313th fed us a full-course breakfast in their chow hall, with powdered eggs, bacon, hot cakes, toast, and gallons of coffee. The thought crossed my mind that it might be the last meal for the condemned, so I said a quick prayer.

Since our take-off time was past noon, officers and NCOs were ordered to assemble at 1000 in the hangers for a final mission briefing to explain the current tactical, at least as far as our commanders knew it. I got my first close-up look at the most recent aerial reconnaissance photos. The constantly changing timetable had not allowed time for creating sand-table models as the intelligence staff had prepared for Normandy. The situation on the ground in Holland was fluid, changing by the hour.

The battalion intelligence officer, the G-2, stepped forward and kicked off the briefing with a pointer and a series of small-to-large scale maps to illustrate. Knowing that our lives would depend upon the information, each of us listened attentively. I have refreshed my memory from the actual 82nd Airborne documents, and it went something like this:

"Gentlemen, the meteorologists tell us we have a brief weather window today, with partly cloudy conditions in the objective area. You wouldn't know it by the weather here, but it's better in Holland.

"The British 1st Airborne Corps paratroopers that landed at Arnhem on the seventeenth have been isolated and surrounded by German forces. Likewise, the glider troops that landed near Oosterbeek, on the west side of Arnhem, are surrounded. We have been unable to break through yet to relieve them. To the south, the 82nd Airborne paratroopers have taken the road and rail bridges over the River Meuse at Grave and the Lower Rhine at Nijmegen. They are heavily engaged by armor and artillery of German SS, Fallschirmjaeger, and Panzer grenadier units.

"Closer to the Belgian-Dutch border, the 101st Airborne dropped on the village of Son, then proceeded to take the city of Eindhoven. Retreating German troops have blown the critical bridges over the Wilhelmina Canal, but British engineers have laid down Bailey bridges to sustain their advance and keep the supply line open.

"Veghel, just to the north of Eindhoven, is under heavy siege by German artillery east of the highway and getting pressure from Fallschirmjaeger units on the west.

"The British advance has been slower than anticipated and German resistance has been stiff. Intelligence from the Dutch resistance indicates that the Germans have organized their defensive forces into makeshift Kampfgruppe, or battle groups. These composite armor and mechanized infantry units were recovering and rearming after we hammered them in Normandy. German artillery has been raining hell on Veghel for nearly two days. Our troops there report it to be the heaviest shelling they have ever encountered, and a strong German attack from the east has temporarily cut the highway to Arnhem just north of Veghel."

He shifted over to a larger scale map of the area just west of the German border and slapped the pointer on a circled position marked LZ-O.

"The 325th will land at LZ-Oscar, at Overasselt, along with the remaining units of the 307th Engineers and the 80th Anti-Aircraft Battalion. The plan is for you to relieve the 505th Parachute Infantry, who has been defending a line just to the south of Groesbeek facing the Reichswald Forest. So close to the German Reich, you can expect resistance to be fierce."

Switching to a much smaller-scale map that spanned the entire width of the briefing board, he traced out the air route from England to LZ-Oscar, turns marked with pins, and the flight path with red string.

The G-2 briefer continued: "We will be flying in via the southern route, crossing the Channel into Northern France, then turning north across Belgium, roughly parallel to the main north-south highway and XXX Corps. The road is only two-lane and mostly elevated above the surrounding terrain.

"The first airlift of the 82nd on the 17th used the northern route, which exposed them to heavy concentrations of German anti-aircraft fire. This final lift will take the southern route. This route was used earlier for the airlift of the 327th on the 19th. Because German units are counter-attacking Allied positions on the highway, you can expect anti-aircraft fire around Eindhoven and Veghel."

At this point, he again shifted to aerial photographs of the landing zone, circled and labeled with a bold LZ-O. He waved his pointer in a circle around the area, and I could see the little silhouettes of landed gliders from the earlier airlifts. He shuffled some notes and continued.

"LZ-Oscar is a huge grassy area, roughly two miles wide and three and a half miles long. It is near Overasselt on the north bank of the Maas River, close to the Rhine River and Germany. The 504th Parachute Infantry dropped there six days ago and is firmly under our control.

The airlift today will consist of 406 Waco gliders carrying almost 3,500 men. You will also be taking 104 jeeps, 25 howitzers, and 59 trailers of ammunition, mostly from the 325th."

I was amazed at the size of the invasion forces and followed his briefing with rapt attention. He lowered his pointer, shifted his feet, and referred to his notes.

"Now, for the terrain. Once on the ground, you can expect it to be flat but rising towards the Reichswald, the forest on the German border. The area is damp and densely cultivated and crisscrossed by drainage ditches. The scattered woods are thick, with both coniferous and deciduous trees. The soil there is sand and gravel. Drainage ditches are two to six feet deep and five to twelve feet wide. The soil in the cultivated fields has a clay consistency, so expect some ditches to have standing water. The paved roads are two-lane, raised on embankments, and most secondary roads are single-lane and unpaved. Off-road vehicle travel in low areas is difficult."

Turning to the company commanders, he looked at his watch, then finished up. "Take-off begins at 1300 hours. Expect to reach LZ-Oscar at 1645 hours. Sunset is at 1837 hours, with full darkness at 1948 hours." (All times are British Double-Summer Time, which was one hour behind the German local time.)

As the briefing broke up, Captain Sauls motioned for the George Company leaders to gather around him for some last-minute words.

"As you probably realize, the dangerous part of the flight will be after we cross the French-Belgian border. We will be flying east of Eindhoven, but we can expect heavy anti-aircraft fire in the vicinity of Erp and Veghel. The landing itself should be routine since we hold the landing zone. Be sure your men have drawn whatever items they need from the quartermasters, then stand by your gliders. Load up by 1230 hours. Good luck to you all, and I'll see you on the ground."

After the briefing, I met again with First Platoon. Our one veteran from Normandy, PFC Richard D. Cator, was quiet and attentive, probably thinking about Normandy, where he was wounded at the Merderet River causeway. The inexperienced troopers were nervous, not knowing what to expect. Some were talkative, joking nervously amongst themselves, and as I laid out my silk escape-and-evasion map on the ground, they all crowded around. I told them to listen up and pay attention, then outlined the situation from what the G-2 had briefed. When I finished, we still had about an hour to wait. Once again, I told them this was the last chance to draw any extra equipment, weapons, rations, and whatever else they thought necessary

I spent the remainder of the morning double-checking my equipment. I cleaned the Thompson and checked its function, emptied my pockets and sorted out all my stuff one last time, then reloaded my pockets, musette bag, and gas mask bag with all the extra gear. Nobody kept the gas mask, but the bag was handy for extra grenades, ammo, rations, and personal items.

Our glider, serial number 43-41467, was easy to identify. It had a foot-high number "13" hand-painted on the side of the cockpit, which I assumed was the sequence number for George Company's ships. Coincidentally, it was the number of glidermen on board. I hoped it wouldn't be bad luck. I would be flying with my first squad, led by SGT Walter Barc. Since Walt had been with me since Camp Livingston, I had the utmost confidence in him, and I knew his squad was as good as any in the 325th.

Our platoon leader, 2nd Lieutenant Irvin C. "Andy" Anderson, would ride with us. Just twenty-three, two years younger than me, Lieutenant Andy was from Gloucester, Massachusetts. He had light brown hair, hazel eyes, and a scar on his chin that gave him a bit of an aura of toughness. Despite being a ninety-day wonder and only five-feet two-inches tall, probably the shortest soldier in the battalion, we liked his enthusiasm. During the past three months, we gained confidence in his leadership abilities, and I learned a bit about his background. One day during a lunch break during a map-reading exercise, he told me that his family owned a laundry and dry-cleaning business in Gloucester, Massachusetts. Still, he wasn't interested in taking over the family business. Instead, he decided to join the army during high school. At the first opportunity, he joined the junior officer training corps and the rifle drill team and planned to make a career in the army. He had trained with us for months now and had demonstrated common sense, as well as a willingness to listen and learn from the Normandy veterans.

At about 1100 hours, the canteen trucks showed up, staffed by young English and American Red Cross girls. As they made their way around the flight line, we fueled up with coffee, donuts, and sandwiches. We waited, stretched, and sat around as the sun emerged and began to dry things out. At noon we began to gather back at our assigned glider.

Our tow plane, a Douglas C-47 Skytrain, a "Dakota" to the British, was marked with the squadron code letters "N3" on the nose and "A" on the tail for the aircraft identity. Seeing forty-nine C-47s lined up nose-to-tail on the runway centerline was impressive. The forty-nine gliders that would carry Easy, Fox, and George Companies and the HQ and HQ Company of the battalion were positioned at a 45-degree angle on the left side of the tarmac, each about twenty yards away from its C-47 tug. The towline for each glider was carefully "flaked" out on the ground between the glider and the tow plane in a looping pattern that would play out without tangling as the tugs moved into the take-off position and began to take up the slack. The entire formation was packed so tightly that wingtips almost overlapped, and C-47 tails almost touched the noses of the plane behind.

A tall, skinny, dark-haired fellow with a receding chin walked over to join us. He carried a .38 caliber revolver in a shoulder holster, and the rank pinned to his garrison cap identified him as our glider pilot. He introduced himself as Flight Officer Alvin C. Jones, from upstate New York. He was about my age, but I thought he looked younger. After Lieutenant Andy and I introduced ourselves, he told us that because of a shortage of glider pilots, he was on loan from the 315th Troop Carrier Group. Jones assured us that he had made numerous glider flights. "Don't worry. You're in good hands. I haven't wrecked a glider yet or lost anyone." I noted that he hadn't said any of his flights were combat missions, which added to my apprehension. I had heard that many of the glider pilots were flight school washouts.

"Have you spoken to the crew of our tug?" asked Lieutenant Andy.

Jones motioned towards the five-man C-47 crew gathered at the aft door of their ship, pilot, copilot, navigator, radio operator, and crew chief.

"Yessir, I have. The pilot is Lieutenant Day Oxford. He flew the earlier airlifts on the seventeenth and nineteenth. I know the copilot, Bob Greite, pretty well, and he's also on loan from my group. Bob told me that the southern route didn't get such heavy flak as the northern one, but the Germans had plenty of time to move artillery closer to our flight path. They've finished their pre-flight checks. We're ready to go as soon as we get the word."

At 1230 hours, the order came to load up. Without further ado, we shouldered our gear, made final adjustments, and began climbing into the glider through the rear doors. The CG-4A Waco glider had a flexible interior arrangement. Seating for troopers consisted of parallel three-man-wide plywood boxes arranged on both sides of the cargo bay. The box seats, with storage inside, were attached to the honeycombed plywood decking with over-center latches, like trunk latches, that made them easy to remove to accommodate jeeps, trailers, and artillery. Each man had a wide lap belt, and they strapped in facing each other, rifles held vertically in front of them, with cargo boxes between their feet. We were carrying a crate of bazooka rockets, two of .30-06 ammunition, and one of fragmentation grenades.

Because of the enormous number of gliders employed in Operation Market, the airborne portion of Market-Garden, 9th Troop Transport Command was critically short of qualified glider pilots. Soldiers were pressed into service to act as ad hoc copilots on virtually every glider. It had already become a source of friction between the Troop Carrier Command and General Gavin. He felt strongly that glider pilots should be integral to the airborne units and trained alongside us, but the War Department overruled him. The glider pilots always denied that the soldiers seated next to them were copilots, just extra passengers.

As I climbed on board, Lieutenant Andy grasped my right arm and held me back. "Wait, Sarge, you take the front seat today."

I had expected Lieutenant Andy to take the copilot's seat, and I questioned him as he motioned me toward the front. "Lieutenant, shouldn't you take the front seat as the senior man?"

He smiled briefly and replied, "No, I have confidence in you. Take the seat, and I'll sit with the men in the back."

I hadn't warmed up to flying, and to say I was apprehensive would be a huge understatement. But I shrugged, climbed aboard, and worked my way forward into the copilot's seat.

Flight Officer Jones assured me he would show me how to control the glider after we got airborne. "It's a piece of cake, sergeant," he claimed. Of course, it was, I thought sarcastically. That's why he went through months of training and earned pilot's wings.

I have never been particularly anxious to fly, and my first flight had been at Chilton Foliat, where I nearly became a eunuch. To be ordered to act as a backup pilot in the event of Jones' incapacitation was crazy and sent chills down my spine. If that happened, we were dead men. I had never even held the control yoke before, and now I could have more than a dozen lives depending on my performance as a neophyte aviator.

The lieutenant took the foremost bench seat behind Jones, and the others buckled up on either side, with Walter Barc taking the last seat on the right side. The first man behind the lieutenant was our radioman, a big, strong kid, PVT Cecil L. Blood. He was just nineteen but looked more mature because of his size and trim physique. He was the middle of three kids and came from Chicago, Minnesota.

Next came PFC Richard D. Cator, a twenty-two-year-old and our only Normandy veteran. He was a quiet fellow, perhaps because of what he had experienced in Normandy. He had earned the coveted Combat Infantry Badge (the CIB) and a Purple Heart for wounds he received at the Merderet River causeway. We all respected him for his proven combat experience and courage. Like our pilot, he was from upstate New York at Seneca Falls, where he had been a light tender on the Erie Canal.

Next in line was our smallest trooper, PFC John T. Clark, Jr., son of a railroad conductor. At the ancient age of twenty-eight and short in stature, only five-foot-four, it was easy to underestimate John's tenacity. He had quickly teamed up with his "battle buddy," PVT Louis A. "Art" Delosh, who carried our squad's Browning Automatic Rifle. John's role was to lug the ammunition for the bullet-hungry BAR.

Art Delosh was from Watertown, New Jersey, and was my age. He was a big fellow, nearly six-foot, muscular and broad-shouldered. Art made handling the nineteen-pound BAR look easy, and he could fire 650 rounds per minute in full auto, single shot, or short bursts with great accuracy. Art was a bit of a joker and a popular squad member.

PFC Carl L. Ellis was a country boy from Jackson, Tennessee. He was also one of our tallest men at six feet. He had a great country drawl and an endless number of funny stories. At first, I thought that his age, thirty-three, and the oldest in the squad, might be a handicap. But Carl had been a farm hand since his teenage years and was strong, used to hard labor, and in good condition. My biggest concern was his ability to exit the glider through the small side doors quickly.

We had another trooper from Tennessee, PFC Robert C. Miller, a twenty-four-year-old. Unlike me, he had finished high school and had worked the family farm. He and Ellis naturally bonded, but he was a taciturn fellow, very average looking, and easy to overlook. I hadn't had much time to get to know him.

PVT Julian E. Gorski, a twenty-two-year-old Polish kid from Chicago, was our newest replacement, but he fit in well. His family had emigrated when he was just a youngster, and he spoke English with a heavy accent that was amusing at times, and he came in for a lot of ribbing because of it. He also knew a bit of German.

PFC Galen Overholser was also twenty-two. He had been a roofer before the war and hailed from South Bend, Indiana. Galen was our field radio lineman, and at nearly six-foot and broad-shouldered, he was the perfect pairing for Cecil Blood. His job was handling the heavy spools of communication wire and equipment.

Another farm boy was PVT Robert H. Wood, twenty-one, from Wabash, Indiana. He naturally teamed up with Galen Overholser, his fellow Hoosier. With German heritage and adequate knowledge of the language, I hoped he'd come in handy if we captured any Krauts.

Last came twenty-six-year-old T5 James C. Dunlap from Jack County, Texas. As a T5, a specialist technician, James was Walt's assistant squad leader. A year older than me, James looked like the stereotypical cowboy, five feet nine inches tall and all lean muscle. He was slow to speak and had a bit of a drawl. But looks could be deceiving. He had been a hotel clerk and had a wife back home (or perhaps that was history, I never knew). He was the fifth of six children, left home early, and had been in the army almost as long as I had. He could easily take over the squad if Walt became a casualty.

As the squad settled onto the bench seats, I buckled into the copilot's seat, which took a big step over the V-shaped bracing between the two front seats. Flight Officer Jones had walked back to the C-47 for some final words with the crew but quickly returned and climbed into his seat.

"I've already done the pre-flight inspection," he said. "If everyone is all belted-up in back, it's just a matter of waiting our turn. Take-off is scheduled for 1300. As number thirteen, we should be rolling by about 1310. Our flight time on the southern route is a bit less than four hours. Our drop time at LZ-Oscar is 1645 hours." He paused and gave me a grin. "Are you ready to learn how to fly?"

"That's not funny," I replied. "I guess I don't have much choice. You can show me, but I think if anything happens to you, we're done for."

"I get it," he replied, "but I'll explain the basics. I can talk you down even if I get hurt. Once we get in the air, follow me as I explain the controls and the landing procedure, but first, let me tell you the basics of flying the glider."

Jones told me what he thought I should know about flying a glider. With a 12-to-1 glide ratio, the CG-4A would glide for over two miles from 1,000 feet. He explained how to set up an approach by holding an airspeed of about sixty miles per hour and keeping the desired touch-down point at a constant position relative to a spot on the glider's nose frame. Approaching the landing zone at the planned release altitude of 200 feet, we could coast to a landing in about a half-mile, then level off just above the ground and deploy the spoilers by pulling up the handle alongside the seat. He made it sound simple, but I was sure I would kill everybody on board.

The glider instrumentation was basic: airspeed indicator, altimeter, rate of climb indicator, turn and bank indicator, and magnetic compass. After explaining how to read each of the strange instruments, Jones demonstrated the functions of the control wheel and rudder pedals, then described our position in the glider "serial," the term for the formation. The tugs and gliders flew in flights of four pairs, each glider flying slightly above the C-47 to stay above the slipstream, with the tow line and its communication cable forming a 300-foot catenary between us. As number thirteen of the fifteen gliders assigned to George Company, we were in the lead position of the fourth echelon, and each aircraft pair was stepped slightly behind and above the pair to its left, which gave pilots the best view of the ships in the formation.

By the time Jones began to describe the landing, I was getting information overload. With the glider's descent rate of 600 feet per minute, releasing at 200 feet would give just seconds to make decisions. All I remembered was to head into the wind, probably from the west-northwest, try to maintain about 60 knots of airspeed, keep the nose pointed at the front edge of the landing field, and pull up to flair or level off (he demonstrated with his hand) when we were about 20 feet above the ground. He assured me that the rudder pedals would help keep the glider lined up on the landing heading, but I had some serious doubts and was horrified to think of what could happen.

He smiled as he finished the lesson. "Take heart. You're in good company. I don't think any of the other gliders have copilots either." It was not reassuring, and I just prayed that Jones wouldn't get hurt. If he did, we could all end up scattered across Holland.

As the minutes dragged on, the stuffy cockpit became warmer and warmer. The sweat beaded my forehead and trickled down my spine. Lieutenant Anderson opened the forward fuselage door for air, but it didn't do much good. Jones watched me and assured me we would cool down quickly once airborne. Fighting my nervousness, I asked him a bit about his flight experience

"I've been flying for over a year," he explained. "We all trained for Normandy for months. I brought over a dozen gliders back from Normandy using a snatch-and-grab system. Some of those gliders were in less-than-ideal condition. I've probably made nearly a hundred landings by now."

I thought about what he said, and it occurred to me that he didn't say he had made a combat landing. Was it significant, or should I just let it pass? I decided not to press the issue, but I was curious about what he was supposed to do after landing. "So, once we're down," I asked, "what are you supposed to do? Do you stay with the glider or join the squad? Are you supposed to be evacuated right away?"

His reply sounded like a "best case" scenario. "All the pilots are supposed to be evacuated back to England, but it will take a few days. We're supposed to assemble into a reserve unit. We've all had basic infantry training. It's like your training, but more compressed. I'll take care of you in the air, and you infantry guys can take care of me on the ground."

As the wait dragged on, I examined the interior of the glider and took notice of the data plate fixed to my side of the instrument panel. I was amused to read that this particular glider was made by the Gibson Company of Greenville, Michigan, just a few hours' drive from my home. What a small world, I thought. I hoped it was a good omen.

Finally, as my watch ticked past 1245 hours, we watched with growing excitement as the C-47s fired up their Pratt & Whitney radial engines. The noise became deafening, not just a roar but a reverberating thunder that caused the glider to vibrate in harmony. Green flares popped up from the airfield control tower at precisely 1300, then the first ship began to move forward, went to full power, and started the take-off roll. Once again fascinated by the process, I watched each of the tug and glider pairs roll forward and take off. As each C-47 revved its engines and began to move, the tow rope slowly straightened out and the glider jerked into motion.

Chapter 14

Into the Chaos

When it became our turn, I watched the 350-foot tow rope pay out behind our C-47, one long loop at a time, until finally, we felt a jerk and acceleration as we began to roll onto the runway. The excitement was palpable, and I divided my attention between watching Jones' motions on the controls and the panorama of the group take-off. I had experienced a glider flight like this just a few weeks before, but this was the real deal.

We began to accelerate at 1310 hours, and the glider lifted off before the tug, and Jones had to react quickly to hold us low until the C-47's tail lifted. Once the C-47 became airborne, Jones maneuvered us to our perch, just above and slightly to the right of the tug. Too high or too wide to either side, we would interfere with the control of the tow plane, and if directly astern, we would get into the turbulence of his propeller wash. As we climbed away from the field and circled, other aircraft pairs in our four-ship echelon formed on us. I watched a long procession of tugs and gliders moving together and assembling into waves of echelon formations.

Once we leveled out, I relaxed and took a good long look around. The view was breathtaking, a cerulean sky broken by massive, brilliant cotton balls of cumulus. Below us was a multi-hued, green-yellow-brown checkerboard of farms. The landscape was dotted with dozens of villages, all connected by a web of narrow roads. As our formation assembled, we began the first leg to the coast. I was stunned by the size of the air flotilla. It seemed as though the entire sky had filled with aircraft. As far as I could see, there were tugs with gliders. Escorting fighters weaved above and below as the separate formations began to close up into massive waves of aircraft. I found it hard to take my eyes off the panorama unfolding around us.

We neared the English Channel coast within thirty minutes, and Dover's iconic white chalk cliffs passed beneath us. But not everyone was enjoying the view. I heard some retching from behind me as a few men became airsick, but most were quietly joking and talking to relieve their anxiety. But for me, sitting forward, most of the conversation was muted by the hiss of the airflow and the subdued roar of aircraft engines. For a few minutes, I forgot about the dangers waiting for us and just enjoyed the view as we flew over the English Channel, and the French coastline appeared out of the haze ahead of us.

The channel crossing was uneventful, and we stayed at a low altitude, perhaps 1,500 or 2,000 feet. The scattered cloud base loomed above us at just 3,000 feet, and we repeatedly passed from sunlight to shadow. Jones seemed calm, holding the glider in position with minor adjustments while I daydreamed of home. It was Sunday, and I tried to calculate the time difference. My family was probably at church. I wondered where my brothers John and Andy were and whether they were in action in the Pacific.

The armada droned on over the sea, and my thoughts returned to reality. I was finally going to face the enemy. I wondered if I would measure up. My former role as a sergeant in California was nothing compared to the responsibility of leading my platoon into action. I felt a nagging fear, not of death, but of failing as a leader, or worse yet, letting fear get the better of me. Did I have the skill and guts to be aggressive, to make the right tactical decisions? Or would I hesitate, give in to fear, or even worse, would poor decisions get men killed? I would soon find out. I silently prayed for strength, courage, and wisdom. I admit that I was afraid of what lay ahead. My mouth became so dry that I pulled out my canteen and took a quick swig of water.

The minutes ticked by, and we made landfall over France. The formation descended to about 1000 feet. At this low altitude, the broad patches of cloud shadow on the French farmland created some mild turbulence. Looking down, I could see Allied troop movements on the roads and clusters of vehicles on open ground. The situation seemed almost idyllic, and visibility was excellent. I couldn't resist unfolding my escape map and following our progress, identifying landmarks on our route. I was so fixated on this that the left turn over Belgium and across the Escaut Canal into Holland caught me by surprise.

I turned in my seat for a brief final check on the troopers and gear, but as I was about to speak to Lieutenant Andy, Jones exclaimed, "Look up ahead! It's going to be a rough ride from here on in." We were hardly past the Belgian-Dutch border when the lead aircraft began to draw German anti-aircraft fire with a vengeance. Glowing balls of green and red tracers from twenty- and forty-millimeter weapons arced into the formation. Larger eighty-eight-millimeter shells exploded in puffs of brown-black, creating dirty punctuation marks in the sky with hot, yellow-orange cores. I turned once more to glance back at Lieutenant Andy, and as we locked eyes, I could see the fear and anxiety on his face. I'm sure he saw it in my face as well. There was nothing to say.

As the flak bursts drifted towards us, it was mesmerizing. They blossomed and appeared motionless in the sky, like serried ranks of soldiers standing to attention, continuously reinforced as we flew through them, interlaced with smaller caliber tracer fire. It seemed surreal, with the bright late summer sky a rich blue and white, juxtaposed with the dirty black puffs. Fear tightened my throat as the German anti-aircraft gunners quickly found the altitude of the formation, and shrapnel began to pepper the planes and their trailing gliders.

The barrage continued for at least eight or ten minutes, and I occasionally felt and heard the shock and popping sound of shrapnel or smaller caliber bullets piercing the aircraft. Helpless to do anything except endure it, I was scared to death. Jones announced that we were approaching Veghel, and the intensity of the ground fire, which I already thought was heavy, increased noticeably. Suddenly our tow plane took a direct hit in the left engine. A ball of flame engulfed the engine nacelle, and cowling fragments and engine oil streamed back beneath us. Flight Officer Jones reacted immediately, reached up, and tripped the lever to release the towline. In a second, it detached from the tail of the tow plane and snaked its way towards the ground. The C-47 struggled for several seconds to maintain altitude and stay wings-level, but it slowly began a smoking descent, fighting the drag of the dead engine. I lost sight of it when it banked to the right to stay clear of the aircraft in formation on our left.

As we dropped below the formation, Jones banked our glider back slightly to the left to clear the formation behind us, then he set up his best glide speed, and both of us began an anxious search for a clear landing site. For a moment, it felt like an out-of-body experience. Was this happening to me? With just a few hundred feet remaining, Jones leaned over towards me, pointed to the left of our nose, and calmly said, "See that little field next to the woods? I think that's as good a place as any to set us down."

It looked like a postage stamp, but I said, "If you say so. Just land us in one piece." I stared at the field as visions flashed through my mind, a glider crashing into a tangle of wood, tubing, and broken bodies. As it passed down our left side, I remember an impression of a small, level field with a low crop of something or other. A drainage or irrigation ditch appeared to bisect the field, almost parallel with our flight path. A thick woods passed on our left, and Jones began a left turn into the wind to line up on the field.

I just had time to holler to Lieutenant Andy and the others to brace for landing, and I shouted the reminder, "Pick up your feet!"

I flinched as I both heard and felt popping sounds as German small arms fire punched through the doped fabric skin of the glider. One struck the steel tube framework in front of me, sparked, and sent steel shrapnel flying across the cockpit.

Flight Officer Jones concentrated on the landing, ignoring the distracting tracer fire from the ground. He was flying for his life as well as ours. I had a brief flash-back to Folkingham when one of our troopers sarcastically joked, "Don't worry, the pilot will hit the ground first!" Time seemed to slow, and I still have memory flashes, like still-frames of a movie: Jones making minute course adjustments to line up perfectly parallel just to the left of the ditch that ran down the center of the field; crop furrows aligned with the ditch; at the right side of the field a narrow dirt road just beyond a thin line of trees; wings level; and then the woods flashing below.

I braced myself, crossed my fingers, and the ground rushed up at us. Jones pulled up on the spoiler lever, and we grounded with a sudden shock. Crops went flying everywhere as the skids dug into the ground in a shower of dirt, and as the glider's tail lifted and then fell back, we came to a stop.

Either my seat belt broke, or the buckle failed. I was thrown forward into the instrument panel and the tubular framework supporting it, but my helmet took the brunt of the impact, and I ended up slumped on my right side, my legs between the seats, and momentarily stunned.

As I regained my senses, my only thought was to get out of the glider as quickly as possible. I pulled myself back onto the seat, turned, and climbed across tangled legs and boxes of ammo. As I stumbled aft, I released the seat belts of five of my men, then staggered to the small V-shaped emergency exit door on the right side. Bullets were still ripping through the wings and upper fuselage of the glider, stitching bright holes in the fabric interior. We'd all be killed if we didn't move quickly.

I shouted, "On your feet! Get the hell out of here! GO, GO, GO . . . EVERYONE OUT!"

I jerked the door handle and threw my weight against it, nearly tearing the flimsy plywood and canvas door off its hinges, falling through the opening onto the turf, flat on my face. If I hadn't been so scared, I would have gone out the much larger left-hand door, which might have screened my movements from the Germans. But in my single-minded rush to escape the glider, I went for the nearest exit, putting me on the exposed side, a perfect target for German gunfire from the woods. But I was only a few yards from the ditch.

I no sooner stood up and stepped out from under the wing than I took a tremendous "whack" to my left leg. It felt like someone had struck me with a baseball bat, and I dropped back onto the ground with my face in the dirt again. I instinctively knew I'd been shot, and my leg felt numb. I wished the earth would swallow me up, but I had to move. I pulled myself back onto my feet, staggered around the nose of the glider, and hobbled to the relative safety of the shallow ditch. I pitched headlong into the bottom, relieved to find it was about twenty-four, perhaps thirty inches deep, and at least four or five feet wide.

I rolled over and peered over the crops on the ditch's rim; I could see smoke coming from holes in the fabric of the rear fuselage. No one had followed me yet, so I shouted again, "Get the hell out of there and into the ditch, or you're gonna die in there!"

I cocked the bolt of my gun and squeezed off a short spray of gunfire at the woods that I thought must be concealing the Germans. Beyond the glider's tail was the more extensive woods to the east, perhaps 150 yards away, but another, smaller wood was in the southeast. At first, I wasn't sure where the gunfire originated. I scanned the entire area and saw a group of Germans coming from the field's access road and northeast corner. A return burst of tracer fire confirmed that they were the likely source.

After what seemed like minutes but probably seconds, the right rear door burst open, and the rest of the squad emerged in a rush of bodies, with Lieutenant Andy bringing up the rear, urging the men into the ditch. A few were wounded, and their buddies helped them in the dash as I emptied the magazine into the trees in short bursts.

Flight Officer Jones was one of the last men out. He emerged from the small emergency door behind his seat. Running around the nose of the glider in a crouch, M-1 carbine in his hands, he jumped into the ditch. I counted heads and came up with thirteen, plus me. Several men began to search for targets, firing at the Germans, while the wounded started opening first aid packs to bandage their wounds.

Automatic weapon fire from the woods to the southeast startled me, and I was sickened to realize we were at risk of being caught in a crossfire. I guessed that we had taken the Germans by surprise, and it took them several minutes to reach the edge of the field in any number, but we were in a desperate situation. All of us began to return fire, anticipating an imminent attack.

But nothing happened, and the gunfire died out. I thumbed the magazine release, pulled the empty mag out, and fished a replacement from the pouch on my web gear. As I did, I noticed blood on both my gloved hands. Damn, I thought, when did that happen? I must have taken shrapnel from hits to the glider's steel tubing, but I hadn't noticed it. I flexed the fingers of both hands, but other than rips in the thin leather gloves and the blood, I couldn't see or feel any damage. My leg wound was another story. I had taken a bullet just above my left boot. It hadn't broken the bone, but it hurt like hell. It would have to wait.

The Germans seemed to have gone to ground at the edge of the field. A narrow area of scrub or grass lay between our fodder beet field and the woods and I wondered if that was where the Germans were. If so, they were only fifty or sixty yards from our sheltered position, but they couldn't get a clear shot at us without briefly exposing themselves. But that didn't stop them from trying one frontal assault, and five or six soldiers began quickly moving towards us.

I don't think they knew how many of us were in the ditch. Our gunfire took its toll whenever a German exposed himself. One German soldier who advanced from the woods took a burst from my Thompson and pitched forward onto his face, not twenty yards away, and I was sure we hit a few others. He was the first man I had ever shot, and I felt an overwhelming but irrational fear that he would get up and keep coming at me. I instinctively gave him a second burst of fire. He was so close I saw several bullets punch holes in the top of his helmet, perforating the steel, but he didn't move.

I suddenly felt sick to my stomach, aware of what I had done to the man. The Thompson fired the same .45 ACP round as the Colt pistol. It's a slower, subsonic, and heavy round, nearly a half-inch in diameter. It packs a solid punch, and a hit can lift a good-sized man off his feet, throw him backward, or at least spin him around, if not drop him. It didn't bear thinking about what a few rounds would do to a man's head. It became a recurring nightmare that would haunt me for decades to come.

The Germans disappeared, and as the gunfire slacked off, I looked for Lieutenant Anderson. Of the fourteen of us, it appeared as though Lieutenant Andy was injured the worst, taking a bullet to his shoulder while he was still the glider. He lay on his side against the berm of the ditch. I cautiously crabbed over to him and saw that he was ashen-faced and had his eyes closed.

"Lieutenant," I said, "You took a bad hit. We need to get something on that. Let's get your gear off." I unclipped his pistol belt, and the trooper on his other side pulled the combat suspenders off, then took out the lieutenant's first aid pack, ripped it open, and took out the gauze dressing. He used his trench knife to slit the back of the jacket and dress the wound as best he could, then gave him a syrette of morpheme and stuck it in his jacket lapel, all while lying on his side as flat as possible.

I asked the lieutenant, "Do you think you can hold on for a few hours until dark?"

He opened his eyes and replied, "Yeah, I think I can." He pulled his carbine up and cocked it with one hand, buttstock on his thigh, and eased himself up to the lip of the ditch to squeeze off a few shots, then lowered himself down. I could see the pain on his face, but he was a plucky guy.

I was carefully scanning the field's eastern edge when two men nearest the glider's tail signaled to me that they saw movement from the small woods. Suddenly they stood and fired past the tail and then dropped back down. They crawled back toward me.

I asked, "How many? Did you get them?"

"Yeah," answered Cator, "we got at least two, and the others withdrew."

By now, the glider began to burn, flames licking out of the fabric and spreading quickly. The bazooka rounds and grenades were in wooden crates that would burn quickly, but the .30-06 rifle ammunition would take longer to cook off. With Germans in multiple positions, I abandoned any thought of retrieving any of it. We would be exposing ourselves to direct fire. In any case, the fire was rapidly consuming the aircraft.

I called out so all the squad could hear me. "Move down the ditch to the west, slowly, away from the glider, and for God's sake, stay low. The ammo inside is going to go off. Try to dig yourselves in." We crabbed slowly, one man at a time until we reached another ditch, this one perpendicular and running the width of the field with heavy shrubs to our back. We pulled out our trenching tools and began to dig carefully at the damp soil of the ditch to give ourselves a bit more protection.

Within a few minutes, the flames reached the explosive cargo, and the glider was rocked by either a bazooka round or grenade exploding; then, the bulk of the load went off in sympathetic detonations. Pieces flew everywhere in a series of blasts, raining scraps of burning fabric, melted Plexiglas, steel tubing, and scorched plywood honeycomb all around the field. In a few minutes, the rifle ammunition began to pop off in ragged bursts, then died out completely. Within ten minutes, the glider was a shattered, smoldering skeleton. The thought suddenly struck me that my silk escape map was in there!

After the flames subsided, things became quiet for a while. I became aware of the "crump" of heavy artillery firing in the woods to the east for the first time. Rolling onto my back, looking up, I could see the sky was clear of aircraft, so it wasn't anti-aircraft fire. I guessed that it was a German artillery battery deep in the woods shelling the Allied positions along "Hell's Highway" and that the troops we faced may have come from the artillery unit. It was just our luck to land in this field, smack dab in the middle of a bunch of Krauts.

I decided to check on all the men and started crawling down the ditch. I hadn't moved more than five feet when I felt a jerk to the back of my jacket and heard a gunshot. I dropped flat, reached back, and felt a hole but no blood. I figured it was a less-than-friendly reminder from the Germans to keep my ass down!

I kept moving, as low as possible, and came to one of my men that looked dead, lying on his back with his eyes closed. It was Private Art Delosh, our BAR gunner. As my face passed close to Art's dirt-smeared face, he opened his eyes and muttered, "Hi, Sarge."

"Are you hit," I asked him?

"Naw, I don't think so . . . just so dammed scared I must have fallen asleep!"

I had never heard of such a thing and thought he was joking. I learned later that it was a rare but genuine reaction for troops in shock, severely wounded, or under sudden, nearly overwhelming fear. The theory is that when the human mind is over-stressed, it just shuts down temporarily. As I looked him over, I could see that despite what he said, Art had been severely wounded in his upper left shoulder, very close to the base of his neck, and in both legs. I didn't see any arterial blood, but he was a mess. I was sure he was in shock.

"You're hit pretty bad, Art," I told him. "Give me your first-aid pack, and I'll try to dress it for you."

"I must have gotten careless," Delosh replied. With his right arm, he handed over the small Carlisle first aid tin from his belt pouch. I helped him pull off his combat suspenders to expose the shoulder, peeled the seal off the container, took out the dressing, and did my best to wrap it around his left shoulder and under his right armpit. It was a lousy job, but I took a clean handkerchief and stuffed it under the wrap to put more pressure on the wound. It still wasn't perfect, but it was all I could do. I told PFC Clark, Art's assistant, to do what he could for the leg wounds.

"Can you move your right arm?" I asked him. As our BAR gunner, if he were out of action, he'd need to pass the BAR to Clark, who was on his far side.

"It still works, and I can still shoot," he replied, "as long as I can get the damn magazines out of my belt."

The Browning Automatic Rifle is an excellent squad weapon. The renowned gunmaker John Browning developed it during the First World War as an easily portable automatic weapon for clearing enemy trenches. The BAR weighs nearly 20 pounds empty, plus the weight of the 20-round box magazine and the added weight of a muzzle-mounted bipod. It fires the same .30-06 round as the Garand and Springfield rifles and puts bullets downrange at a blistering 2,700 feet per second, more than twice the speed of sound. Art could squeeze off aimed bursts of 3-5 rounds with the selective fire capability. With several magazines, and if he was sparing with his firing, he could keep the Germans in the woods hunkered down for well over an hour.

While Clark worked to bandage Art's leg wounds, I got the box magazines out of his cartridge belt and placed them in a row on the ground next to him. "Don't waste them. We need to hold out until dark if we can," I reminded him. "Let Clark do the shooting."

Smoke still emanated from the glider wreckage, and we had worked our way down the ditch as far as we could to escape it. From this position, I could see a couple of Germans moving, attempting to flank us within that sparse tree line on our left. Their dark forms scuttled from tree to tree, seeking cover behind the trunks and shrubs. The guys on my left could keep the Germans from moving too close.

There was a prolonged lull in the shooting for more than a half-hour, and we observed several German soldiers cautiously approaching from the northeast corner, off the access road. They were taking their time, and one had his weapon slung over their shoulder, seemingly unaware of us. The other two appeared to be officers. I wondered what the hell they were doing. Perhaps the smoke from the glider masked our position, but we were low, well away from the glider. Were they from a different unit and unaware that anyone had escaped the glider?

When the trio got within a dozen yards of the wreckage, several of my guys opened fire, dropping all three in their tracks. I don't think they even knew what hit them. But I was worried that the Germans might have flanked or gotten behind us. Or were they just investigating the glider wreckage?

As if on cue, new German submachine gun fire opened up from the southeast woods, and bright tracers passed over our heads. Rifle rounds threw up clods of dirt that rained down on us. My greatest fear was that the Germans might employ an MG-42 machine gun. I had fired one back at Scraptoft, and it was a superb squad weapon. It fired belted ammunition at a rate of 1,200 rounds per minute, so fast that it's almost impossible to distinguish the individual muzzle blasts. So far, all the opposing fire had been from personal weapons, but our situation had gone from bad to worse.

Exposing as little of myself as possible, I fired a few random bursts at the tree line, hoping I might hit the man with the submachine gun. It seemed as though I was the only one shooting, but the adrenaline takes over in combat, and your focus narrows to just what is in front of you. At long range, my Thompson was pretty ineffective, but we had some excellent rifle marksmen in the squad.

"C'mon, you guys, lock and load, and get shooting," I hollered. Almost as one, each man in the ditch began returning the German fire. The submachine gun stopped firing.

The Germans intended to keep our heads down so we would not observe their maneuvers, but within a short time, Lieutenant Anderson shouted out that there was movement in the trees again. They were approaching our left flank again, carefully leapfrogging down the thin tree line on the road. We laid down a good burst, including Private Delosh with his BAR, and the Germans went to the ground, or maybe we hit them. We kept up sporadic fire whenever we saw movement in the trees or tall grass. Gradually, the shooting slowed and stopped again, suggesting that the Germans were content with the status quo. I was pretty sure they didn't know how many of us were in the ditch.

Unable to see the German artillery and the direction of their firing, I could not tell where the nearest Allied position might be. I knew we were many miles short of LZ-Oscar and tried to orient myself. On my back, I fished out my pocket compass and tried to study the view to the west. I could see a smokestack, tower, or steeple of some sort just above some treetops, perhaps a quarter of a mile away or a bit more. There was supposed to be a milk processing plant near the Overasselt landing zone, but we had never gotten that far north.

As I lay back, I tried to do some calculations. Our tow plane had been hit shortly after crossing the border, and with a towed speed of no more than 150 miles per hour, we had covered 2.5 miles each minute. I calculated that we were hit about 8 to 10 minutes after crossing the Escaut Canal on the Belgian-Dutch border. That meant we could be somewhere around 20 to 25 miles into Holland. During our flight, I studied the escape map and tried to recall the distances between cities on our flight path. From the Belgian-Holland border, Eindhoven was about 15 miles up Hell's Highway, Nijmegen another 30 past that, and Arnhem another 15 miles or so. Ten minutes' flight into Holland would put us slightly to the north of Eindhoven and the 101st Airborne. Since our course was east of the highway, we were probably more than ten or twelve miles from the nearest Allied positions. I tried to recall what towns were in that area. Erp? Gemert? Veghel? It was anyone's guess, but I was pretty sure we were well east of the highway, miles into German-held territory. Veghel was supposed to be in the hands of the 101st, or at least it was at the morning briefing.

I crawled close to Lieutenant Andy to discuss it with him. I tried to establish the rough direction towards where I guessed Veghel would be. In the daylight, the Germans had us pinned down, gradually running out of ammunition and slowly being surrounded by enemy soldiers. If they got behind us, we were done. We landed at about 1615 hours, it was now approaching 1800 hours, and I recalled that sunset would be in about thirty minutes. But we still had over an hour and a half until it would be fully dark. Even then, we might not be able to slip away. It was not looking good for us.

I wriggled my way down the ditch, crawling over a couple of the men to get to Sergeant Barc. Walt was busy dealing with a wound to his left forearm. He had passed his submachine gun and spare magazines to Private Gorski, who was next to him, and he was applying a dressing as well as he could. Gorski began to squeeze off occasional short bursts at the woods.

I asked Barc, "Walt, how bad are you hit?"

"Not too bad, but it's starting to hurt like hell," he responded.

I shared my thoughts with him. "If we can hold out until dark, we might have a chance to slip away. It's nearly 1800 now. It won't be dark enough for at least two more hours. Do you have any idea where we are? I think we're east of the main highway, which means we'll need to head west. We're miles short of the LZ and might be near the 101st guys in Veghel."

"I think you're right about that," replied Walt. "But we'll never last that long."

"I'm afraid you're right, but we don't have much choice unless we decide to surrender soon. We're running out of ammo," I added.

The firefight had dragged on for nearly two hours. As we tried to shoot at the Germans on our left flank, the soldiers in the woods would open fire, forcing us to keep our heads down. It was a stalemate. I had repeatedly changed magazines, firing short three-round bursts as Germans exposed themselves or to spots where I saw a muzzle flash, but the range was too far for accuracy. I couldn't believe the Germans would try another frontal attack, but just to discourage them, several of us had lobbed hand grenades at spots where we thought Krauts hid in the narrow tree line. With my boxing conditioning, I had a strong arm and could throw a grenade pretty far, but not from a prone position. As it was, the range was just too far, but at least it kept them at bay.

As the shadows began to lengthen, we were nearly out of what little ammunition remained. I was almost through my last magazine of Thompson ammo and still had one grenade and my pistol. I prayed we could just hold out until dark, then perhaps a few might be able to slip away and make it to our troops.

I slowly worked my way down the muddy ditch towards the lieutenant, only vaguely aware of the danger from German gunfire, partially deafened by our own.

We watched helplessly as the Germans finally edged closer and closer to our left flank. They had too much cover, and we had too little ammunition to survive an assault from both the wood and our left flank. I thought that our saving grace was that the Germans were in the situation of a circular firing squad, where reckless gunfire risked hitting their men. As the shadows of the few pine trees to our west reached our position in the ditch, I called for everyone to check their ammunition. No one had more than one eight-round clip left for their M-1s. Barc and Delosh were out, and I was down to my last few rounds of ammo. My pistol was only good for close-quarters shooting, and I still had a full magazine in the Colt. I thought of the spare pistol mags in my pockets and considered stripping off the rounds, just fourteen, and loading them into an empty Thompson magazine.

At this point, one of the men hissed and pointed to our rear. The brush about twenty yards away obscured our sightline in that direction. Peering under it, I saw a couple of enemy soldiers approaching. They had us surrounded, and any further fighting would be futile. I crabbed back to Lieutenant Andy.

"We're almost out of ammo, and they've surrounded us. We could give them one more volley, but then it'll be a knife fight. I think we should throw in the towel now. If they rush us now, it would be a blood bath."

The look on his face was a mix of resignation and pain. "Sarge, I concur. If we try to hit them again, it might just make things worse. We'd be wiped out for no good reason." He paused before adding, "I can't raise my arms. Think you can surrender without getting shot?"

He was right. The choice was obvious. If we shot some of them up and then tried to surrender, they'd likely just chop us up. If we surrender now, perhaps we would be taken prisoner and not killed outright.

"Okay," I replied.

"Hold fire," shouted Lieutenant Andy.

Here goes nothing, I thought. I put down my weapon and shouted as loudly as possible, "Don't shoot. We surrender!"

I cautiously rose to my feet, hands about shoulder high, hoping not to be shredded by a hail of gunfire. I faced what I believed to be the closest Germans emerging from the trees on our left flank. I tensed, expecting to feel the impact of bullets before I even heard the blast, but nothing happened.

I hollered again to the Germans, "Don't shoot!" Thankfully, they held their fire as they cautiously approached. The rest of our squad put down their weapons and struggled to their feet, following my lead.

Chapter 15

For You, the War is Over!

I watched a half-dozen Germans emerge from the trees and underbrush. Two held Schmeisser MP-40 "burp guns" leveled at me. As they came closer, I saw that one was an officer, wearing a peaked cap and holding a pistol. Another was an NCO, identified by his silver-edged collar. No one fired, although I'm sure their emotions were running as high as ours, if not higher, since I was confident that we had killed a few of their men. The officer, an older man whom I guessed to be about forty, spoke clear English. "Put down your weapons!" he ordered. "For you, the war is over."

With much gesturing to reinforce the officer's orders, the German soldiers moved us away from the ditch into the center of the field and made it clear that we were to drop our weapons where we were. One of the younger-looking Germans, a particularly unpleasant-looking fellow with an assault rifle, hollered something at me in German.

I guess I was resentful at our capture and maybe sort of cocky just to be alive, so I snapped back at him.

"I don't speak Kraut, so don't bother shouting at me!"

It just made him angry, for he instantly swung his rifle around and gave me a solid butt-stroke to the chest in the blink of an eye. I went down on my ass, gasping for breath, and he quickly reversed the weapon and shoved the muzzle in my face. "Easy for him to be tough, with his finger on the trigger," I thought. And he might have pulled the trigger if it wasn't for the officer at his side. The Germans had shot paratroopers in Normandy, hung up in trees, helpless to fire back, getting no quarter. Thankfully, the officer kept a tight rein on his men, and no one else was injured.

Some of us had collapsed onto the ground, wounded, and exhausted, but they hauled us to our feet and prodded us towards the trees. Two men helped Art Delosh up, and I put Lieutenant Andy's good arm over my shoulder and one arm around his waist, and together we limped across the field in the fading light into the darkness of the woods. The intermittent flash of heavy gunfire from the artillery deeper in the woods briefly illuminated everything, casting intense shadows and almost blinding me if I looked toward it. I was exhausted and hurting, and in the momentary light, I could see that all of us were in the same condition.

After shuffling about thirty yards, we entered a small clearing, and curious Germans surrounded us. Most appeared to be about our age, but a few who were probably still in their teens came close, just staring at us while the ones that rounded us up kept us covered with their weapons. The officer motioned for us to sit and addressed us in clear, barely accented English, "Sit and wait."

We all just dropped to the ground where we were. We looked each other over for injuries, which wasn't easy because of the darkness, dirt, and grime that covered us. Our captors allowed us a few minutes to dress our wounds while they conferred, apparently waiting for instructions. We didn't see if they recovered any of their casualties from the firefight.

Ten of the fourteen of us were wounded, with Lieutenant Andy and Private Delosh the worst. I gingerly pulled up my blood-soaked trouser leg to examine my leg wound. I found a puncture on the inside of my calf, but curiously there was no exit wound. Most of the bleeding had stopped, so I poured sulfa powder on it and wrapped it with a field dressing. As the temperature fell with the onset of darkness, I began to shiver uncontrollably. I suppose shock had set in as well. I wasn't the only one in rough shape. We all looked like crap: wet, bloodstained, sweaty, and muddy.

I sat back and looked up at the night sky but couldn't see stars. It had clouded over and looked like it was going to rain again. As I looked around the clearing, it suddenly occurred to me that it was quiet. The artillery firing had stopped, and it was strangely silent in the forest, with just the soft murmur of German voices and the dripping of the leaves. In the distance, I could hear the clanking of armored vehicles moving down a road.

In a few minutes, the German officer returned with instructions. "You may keep personal items, but the bags stay here. Be quick about it. We leave in just a few minutes." He cupped his hands to light a cigarette, and I could see his illuminated face, unshaven, with exhaustion in his eyes. As he puffed, he carefully watched to ensure we complied. As if to answer our unspoken thoughts, he smiled and added, "I studied at Oxford before the war."

We peeled off our field gear and emptied our packs and bags. We dumped what we could do without, or couldn't carry, then stuffed our pockets with personal items. I kept my toothbrush, a small pen knife, a pair of socks, underwear shorts, a t-shirt, a couple of chocolate bars, a pack of Blackjack gum, a pack of Charms hard candies, a comb, a razor, a small bar of soap and a packet of toilet paper. When I tried to pick up a couple of K-ration boxes, a German guard bent down and grabbed my wrist to stop me, so I tossed them onto the growing pile of gear to be left behind. I kept my bloody gloves on because my hands didn't hurt much, at least not yet. It was getting too dark to see much anyway.

"What's next?" I asked Lieutenant Andy. "Think they'll shoot us, keep us here 'til morning, or take us somewhere else?"

The German officer quickly snapped, "No talking!" Then he stubbed out his smoke and signaled for us to stand. Using their weapons, our guards prodded us to our feet, then started us moving out. Stiffness and pain were setting in for all of us who were injured. It took us a few minutes to struggle up, and flex our limbs to stimulate circulation, then we limped out of the clearing, through the trees, and out to a rutted dirt road that led from the field to a narrow-paved road. Once on the pavement, we turned right, with guards on either side and a sergeant bringing up the rear with his Schmeisser machine pistol slung across his chest.

If you could call our staggering gait a march, our march seemed to go on forever. It was difficult to determine what direction we were headed, but I was pretty sure it was to the east or possibly the southeast., which I knew was toward Germany. Could the Germans be retreating, or were they just consolidating their position? The road was busy with vehicle traffic, mostly moving in the same direction. The shielded driving lights cast a feeble glow on the pavement as they passed. We walked on the right shoulder, tired, dizzy, and weak from our wounds and the post-adrenaline letdown after the firefight. Delosh, with wounds to both legs, was half-carried between two of the uninjured guys who rotated with others every half-mile or so.

Despite being fixated on my pain, trying to put one foot in front of the other and not trip on the edge of the pavement, I was aware of staff cars, bicycles, motorcycles, trucks, self-propelled guns, half-tracks, armored vehicles, and even a few Panther tanks, almost all headed our way in an apparent German withdrawal. A few staff cars and motorcycles threaded their way back to the west, probably to direct the pullback or carry dispatches back to the units covering the retreat. The sheer number of artillery pieces, both self-propelled and towed, was evidence of the hell that rained on our troops during the preceding days.

Finally, after several hours, we approached a small town, and the pavement gave way to cobbled streets. In the dark, I was dimly aware of multi-story buildings on both sides of me, but I couldn't make out any signs or details. We made several turns, then halted in the middle of the road as one of our guards crossed to a large brick building, climbed a short flight of stone steps, and knocked on a heavy wooden door. In a moment or two, the door was opened, casting a shaft of light across the threshold, and illuminating our German guard. He spoke briefly to whoever answered, then motioned for us to move inside.

We found ourselves in a large, sparsely decorated vestibule with closed doors on the right and left. A long, wide staircase on the wall in front of us led up to a second floor. A carved wooden credenza against the left wall was the only furnishing, and the white plaster walls were bare except for a large crucifix on the wall to our right. I concluded that we were in a monastery or convent, but the occupants were nowhere to be seen. Our lead German, who I now recognized as a sergeant by his collar edging, opened the door on the right. Two of his men shoved us into another much larger room with a higher ceiling and several wall sconces for illumination. There was a table against one wall with two straight-backed chairs, one on either side, and a large rug on the floor, which we proceeded to muddy up and bleed all over. One of our guards checked another door that I had not noticed. Finding it locked, he seemed satisfied. Without a word, the NCO motioned us to sit, and then both Germans departed, closing the entry door behind them, the thud of the heavy door conveying a sense of finality.

We were bone tired, dirty, and still in a state of shock from the adrenaline rush of the previous afternoon, and we all slumped against the wall and slid to the floor. I suddenly realized that I was famished and fished a chocolate D-bar out of my jacket pocket, unwrapped it, and tried to chew it slowly. We spoke quietly among ourselves for a while, reexamining our wounds and treating them as well as we could.

I sat between Lieutenant Andy and Art Delosh so that I could keep an eye on them, and both men were stretched out flat on the floor. Their eyes were closed, and they were exhausted and in pain from their shoulder wounds and Art had leg wounds as well. I felt that we should be able to do something for them. As I finished the chocolate bar, I looked around the room to see how everyone else was fairing. Most had minor wounds, but none were life-threatening.

"Hey," I called out, waving the morphine tin. "Who's got any spare dressings and morphine? We need to treat everyone's injuries and make Art and the lieutenant more comfortable."

Five or six of the guys offered up first aid packs, and several had morphine syrettes to offer, so I asked Private Cator, who was not wounded, to collect them and bring them over. He collected them, and when I stood to make room, he knelt between the two men, then injected them. Finally, following standard operation procedures, he stuck the spent needles into their jacket collars to indicate that they had been injected with morphine. As carefully as they could, Cator and Blood changed the dressings of the wounded. I sat against the wall next to the lieutenant and to numb the pain of my leg wound, I took a syrette and injected myself, then stuck the needle through my jacket collar. It was all we could do for now.

I finished chewing the bite of chocolate. I was exhausted but still keyed up, so I shrugged out of my damp field jacket, wadded it up for a pillow, and laid down. My thoughts were random and confused. I couldn't help but feel frustrated and disgusted at being captured during my first contact with the enemy, but I tried to reassure myself that we had all done as well as we could, and none had been killed. I had done my best, even though it was not enough.

I learned many decades later that our situation had been untenable. We were surrounded by elements of Kampfgruppe Walther, one of several hastily collected battle groups composed of SS, Luftwaffe, Wehrmacht, Panzer units, military police, reserves, and young replacements that rushed into action. Our unscheduled landing, as well as that of at least eighteen other gliders, persuaded Colonel Walther, a Luftwaffe officer, that it was time to abandon the repeated attempts to retake Veghel. Late on the afternoon of September 23, he reported to General Obstfelder, commanding the LXXXVI Corps, that new Allied landings from the air forced him to pull back to a line running from Handel to Gemert and abandon Erp, the village closest to our landing. Had I known that we had contributed to the German withdrawal, I might not have been so disheartened.

But I knew nothing of that, and my thoughts turned to the future. Would the Germans treat the wounded tomorrow? Will my parents think I'm dead? I popped a Charms candy into my mouth, sucked slowly to savor the sweetness, and as the pain faded, my thoughts wandered back to my childhood. Sometime later, I fell into a dreamless sleep.

Morning came all too soon as the door was thrown open with shouts of, "Raus! Raus!" We struggled to our feet, but my left leg was so sore and stiff that I could hardly put weight on it. I hobbled to the doorway, and as I leaned against the frame, I slowly put more weight on the leg and nearly collapsed.

A voice behind me said, "Sarge, let me give you a hand." Private Overholser put an arm around my waist to help me walk around in circles until my leg muscles warmed up. When we were all on our feet, the Germans herded us out the front door. As I stood for a moment on the top of the porch landing, a drizzle of cool rain washed my face. It felt good, and I tried to wipe the grime off my cheeks and my beard stubble. We descended the steps and about a block or two into what seemed to be the courtyard of a large church, castle, or monastery. We were joined by a couple dozen more captives, a motley collection of American paratroopers, fellow glidermen, and several British soldiers.

We all seemed to be equally gloomy, and there was little talking. The Germans made a quick head count, then ordered us onto several waiting trucks with engines already running. I climbed and crawled into the covered truck bed with about twenty others. Two German guards with submachine guns climbed in with us and sat next to the tailgate. The engines revved, the guards pulled down the rear tarp, and with gears grinding, we were off, rumbling over cobbled streets and turning onto the smoother pavement of a major road.

As my eyes adjusted to the gloom, I asked my companions how each was doing. I immediately got a gun muzzle stuck in my face, and the guard growled, "Nicht sprechen!" It was abundantly clear that we were not to talk, so we rode in silence, most of us dozing off, stirred only by the bumping and lurching of the truck. It was painful for the guys with severe wounds because a couple cried out when we hit big bumps. Several of the younger ones sobbed a bit. I don't know if that was from pain or just despair.

For my part, I was apprehensive about what lay in store and rehashed my thoughts from the night before, still bitterly frustrated and angry at the turn of events. Again, I wondered if there was more I could have done. Here I was, a prisoner of war, while the rest of the regiment was taking the fight to the enemy. Even though I knew we were dealt a bad hand, I couldn't help but feel a failure. At least we were still alive, for now, anyway. I kept my mouth shut and closed my eyes.

American and British POWs being moved out of the Gemert monastery to waiting German trucks on the morning of September 24, 1944. (By permission of Pater Loffeld)

We traveled for several hours, alternately making good time, then slowing or stopping as we moved off to the shoulder of the road to let higher priority traffic pass. Sometime near midday, the truck turned off, and we stopped. Our guards climbed down and reported to an NCO who motioned for us to dismount and then ushered us into a German field hospital. A German doctor, wearing a bloodstained white smock, gave each of us a once-over, then directed a couple of soldiers to move the more seriously wounded, including Lieutenant Andy and Art

Delosh, into a different room to have their wounds examined and redressed. One at a time, the guards took us across a hallway to be interrogated.

As the senior man in the group, I was first, roughly hauled into a dimly lit, sparsely furnished room, where I stood in front of a desk behind which sat a young SS officer. He ignored me for a moment, and I took a glance around. A chalkboard was mounted on one wall and assumed this was a commandeered schoolhouse. I studied the officer, but I couldn't figure out his rank. He seemed almost as tired as me, with dark spots under his eyes. His dark brown hair, combed back and parted just off-center, was a bit disheveled. He wore eyeglasses low on his nose, and a cigarette hung from his mouth. After a minute or two, he looked up to acknowledge me but then put his head back down and continued smoking. I took notice of a pack of Lucky Strikes on the table next to a full ashtray. He shuffled through a few files, opened one, and examined a sheet of paper. My God, I thought to myself, this is like the movies! I wondered if I would get the light-in-the-face treatment and be beaten with a rubber hose?

Finally, after several minutes, the officer looked up again and gave me a cursory once-over. I still looked like a mess.

"So, why is America fighting Germany?" he asked me in clear English.

According to the Geneva Convention, I only had to give him my name, rank, and serial number, but it seemed a stupid question that deserved an equally stupid answer. Germany had declared war on America first.

"We're fighting for our American cigarettes," I replied, motioning to the pack on his desk.

"Perhaps you would like one?" he asked, a slight smile on his face. I would have loved to give him a stiff punch in the nose, but I just stood there.

"No thanks," I responded, trying to act like I was nonchalant. I lied and said, "I'm trying to quit."

He stared at me for a moment, then looked back down to the papers on his desk as though he had a file on me. "You were in a glider, were you not, Staff Sergeant? What was your mission?"

Okay, I had said about enough. I recited what the Geneva Convention required. "Condon, Billy, Staff Sergeant, three-six, one-zero-four, four-zero-one."

"Come now, Sergeant Condon, I know all about you and your men. You're with the 325th Glider Infantry Regiment, and you were supposed to reinforce your paratroopers at Groesbeek, were you not? It was a foolish strategy. Your armored column is stalled and isolated, and your American airborne is surrounded and will have to surrender within days. You have nowhere to go."

I thought he was full of crap and kept my mouth shut. I didn't know much anyway. He persisted with questions about where I came from, who my commanding officer was, and trivia like that. He probably knew the answers anyway. From the information on my dog tags, he knew my name, serial number, blood type, and home address, but nothing more personal and certainly nothing of any intelligence value. I just continued with the name-rank-serial-number reply.

Finally, after about ten minutes of this charade, he shouted for the guard, dropped his papers, and just snapped, "Get out, sergeant! I hope you like being a prisoner of war."

After about a half-hour standing idle in the corridor, it was my turn to see the German doctors. A guard escorted me into a large room at the end of the hall, and a doctor examined my leg and the wounds on my hands. They probed the leg wound without anesthesia, then swabbed it with iodine. It hurt like hell, and the doctors just laughed when I winced and sucked in my breath. They applied simple dressings, then motioned for me to peel off my gloves. They were stiff with dried blood, making it difficult to get them off. Each hand had a laceration, one to the forefinger of my right hand and the other to the heel of my left hand. A medic soaked my hands in a water basin, saw nothing was broken, swabbed each hand with more iodine, and wrapped them in gauze. Surprisingly, my hand injuries were the most painful, and I nearly screamed!

When they finished their cursory treatments and interrogations, we were hustled out of the aid station and ordered onto a new truck. This one had an open stake bed. Our new guards were soldiers in camouflage field uniforms—Waffen SS by their collar insignia runes—and we moved out. They were a hard-looking pair, probably in their mid-twenties, and they looked like no-nonsense combat veterans, either from the Eastern Front, Normandy, or both. They joked and laughed with each other as they smoked American Chesterfield cigarettes, generally ignoring us as though we were just cargo.

We had not gone more than a few miles when the truck pulled to a stop at a crossroads. The driver was confused and had to get directions or possibly local authorization to proceed.

As we heard but couldn't understand the exchange between the guards and driver, two young girls came walking down the road carrying baskets. The youngest one looked to be about eleven or twelve years old, and the elder perhaps fourteen. I had no idea where we were, so I don't know if they were Dutch, but as they walked past the truck's rear, they saw us crowded in the back. Recognizing the olive drab American uniforms, easily distinguished by the American flag sewn onto the right shoulder of our field jackets, they each smiled, and the older girl waved at us. Several of us smiled and waved back.

The off-side guard, facing the girls, became visibly angry, promptly cocked his MP-40 machine pistol, and pulled the trigger. To our horror, both girls were spun around in a bloody welter of arms, legs, and baskets as dozens of 9mm slugs chopped them to pieces. I was speechless and wanted to vomit, but all we could do was glare at the Nazi bastard in disbelief! He gave us a sneer, waved his weapon at us as though inviting anyone to make a move, then said something his companion thought was funny. I could have killed him with my bare hands. Although I witnessed a lot of heartless cruelty in the coming year, nothing I saw after this shocked me as much. The wanton killing of innocent children like this became another source of nightmares for years to come. Everything else paled in comparison. More than anything else, the cold-blooded murders brought the realization that my life wasn't worth a damn now.

Chapter 16

Kriegesfangenen, Stalag VI-G

We continued our slow truck journey for the next two days, occasionally stopping for fuel, water, and food, usually stale black bread, hard cheese, or a cup of bland stew. The blackout kept most vehicles off the roads at night, so we were locked inside whatever buildings were available. The first night we spent locked in a chilly, drafty barn. The second night, probably somewhere in Germany by now, we slept in an abandoned, bomb-damaged factory.

Finally, late on September 27, we pulled into a fenced compound with a large sign over the gateway that proclaimed it to be Stalag VI-G. One of the other fellows said he had seen a sign on the road that pointed towards Cologne, so at last, we had some vague idea of where we were. We stopped and unloaded, stood in formation for a head count, then we were ordered to deposit our helmets in a pile beside the gate. I felt relieved when our Waffen SS escort turned us over to the camp guard detachment. Mostly, these fellows looked like older Wehrmacht soldiers, which gave me some hope that our conditions might improve.

We were ushered into a large stucco, three-story headquarters building, where the guards lined us single-file along the main corridor with doors on either side, which I assumed were administrative offices. One by one, we were escorted into a reception hall, about fifteen feet wide and thirty feet long, with tables along one wall and a large portrait of Adolf Hitler on the end wall. Clerks seated at the tables, both male and female soldiers, formally processed us as POWs. After being given a cursory physical check for height, weight, hair, and eye color, we were fingerprinted and photographed while holding a chalkboard with our name, rank, and serial number.

A couple of German civilians stamped our names and POW identification number onto a rectangular tin dog tag. This German version measured one-and-a-quarter inch by three inches and was perforated down the center of the long axis, with identical information on each half. In the event of my death, half of the tag would be broken off to record our demise. (I still have it in my collection of memorabilia.)

My first impression of Stammlager VI-G, or stalag for short, was that it may have been a hospital before the war, now serving as a German army hospital for the less seriously wounded, with an attached prisoner of war compound. For the sake of Lieutenant Anderson and Art Delosh, our more seriously wounded men, I hoped we would be given additional medical treatment.

With the check-in complete, we were separated by rank, with our officers, Lieutenant Anderson and Flight Officer Jones, going to one compound, Walter Barc and me as senior NCOs to another, and the remainder of the men to an enlisted compound. I never saw either the officers or privates again.

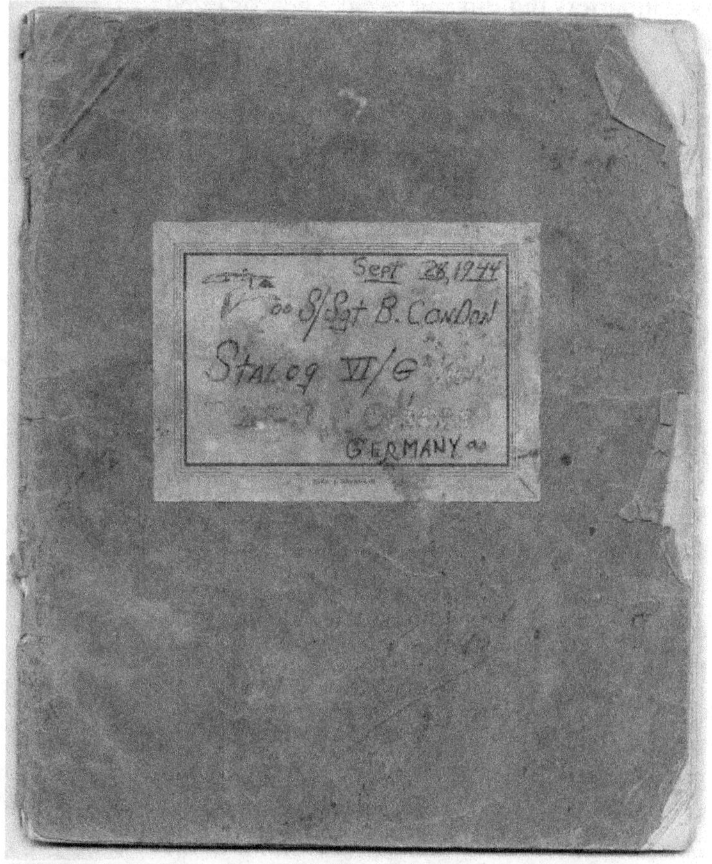

Billy Condon's slim and worn POW journal. (Author's collection)

Stalag VI-G turned out to be an enormous, well-established facility with several brick and concrete buildings and scores of more recently constructed wooden barrack huts. Walt and I were assigned to one of the wooden huts and found our way to a nearly empty cubicle. As we entered, I nearly collapsed with exhaustion and the pain from my leg wound.

"Home, sweet home!" Walt exclaimed, trying to cheer me up as I shrugged out of my jacket and tossed it on the bottom bunk. Because my leg had not yet healed and was giving me trouble, I wanted Walt to take the upper bunk. Our room filled up the next hour with other newly arrived men. One of my roommates gave me a small composition book that I decided to use as a journal to record my time as a POW. I knew then that the memories would fade; if I didn't survive, perhaps one of the other guys would see that it got to my family. I was careful to keep entries brief, in case the guards confiscated and read it, but I decided I would record every event of interest by date.

We inspected our new home, but there wasn't much to see. The typical POW hut was about 40 x 130 feet, with a central hallway, ten cubicles, each about 15 x 23 feet, and bunks for sixteen men until our captors added more bunks to accommodate twenty men. Each room had a row of bunks along the two long walls. A door and a small, shuttered window were centered on opposing walls, and the center space of the room, about six feet wide, was bare. The bunks were simple wood construction, with six slats, no more and no less, supporting thin, lumpy, tick mattresses filled with straw or wood shavings.

In VI-G, there were no tables or chairs and only a single light bulb, not more than 40 watts, to illuminate the room, but it was only switched on for a few hours each night after the shutters were closed. Perpetual gloom pervaded the space, and the smell of unwashed bodies was enough to make me gag, at least at first. Within days I grew accustomed to the odors and smelled just as bad myself. It would be weeks before I could take my clothes off or wash them, proving to be a rare event for the next nine months. I was thankful that I had kept my toothbrush, and for the duration of my captivity, I brushed daily with a pinch of sand, rinsing my mouth with my morning ration of ersatz coffee. It wasn't pleasant, but I never suffered a toothache or lost any teeth.

By this point in the war, the camp population was approaching 30,000 men, with new POWs arriving daily. (Records show it blossomed to over 50,000 after the Battle of the Bulge.) The various nationalities each had separate compounds, and we had about 1300 Americans in our compound. The German "posterns," or guards, lived in their own "vorlager," a substantially better barracks complex. At the same time, the POWs lived in "lagers," or compounds with wooden barracks clustered around a central assembly area.

All of this was surrounded by two parallel barbed wire fences, each about six feet high and spaced five or six feet apart. This gap was a no-man's zone, often patrolled by guards with dogs. A bare warning wire was strung another six feet inside the perimeter of the inner fence. A foot-high trip wire marked the death zone: crossing it meant that the guards would shoot to kill, and we were cautioned about this regularly.

To give the guards a clear and unobstructed view of the entire compound, the guard towers, about fifteen feet high, were positioned at each corner and about fifty yards apart. The guards in each tower had MG-34 machine guns, rifles, and searchlights that scanned the camp continuously at night. Each guard carried an automatic weapon when they walked the compound perimeter. They say that you can get used to anything, but it took a long while to get accustomed to being under the constant scrutiny of armed guards. I admit that I got accustomed to it but was never comfortable. It just works on your mind, like a sore that won't heal.

The prison population of Stalag VI-G consisted primarily of British, Polish, Russian, and American soldiers, but there were prisoners from virtually every country in Europe and several from overseas, such as India, South Africa, New Zealand, and Canada. The Russians were confined to a lager next to ours, and I quickly saw that they received particularly harsh, even brutal, treatment because Nazi propaganda portrayed them as subhuman.

To my surprise, I learned that some of my fellow American inmates had been prisoners for over four years and were desperately anxious for news about the war. Among the first few batches of POWs from Market-Garden, we were questioned repeatedly by the other "kriegies," our POW abbreviation for the German term "kriegesfangenen." Having been captured within hours of landing, I knew little of the progress in Holland. Still, I shared what I had read about Patton's push across northern France, the island assaults in the Pacific, and the collapse of Italy, but there was little else I could tell them that was newsworthy.

Although the Germans controlled the POW camps and doled out the meager resources of life, the camps I was held in were all organized by the internees themselves. Each camp had a hierarchy, whether the compound was designated for officers, NCOs, or privates. Within each building, hut, or tent, there was a senior man, usually based on seniority but just as often chosen by the occupants. As a transitory camp or hospital camp for the newest American prisoners, the population of Stalag VI-G changed weekly, giving American POWs little opportunity to organize completely.

I didn't know what the Germans had planned for us, and I was never even registered as a POW with the Red Cross until I moved to the next camp. By comparison, the Commonwealth prisoners (mostly Indians and Sikhs), as well as the Norwegian, French, and Belgian prisoners who had been incarcerated here for years, were well organized and had found ways to keep their huts cleaner and better appointed. They had their own organized activities: sports, a library, and even a theater where they put on plays. But with the total segregation by nationality, we only had glimpses of it across the wire fences.

Our diet at Stalag VI-G was poor and disgusting. A post-War investigation assessed it as somewhere around 700 calories per day. Although the Red Cross shipped food packages for registered prisoners of war at the rate of one per man every two weeks, getting one was rare. When one did appear, it was shared among at least four men. I received just one while at Stalag VI-G.

Our daily menu, which never varied, consisted of nasty ersatz coffee made from ground acorns or sometimes weak tea in the morning, followed at noon by a thin grass soup and a small, stale, wormy loaf of black bread rolled in sawdust. Supper was a repeat of breakfast. Occasionally the soup would have a piece of meat thrown

Billy's portrait by Soviet POW. (Author's Collection)

in for flavor, but the rumor was that the meat was from animals killed by Allied bombings and could have been rancid horse, beef, dog, or even rat.

It took only a day in the stalag to realize that the currency in the camps was cigarettes. I had never been a heavy smoker and hoarded my cigarette ration carefully, trading for any food rations even worse than ours, but ironically, many were desperate for cigarettes. I suppose it did something to alleviate their suffering. One day, while walking our compound perimeter that butted up against the Russian lager, I was approached by a filthy and emaciated inmate. For five cigarettes, he offered to paint my portrait. He looked so pathetic I felt sorry for him. I don't think I ever expected he'd paint it, but I did a quick scan to be sure no guards were watching, then surreptitiously passed the fags through the fence.

I almost forgot about the incident, but several days later, he again caught my eye and motioned me over to the wire. Sure enough, he pulled out a small color portrait of me and passed it through the wire. It looked to be painted on a thin piece of cardboard from a Red Cross package. I cannot imagine where he got the brushes and paint to do it, but I was surprised and pleased, even though it bore only a fair resemblance to me. For safekeeping, I slipped it inside my jacket lining with the little journal I had begun to keep. They both came home with me, albeit a bit worn, and I still have them, safely filed with my other GI paperwork.

Food cravings became a constant companion. The issued bread was so hard and stale that it crumbled when cut. One of the fellows claimed his loaf of bread had the date 1938 stamped on the bottom. As hard as they were, I could believe it. These little loaves, not much larger than a softball and half as thick, had to be shared among six POWs. Cutting the loaf became a significant event in our day, and the rule was that the one who cut it got the last piece. As you can imagine, we cut the slices evenly, and even the crumbs were divided carefully. The bread was usually so stale and crumbly that I would put it into the watery soup to thicken it up, then pick the worms out of the concoction as they rose to the top. After a few days, I didn't even bother to pick them out and just ate them for protein. For the duration of my time as a POW, these little black loaves were a dietary staple, sometimes shared among four men rather than six. On one occasion, much later in my captivity, I had a whole loaf to myself. I jealously guarded it and made it last for four days.

On October 3, we had a ringside seat to an aerial dogfight. A flight of three American P-38 Lightnings came in low over the camp and got "bounced" by ten or twelve Messerschmitt Me-109 fighters. The fight, which began at less than 1,000 feet, quickly worked its way up to over 5,000 feet and then back down to nearly ground level. Hundreds of us congregated in the open areas of the compound to watch as the fighters twisted and turned, the unpainted, bare-metal Lightnings flashing in the sunlight and the pale blue and green camouflaged 109s hammering away at them with cannon and machine gun fire. It lasted for several minutes, but the P-38s were heavily outnumbered, and our hearts sank as we saw them shot down, one by one. One of the twin-tailed fighters exploded, sending pieces in all directions, but another just dove into the ground streaming a trail of black smoke. The final P-38 did a quick climb, and the pilot bailed out. We cheered him, but our enthusiasm turned to helpless despair as one of the Messerschmitt fighters strafed him as he hung beneath the parachute canopy, riddling him with bullets. We were outraged at this flagrant exhibition of "Hun" barbarism and talked about it well into the night. We were sure that no Allied fighter pilot would be so callous.

Cologne, not far from our camp, was a high-priority target for the Allied bombing campaign, and on the night of May 30-31, 1942, the British Royal Air Force had launched an intense thousand-plane raid that had nearly leveled sixty percent of the city. On October 13, I witnessed the first of what became almost daily American air raids on the town, as Eighth Air Force B-17s dropped hundreds of 500-pound bombs. Although we were some distance from the city center, the so-called "precision" bombing that progressively pounded the city meant that stray, or jettisoned bombs from stricken planes, would frequently fall near our camp. The famous Norden bombsight was reputedly able to "put a bomb in a pickle barrel from 30,000 feet", but it didn't work that well in practice. We could feel the shock waves as the bombs would detonate, and the clouds of smoke from fires would blacken the sky for hours after the raids.

Watching the contrails of the high-flying formations of hundreds of B-17s and B-24s converge on the target was fascinating. The sky would become dotted with the dark blossoms of German flak, filling the air with hot steel. We quickly learned not to stand out in the open during the raids because the shrapnel from the shells, pieces of aircraft, expended .50 caliber bullets from the bombers, and sometimes even dud antiaircraft rounds would fall to earth. After all, what goes up must come down, and getting struck by a piece of shrapnel could wound or kill as effectively as a bullet. The smaller debris sounded like rain on the hut roofs.

I worried incessantly that some errant plane would drop a load of high explosives in our lap and prayed each time to be spared such a horror. During the middle of one of the RAF's night air raids, a massive bomb struck the ground so close to the camp that the walls shook from the blast, and dust filled the air. A day or two later, while on a firewood collection outing, we passed one of the bomb craters, which I think must have been from a 500-pound bomb. It was about 30 feet across and ten feet deep. I was astonished at its size. You could have buried a small house in it!

By November 11, the temperature had dropped sharply, and winter arrived early. Many of us began spending the time huddled beneath our thin German blankets, trying to keep warm. Meanwhile, the dysentery endemic to the POW camps forced us to use the huts' communal toilet facilities regularly. The stench of this enclosed cesspit was enough to make anyone gag. The only possible alternative was to use the outdoor latrine trench but venturing outdoors meant enduring the biting winds that blew through the camp, so I made my trips to the latrine as quick as possible. I thank God that one of the other fellows had the fortitude to help me when I was almost too weak to make it.

I frequently saw German ambulance-type vehicles going to the Hoffmanstahl Hospital, which was part of the adjacent compound. The name led me to believe Stalag VI-G was originally a German army hospital or rehabilitation center. If so, it may explain why the German doctors never bothered to treat any of the POWs, preferring to conserve medical supplies for the German wounded.

On our side of the wire, the camp medical service was unofficially run by a strict, no-nonsense doctor, a Polish colonel who was himself a POW. His staff consisted of a few civilian German medics who treated wounded and sick officers. Medical care for the enlisted men was meager at best, with captured American field medics doing most of the treatment without anesthesia, medicines, or antibiotics. These wonderful guys would make the rounds each day, trying their best to give treatment and advice, but for wounds, all they could do was wash the area and drain infections. The forefinger on my right hand had swollen to at least twice its normal size, oozing puss, and began to smell. Walt got one of our medics to look at it. He decided that I needed to see an actual doctor, or I would lose my hand, if not my life, to gangrene. He immediately took me to the Hoffmanstahl Hospital to see our Polish guardian angel.

The Polish colonel spoke some English, and as he examined the hand, he asked me where I was from, how long ago I had been wounded and how it happened. After a few minutes of probing, he announced that I still had a tiny fragment lodged against the bone, and he would have to lance the infection, drain it and remove the piece. What little anesthesia existed was reserved for serious surgeries, not minor, infected cuts, and I nearly passed out from the pain as he cut deep into the finger. He washed it by soaking it in hot water, then sprinkled what little sulfa powder he could spare onto the wound. The only bandages available were not gauze, but crepe paper, in rolls like what you might see for holiday decorations. The treatment worked, and the infection quickly subsided. However, changing the bandages was an agonizing experience each time because the paper soaked up the pus and hardened. Then, when the medic peeled the dressing off, the wound reopened, and the pain was intense. In any event, the wound eventually healed cleanly. I was glad just to keep my hand.

I was kept in the camp infirmary for four days until the fever subsided and I regained some strength. In the cot next to me was an American first lieutenant named Vitale, who had suffered a broken arm. His entire arm was encased in plaster from shoulder to wrist, with a brace beneath it to keep it elevated. We got to know each other over the few days we were together. We had fun with a female German nurse who looked more like a wrestler. She had no bedside manner, invariably just ripped dressings off, taking no notice of the patient's acute pain. We addressed her as "bitch", but she didn't know any English. When she quizzed us what the word "bitch" meant, Vitale told her it meant "nice girl." She smiled at that, we all had a good laugh, and then we christened her "Nazi Bitch".

On November 14, just before the doctor discharged me from the infirmary, a badly injured Canadian Flight Officer was brought into camp. Shot down in his Spitfire, his right leg was severely mangled in the crash landing. To save his life, the Polish colonel decided it would be necessary to amputate the leg. From my GI dog tags, the Germans knew that my blood type was O-positive, a match for the Canadian pilot. Since someone with type-O blood can only receive from a type-O donor, I was asked if I would volunteer to give blood during the surgery. Of course, I agreed to do it, and I was immediately taken down the corridor to a room with two beds set up in the center, about three feet apart. Apparently, this would be the operating room.

Stalag VI-G, believed to be the Hoffmanstahl Hospital, October 1944. (Author's Collection)

Six of us POWs had volunteered to give blood, and as the aviator was brought in on a stretcher and shifted onto one of the beds, we sat down along one wall and waited until instructed to get onto the other bed when our turn came. The pilot was pale, in shock, and obviously in great pain. I'm not sure he was even aware of what was happening. The Polish doctor must have had some anesthesia because whatever he gave the pilot knocked him out. One at a time, a medic stuck us with a needle without so much as wiping either the needle or our arms with alcohol. I doubt that they had any in any case. One by one, the six of us gave blood while we watched the procedure.

The doctor cut away the poor pilot's trouser leg and applied a tourniquet to his thigh. Without hesitation, the doctor sliced the flesh to expose the bone, then a common wood saw was used to cut through in a half-dozen swipes. I had to look away to keep from getting sick, but the noise alone was enough to make my skin crawl. The whole thing made me queasy and light-headed, and had I not been lying down, I would have passed out. After transfusing, the doctor's assistant pulled the needle, pressed my fingers on the spot to stop bleeding, and helped me off the bed. Another GI donor then took my position, and when at last it was over, we all filed out. I never saw or heard anything else about the episode, but to this day, I frequently think about the Canadian's ordeal and wonder if the poor man survived. I just thanked God it wasn't me that suffered the amputation. I wonder about the Polish doctor, too. The word in the camp was that he gave the Germans fits, with constant demands for medical supplies, Red Cross packages, and blankets. Without him, I'm sure our conditions would have been much worse. We feared that the Germans would tire of his demands and just shoot him. Many of us owe him our lives, and I hope he survived the war too.

According to my journal, November 14 was the day of the first snowfall. We got about six inches during the day and on into the night. The next morning, thousands of boots turned the stalag into a muddy quagmire, which promptly froze the following night. The temperature continued to fall steadily for the next week.

Four days later, on November 18, we witnessed another dogfight that cheered us up. This time, a lone P-38 Lightning photo reconnaissance plane with the same squadron markings as the previous victims came in fast and made two low passes over the camp. We rushed onto the assembly areas for a better view, then held our breath as five Luftwaffe Focke-Wulf FW-190 fighters dove in to attack the single American. This time, however, it was an ambush. Three British Spitfires screamed in from the west, pounced on the Germans, and the fight was on!

It was like a private air show, and we watched, mesmerized by the fighters as they twisted and turned, climbing and rolling, with the pitch of their engines rising to a howl in a climb, then back to a low roar as they dove and maneuvered to get into a firing position. This time the Germans got the short end of the stick. Even though they held the numerical edge, one by one, three of the Focke-Wulfs exploded in mid-air, broke up into pieces, or plunged into the ground, cartwheeling in a ball of flame and spinning debris. Two tried to escape, trailing smoke, diving away at tree-top level, but the Spits followed in hot pursuit. I don't think any Germans escaped, and we saw no parachutes.

We were ecstatic, whooping, cheering, and slapping each other on the back as each plane crashed. When the third German fighter went down, the camp guards became furious. With frenzied shouting and the firing of pistols and rifles in the air, they tried to force us inside. But we were not to be denied this spectacle, and most of us watched the entire action. As the last Spitfire passed overhead, he did a victory roll, then turned and raced off to the west. We all cheered, clapped, and shouted for joy in a moment of rare ecstasy!

By late November, the camp was getting extremely crowded, new POWs streaming in each day, and on November 24, the guards ordered several hundred of us to collect our belongings and assemble in the yard. Walt and I were included, as well as most of the men in our hut, and we were marched out the front gate, hands over our heads, and escorted by several dozen Kraut guards. Some were armed with Schmeisser machine pistols, and others led guard dogs on leashes. Being close to the dogs was enough to raise the hairs on the back of your neck. These were big, muscular Dobermans and German Shepherds, trained to kill at a one-word command from their handlers. About an hour into our march, I saw one man on the outside of the column ahead of me, perhaps twenty yards away, stagger and fall to the ground. He was immediately set upon by two of the dogs. They went for his throat, and within moments he lay still, a bloody mess, with the dogs licking their chops as the handlers pulled them away. We stepped around the melee, and although it was impossible to tell if the POW was dead yet, I thought he would be better off if he were.

We were led through the outskirts of Cologne, making repeated turns to avoid roads blocked with rubble, until we finally left the city behind. The devastation we saw in Cologne was unbelievable. From the camp, we had watched the bombings at a distance, felt the shockwaves of stray bombs, and saw the pillars of fire in the aftermath, but up close, it was horrifying, much worse than the destruction I had seen in London. Scarcely a building stood in the city, and piles of rubble filled the streets. Buildings were mere stubs of walls, with stairways leading to nowhere, plumbing poking into the air like naked trees, fragments of furniture, books, clothing, and pottery scattered like leaves, and rats everywhere. These were enormous rats, well fed from the corpses buried in the debris, as big as many domestic cats, and they showed no fear of our moving column of humanity. The scarred but still intact cathedral stood like a lone sentinel, keeping watch over the flattened remains of the railway station. It seemed to be a beacon for the Allied bombers, and the smell of ash and death was palpable. We felt as though we were passing an enormous graveyard. I had learned to hate Germans in uniform, but I felt strangely ambivalent towards the few civilians we saw picking through the rubble.

Our march dragged on for three days as the weather deteriorated steadily and snow drifted over the roads. We were still wearing the clothes we were captured in, field jacket, wool pants and shirt, and jump boots. I was frozen to the bone. In hindsight, all the walking was probably better than riding in the back of a freezing truck. At least it kept our circulation going. At night, the wounded prisoners were unloaded from the trucks. At first, I envied them, but they recounted a freezing horror of bouncing down the cratered and rutted road while lying on the naked wood bed of the truck. Most of them quickly began to exhibit signs of frostbitten toes, but the weather had still not turned to full winter.

For those of us on foot, the roads quickly became a river of mud as thousands of boots churned the ground. I had no gloves, regretfully having discarded the bloody leather ones during my first medical exam and interrogation in September, but they were just thin leather and wouldn't have been much good. I just kept my hands in my pockets as much as I could. But my boots were soaked from the snow and slush, and my toes and fingers became frozen, white, and numb. My socks were getting threadbare, but walking kept up my circulation. When we passed through villages and towns, the guards would force us to put our hands on our heads again, fingers locked together, and when we finally stopped, our fingers were so cold and our arms so numb that it took hours to regain any feeling. POWs who had trouble keeping up were left behind. We were always afraid the guards would shoot stragglers, or even worse, leave them to the dogs, so we tried our best to keep up, frequently holding each other up as we staggered down the roads.

On the first night, just before dark, we stopped at a farm and were shoved into the barn for shelter. It wasn't much better than being outside; still terribly cold, but at least we were out of the wind and could huddle together for warmth. The German guards forced us into groups, and we lay in piles on filthy straw mixed with dung, just to share some bodily heat. The outside men rotated into the center of the pile at hourly intervals. The best places were away from the central passage through the barn, where the wind whipped beneath the doors. Those with the strength climbed into the loft, which was probably a bit warmer than the bare dirt floor. My leg wound was giving me pain again, and I opted not to try the ladders. As thin as we had become on our starvation diet, lying on my side caused pain in my hips after just fifteen or twenty minutes. Then I had to either shift my position and get cold all over again, or stay still, suffer in silence, and stay warmer. Usually, I just stayed in one place, hoping my hips would go numb until it was my turn to rotate in the pile. By the end of that torturous night, I could hardly stand up. It took many minutes to get the circulation going again.

Our slow and agonizing march ended after thirty grueling miles on the morning of the fourth day, November 28. We picked our way through the outskirts of Bonn and into the railway yards at Siegburg, littered with the burnt and shattered skeletons of railroad coaches and freight cars, some still on the rails, but many just pushed off into piles. At the same time, civilian laborers worked to clear tracks and fill bomb-damaged areas. We wove our way around the wreckage until we came to a long string of small boxcars, several dozens of them. They were roughly two-thirds the size of an American counterpart, with single axles at each end instead of the four-wheeled trucks common to American railroads. I learned that these were "forty-and-eights," typical European freight cars to carry either forty men or eight horses. They were the traditional mode of travel for European armies on the move. The Germans proceeded to jam nearly eighty of us into each of the cars, double the designed occupancy, then slid the doors closed with a bang and latched them from the outside.

In the gloom, and with so many bodies packed into such a small space, it was difficult to see much detail. The floor of the car was covered with dirty straw, and high up at the ends of each side wall were small openings for ventilation, not windows, but with sliding shutters. They were not much more than a foot square; if opened, we could enjoy daylight or freezing fresh air. One corner of the car with a larger pile of dirty straw was set aside as a latrine. Everyone else huddled together for warmth. I heard later that some freight cars had buckets for latrines, but I never had such luck. The body heat created by the march from camp quickly dissipated, and the cold winds cut through the chinks in the wood sides and dropped the temperature to freezing.

After what seemed like several hours, we could hear and feel a jerk as a locomotive coupled onto the train, and then we slowly began to move out of the yards. We were confined to the boxcars for three days, moving at a snail's pace through bombed-out cities, past villages that seemed untouched, and rail yards filled with cars. Sometimes our train was forced to wait for hours on end, backed onto a siding, waiting for higher priority trains to pass. Through the cracks in the car sides, the POWs at the outer edge of the cluster reported what they saw. Some of the trains were loaded with German army equipment enroute to the front, and the flatcars were loaded with trucks, tanks, and armored cars. A few were passenger trains, but they were rare.

The crush of men in the small freight cars meant those of us who were not sick had to stand, leaning against each other for support and warmth. There was room for only a few to sit down at a time, and no one could lie down. We did our best to accommodate the sick and wounded, giving them as much space as possible to crouch and lean against the car's sides. The comparatively healthy men, including myself, took turns sitting for brief periods, but mostly we just stood, pressed against each other in desperation. Once again, we rotated our positions from time to time so that everyone had a chance to be surrounded by other bodies.

The Germans never bothered to give us water or food for the entire trip. At one stop, it snowed heavily, and by opening the sliding window covers, we collected snow from the top of the car for as far as we could reach. A handful of snow was the only nourishment until we arrived at Limburg on November 26. Sleep was nearly impossible, and I dozed on my feet, hemmed in by fellow prisoners, only to be jarred awake by the lurching of the car or jostling of the other men. The latrine corner became disgustingly foul since almost all of us were suffering from bouts of dysentery, and in the three days we were confined to the boxcar, several men died. We just piled the corpses in another corner and muttered a prayer. They were just nameless faces to me, and I wondered if that was how my life would end. When we finally reached our destination, many men were too weak to move on their own, and the Germans guards had to drag them from the boxcars, where they promptly collapsed on the ground. They struggled to sit up and massage their aching legs back to life. The guards ordered those of us who could still stand to drag the dead bodies to the door and dump them onto the embankment. There were nearly a dozen heaped in a pile. It took over an hour for us to reassemble for the march to camp. We hardly gave them a parting glance as we assembled and began our shambling procession. Their suffering was over, but ours continued.

Chapter 17

Welcome to Hell, Stalag XII-A

In contrast to the hastily built POW facilities of Stalag VI-G, Stammlager XII-A, near the town of Limburg, was a large, well-constructed camp used to register, sort, and process new POWs, as well as to permanently house thousands of enlisted soldiers. After D-Day, it became flooded with POWs, and it took time for newly captured NCOs to be sorted and processed. Unlike VI-G, provisions for medical treatment were virtually non-existent since most POWs were expected to be sorted and reassigned within a few weeks.

When we first shuffled towards the gate, I was relieved to see that the camp was only about 600 yards from the railroad marshaling yards. Suddenly, the absolute horror dawned on me: the yards were a prime target for the Eighth Air Force and RAF Bomber Command, and we were again in a vulnerable spot. (In late December 1944, sixty American officer POWs were killed by an errant bomb during a raid on Limburg's rail yard.) I stared for a

German registration photo of Billy Condon, POW 11071. (Author's Collection)

moment at the enormous Nazi eagle and swastika mounted above the camp gate, more than twelve feet above us. I thanked God that our trip was over and I was still alive, but I added a prayer for preservation from bombs and hoped the Norden bombsight was as good as I had read. A Wehrmacht guard emerged from the little guard shack, a chevron-striped, red, white, and black booth, and raised the red and white striped cross arm. We were ushered between the guard barracks, or vorlager, and formed in front of the main headquarters building. Once again, the Germans segregated us by nationality and then by military ranks into officers, NCOs, and enlisted.

Limburg was the first POW camp where I was formally registered as a POW with the Red Cross. I was sure the Company G Morning Report officially listed all of us in the glider as Missing in Action (MIA) in October, within two weeks of our capture. Still, it took over a month for the information to pass up the chain of command, from the 82nd Airborne Division HQ to the Supreme Headquarters Allied Expeditionary Forces in London, to the U.S. War Department in Washington, D.C., and then to Western Union for transmission to Rochester, Michigan. The tersely worded message offered little hope but promised to inform them of any new information.

We were taken into a large brick building with a formal hall, or vestibule, with several doors that opened onto offices and storerooms. With shoving and cursing, the guards arranged us into several files, each in front of a doorway. I quickly discovered that each room served a different function: camp registration, another photo ID, Red Cross registration, and compound and barracks assignment. As I finished the process at one station, I moved to another. We each filled out the International Red Cross registration postcard that would formally report our capture to the Allied command and entitle us to receive Red Cross parcels at the rate of one per man every fourteen days. These were the lifesaving boxes of foodstuff and small necessities that became important to our existence. It took three months for the postcard to reach my parents.

The Germans sent the International Red Cross registrations to the headquarters in Switzerland and then to the American Red Cross. They, in turn, notified the War Department in Washington, D.C. After that, the Secretary of War ordered a telegram notification sent to the family. The Germans took their time processing the Red Cross registration cards, and the U.S. Army wasn't much faster in getting information out to the next of kin, so it wasn't until after the New Year that my parents finally learned that I was alive and a prisoner of war. My mother, however, had never believed that I was dead. Maybe it was denial or some maternal extra-sensory perception, but my mother was sure I would turn up.

The food ration at Limburg was the same as before: ersatz coffee, the watery concoction that the Germans called soup, and the small loaves of hard, black bread. The only addition was a potato that was occasionally doled out. For variety, we sometimes ate the potato slices raw, like potato chips, or mashed, and sometimes mixed them into the broth to make a simple stew. We rarely received a Red Cross parcel to supplement our meager diet.

While the international convention dictated one package for each man every two weeks, we usually received one package every three or four weeks, again to be shared among four POWs. The boxes from the American Red Cross contained life sustaining products, as well as extras such as playing cards, small bibles, pencils, paperback books, and other handy items to give us a normal existence.

Red Cross Package Basic Contents
1 can of powdered milk (16 oz.)
1 can of spam
1 can of corned beef
1 can of liver paste
1 can of salmon
1 can of cheese
1 can of margarine (16 oz.)
1 K ration of biscuits
1 can Nescafe coffee
1 can of jam or orange preserves
1 can of prunes or raisins
1 box of sugar (8 oz.)
2 chocolate 4 oz. "D" bars
2 bars of soap
5 packs of cigarettes

The slightly bitter chocolate "D" bars were just like the U.S. Army issue bars, so hard that they wouldn't melt in your pocket or mouth. I don't know if it was too much paraffin in the bars, but you could nearly break a tooth trying to bite one if it was cold. I learned the best way to eat one was to shave off small slices with my penknife or sometimes soften it in my tin mess cup next to the stove if it was lit. Of course, as a POW, I was delighted to have anything other than the watery soup the Germans served. We guarded our food jealously and, at the same time, respected each other's shares. The penalty for theft was quite severe, which I was to witness some months later.

Stalag XII-A was an enormous camp with large, separate compounds for each nationality. As at VI-G, in addition to the American lager, there were different lagers for the various Commonwealth countries and others for French, Italian, Norwegian, and Russian POWs. The Russian compound bordered both the British and American lagers.

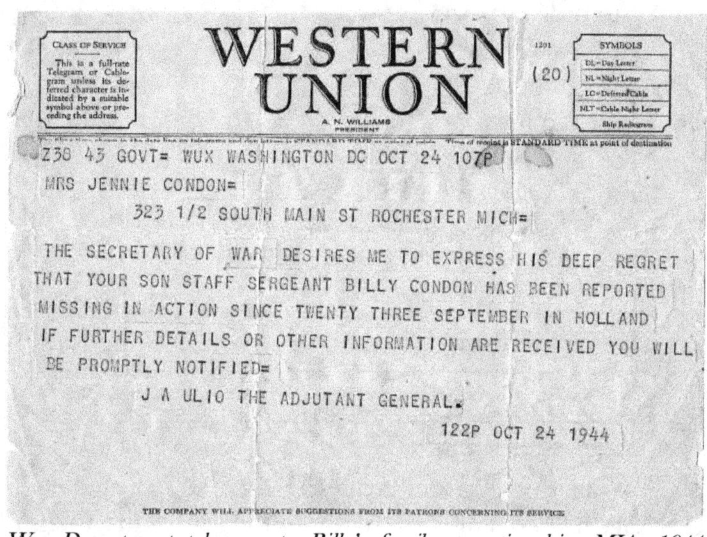

War Department telegram to Billy's family reporting him MIA, 1944. (Author's collection)

The barracks at **XII-A** were of a more permanent construction than those at **VI-G**, but most were still wood and lacked any insulation against the winter cold. They were drafty, and the biting winds drove through cracks in the walls and the window and door frames. Like the huts at **VI-G**, each barrack had ten rooms, five on each side of a central corridor. Each cubicle accommodated about 20 men with triple-tiered bunks along two sides, but these included a couple of tables and perhaps a dozen chairs in the center. Once again, we slept on thin, lumpy, straw-filled mattresses covered with dirty, blue-striped ticking. But we had no lighting and little heat. Walter Barc and I managed to get placed in the same hut, which was at least a small morale booster.

Each hut housed nearly 200 men, but it became more crowded later as the influx of POWs increased. Each barrack had one water spigot and one small stove on which we could cook and generate heat. We were always confined to the barracks after dark, but when the weather conditions were mild, we spent every moment outdoors, soaking up the meager warmth of late-season sunshine or walking in small groups around the soccer field.

Over time, every POW realized that, barring a successful escape attempt, their confinement was for the duration of the war. Most of us were much too weak to contemplate an escape. Even if I could slip past the fence and guards into the countryside, I'd have to avoid any contact because I would stand out like a sore thumb, not to mention that my stink would be a giveaway.

Two groups of POWs seemed to emerge. The first group would do anything to help pass the time and keep busy, whether walking the compound perimeter, playing cards, reading, concocting crazy escape plans, or just talking amongst themselves about their experiences. The talk focused on food, families, and what they would do when the war ended. The second group just withdrew into themselves, huddled under their blankets, and tried to escape reality in sleep. I was among the first group, and once I decided to survive this ordeal, I fared better, although most of us suffered some spells of depression. The mental suffering became the worst. Although you can at least attempt to alleviate physical pain, it is almost impossible to control your thoughts. I witnessed more than one man suffer a total breakdown.

Once each week, a group of men would be detailed to leave camp under close German escort to collect firewood. Since it was impossible to collect as much as we would need for a week, we had to ration our wood use carefully. As an NCO, the Germans couldn't force me to go on work details, but I preferred to keep busy, and to get out of the camp broke the monotony. At this point, I was still marginally fit, so I almost always volunteered for wood collection when the weather wasn't severe. The Germans referred to the work details as "on kommando," but I never understood the term's origin. I was just happy to be outside the barbed wire for a few hours.

The Germans had no mercy regarding the treatment of the Russian POWs. Because the Soviet Union had not signed the Geneva Convention, their POWs were subjected to harsh, even brutal, treatment. The Russian prisoners were marched out of the camp each day on labor details to fill in bomb craters, clear rubble from the town, cut wood, and, before the snow fell, harvest the last of the season's crops. Most non-disabled German men were already in uniform, and the women and children working farms welcomed the help. But the Russians were worked hard, and it was common knowledge that the Germans were satisfied to see the Russians die by the dozen since it meant fewer mouths to feed and bodies to keep imprisoned. We couldn't help but notice that the returning Russian work parties were usually smaller than when they had marched out in the morning. The word spread that any Russian prisoner who fell due to illness or exhaustion was executed.

The Russians were only separated from us by a barbed wire fence on the west side of our compound, so we could edge up close enough to talk to our counterparts on the other side, some of whom spoke a little rough English. As I mentioned before, since I was not a heavy smoker, I built up a small hoard of cigarettes so I could do some bartering for food. Fifteen cigarettes would get us a hundred pounds of potatoes, which the Russians seemed to have in abundance, and just six cigarettes would buy three pounds of onions. Once every few days, they would have a few apples or pears that we bartered for and carefully shared among the men in our room. The onions and potatoes usually went into the soup pot, although occasionally, we thinly sliced the raw potatoes and munched them like chips.

We eagerly bartered just to supplement our meager German rations, and this cigarette trading kept us alive and in some strength, although we all shed weight continually. I weighed about 145 pounds when I was captured, but by the time I returned to U.S. control in May of 1945, my weight had dropped to 98 pounds. Others lost more, some less. Much depended upon your health when you were captured and how well you kept up your daily activity.

One day, a Russian approached me and offered to trade a small ditty bag for four American cigarettes. He claimed it was all he owned and was desperate for a smoke. I agreed, and he tossed the bag over to me. Upon opening it, I discovered that it contained a small roll of German Marks. I was disgusted by what I considered useless paper money and thought I had been cheated! But I was not willing to throw anything away that might be useful, no matter how pointless it seemed. To hide it, I cut a slit in the lining of my jacket and slid the money inside. Not long afterward, I suffered a vile bout of dysentery and used up something like 200 Marks as toilet paper during trips to the latrine.

November 30, 1944, was Thanksgiving Day, and once again, we dined on our usual grass soup. On this day, we sat in small groups talking about home, our family traditions, and what they would be doing. Much of the conversation revolved around foods that we loved: turkey with mashed potatoes and gravy, baked ham, sweet potatoes and yams, cranberry sauce, freshly baked dinner rolls, and of course, pumpkin pie. It was agonizing and satisfying to dwell on such things, but in our relentless starvation, we couldn't help ourselves. None of us knew how long it would be before we would eat anything more nourishing than thin soup, black bread, an occasional potato or onion, and the rare scrap of fetid meat tossed into the soup.

Just a few days after Thanksgiving, during the morning "appel," or roll call, we were told that we would be deloused, given an opportunity to shower, and then given new clothing. It sounded good at first, but then wild rumors started spreading: we were being transferred again, the Germans would shoot us, or while we showered, the Germans would turn the camp upside down, searching for God knew what. We had no choice in the matter, whatever the Krauts intended, but we suspected they were up to no good. As it turned out, we were right. The German High Command was regrouping for a final all-out assault in the west to split the Allied armies poised at the German border and race to retake Antwerp. This offensive became the Battle of the Bulge, due to start in just weeks. The Germans were collecting serviceable uniforms to equip special SS troops as American GIs, to send them behind our lines in the Ardennes to create confusion and sabotage. Of course, we knew nothing and could only go with our suspicions.

I don't know what came over me, but I was outraged at the idea of giving up my uniform. It felt like the guards were stripping me of my identity. They might take the uniform, but I would be damned if I let the Krauts have the Corcoran jump boots I still wore from my abbreviated pathfinder training. I used my penknife and cut the soles off the bottom.

When the German guards saw what I did, they went crazy, waving their arms and screaming at me. One of them rushed over and gave me a butt stroke with his Mauser rifle to the side of my face. I saw black and went down like a sack of potatoes. When I regained consciousness and sat up, the rifle muzzle was in my face. I thought I was a dead man and soiled my pants in fear! Fortunately, the guard seemed satisfied with giving me a bloody cheek and left me sitting there. I wasn't the only GI to destroy uniform items, and several POWs tore up their field jackets.

We were ordered to pick up our clothing, then were marched naked over to the camp shower house, where we piled our uniforms: jackets in one pile, trousers in another, shirts in still another, boots in a fourth, and underwear in the last one. We filed into the shower room and were quickly doused with an ice-cold shower, then left to stomp around, flail our arms, and rub ourselves vigorously as we dried in the frigid air. It was my only shower for the next five months.

Without underwear, boots, jackets, or our woolen GI uniforms, we needed clothing, footwear, and some sort of coat. The Germans brought in several trucks full of old clothes, most of which had French, Italian, or Polish labels and were in poor condition. Some items had bullet holes and blood stains, obviously the scavenged clothing of murdered civilians. We rapidly dug through the piles of clothing, searching first for warm wool trousers and shirts. Most of the trousers were rough-spun wool, almost like burlap, but I found a decent pair of blue wool trousers, underwear, a dark flannel shirt missing some buttons, and a heavy brown wool coat. It was not a fashionable ensemble.

We dressed as warmly as possible, but the only footwear I could find were wooden shoes, just like photos I'd seen Dutch farmers wearing in the National Geographic magazine. After trying several, I found a pair that fit reasonably well. The problem was that I had difficulty keeping them on my feet, and I now had no socks to wear. I quickly experimented and ripped long strips of heavy cloth from an old coat, then wrapped them around my ankles and beneath the instep of the shoes. If I took small steps, almost shuffling, they would stay put.

But the Germans hadn't forgotten my rebellious behavior. Within a few minutes, one of the guards walked over to me, grabbed me by the collar, and dragged me off to the sonderlager, the "cooler," for two days of solitary confinement, with no food, no water, and just a cold cell with a concrete floor on which to sleep. The boredom, penetrating cold, and creeping claustrophobia were awful, not to mention the uncertainty of how long I would be locked in. With my steady weight loss, I had shed much of my natural body padding, and sleeping on the raw concrete was painful. I couldn't imagine how anyone could endure weeks of isolation and misery, but some did.

The one thing that never changed for the entire length of my imprisonment was the body lice. Of all the physical suffering and starvation we endured, I think the vermin that inhabited my clothing and bunks was the worst. It took only a few weeks of sleeping on vermin-infested straw mattresses for the little creatures to work their way through my clothing and into my skin. Moving gave a bit of relief, but as soon as I stopped, either sitting, standing, or lying down, it felt as if my skin was alive. The feeling was awful and nearly drove me crazy. Occasionally several of us stripped down and competed to see who had the most body lice and then crushed them between our fingernails.

Anytime the weather was tolerable outside, and I'm talking about sunny with temperatures in the fifties, hundreds of us would find a sheltered and sunny spot to sit, peel off our clothes and begin the laborious process of picking the little monsters off our clothing and our skin. Those of us cursed with body hair on our chests, backs, and shoulders were especially plagued. Being of Greek heritage, I had plenty of dark body hair for the lice to hide in, but they didn't move fast. When you found them, it was an immensely satisfying feeling to crush them between your fingernails. It was not unusual to sit for a whole afternoon, stark naked, and kill hundreds of them, leaving bloody stains on the ground where you wiped them off. One time, while on a march between prison camps, the Germans gave us a short break, and several of us pulled our pants down and proceeded to dig for lice while German women watched us in amazement and laughed themselves silly. We couldn't have cared less what body parts we exposed as long as we could get some relief.

Chapter 18

Forty and Eights Again

At the morning appel on December 8, we were ordered to collect our meager belongings and paraded out of Stalag XII-A. Either General Patton's advance was threatening to overrun the camp, or perhaps the Germans just wanted to make more room in the camp. We shuffled out of camp, an enormous column of over 1,000 prisoners. Keeping the wooden shoes on my feet was challenging, and it didn't take long to develop blisters where they chafed inside the wooden shoes. It was already cold, well below freezing, but this march to the railroad yard was not as agonizing as our arrival.

To my horror, we were again jammed into the hated "forty and eight" boxcars, and the stench told me that these cars had recently been used to transport POWs. The straw was already well mixed with excrement, and the foul odor made me gag. A helping hand reached down to me, and I pulled myself up into the car and worked my way as far from the latrine corner as possible. I wanted to avoid the smell and, at the same time, minimize my exposure to the icy wind that swept through the chinks in the car siding. We were jammed in tightly, but with not so many of us in this car as on the last trip, we made as much room as possible for the more seriously ill men to sit down.

We waited, unmoving on the rail siding for hours, with all of us huddled together, coughing, sneezing, leaning on each other and the car sides, then slipping out of the pack to defecate in the corner. Finally, we felt a lurch as the locomotive coupled, and we began moving. As the train negotiated its way through the rail yard and onto the main line, I wondered out loud if the cars had the letters "PW" painted on top. As bad as our life was now, the last thing we wanted was to be strafed by our own aircraft. I can almost guarantee that the train had no markings to warn our roving fighter pilots of our presence.

The train's progress was at least as slow and tedious as the earlier ride from Cologne. We stopped often, but I believe that this time it was more often for rerouting around bombed areas than to clear the main line for German troop trains.

Our worst fears were nearly realized on the night of December 11. Earlier in the day, we had pulled into a major switching yard outside of Frankfurt and parked on a siding for several hours. As darkness and the temperature fell, we huddled closer; one moment, I was asleep on my feet, then the next minute, stamping my feet to restart the circulation.

It was close to midnight when we first heard the air raid sirens. Locked in the rail cars, we could do was peer out between the cracks or out the little corner ventilation hatches. First, the searchlights started sweeping the sky, and then we heard the steady "boom, boom, boom" of the antiaircraft guns and the droning of aircraft engines high overhead. When we noticed that the bomb blasts were growing nearer, we realized that the RAF target for the night was the rail yard we were sitting in! The rising wail of the falling bombs made my hair stand on end, like fingernails scraping across a chalkboard, then the blast and concussion of the bombs started to sweep over us.

We felt like pebbles in a tin can, thrown to our knees, slipping in excrement as the boxcar rocked and teetered on the rails. I began to pray loudly, and most of my fellow POWs joined in. We repeated the Lord's Prayer time after time, counting the bomb blasts and trying to determine if they were getting closer or receding. It was the most frightening night of my life. The bombing seemed to go on forever, but it was probably half an hour before things quieted down. Not once did the German guards make an appearance.

I think it was shortly before we pulled out of Frankfurt that we received the only food on the entire trip. The guards pulled back the large sliding door, flooding the interior with bright daylight that blinded us and made us shrink back, then threw in a dozen loaves of the usual black bread and a few links of rotten sausage. In an unusual gesture, the Germans had us dump the dead out the door, and then some civilian workers tossed the bodies into a wagon. The door was slammed, re-bolted, and the train moved on.

Chapter 19

Furstenburg, Stalag III-B

My December 17, 1944, journal entry was very terse – "Arrived at Stalag III-B." By the time we pulled into the rail yard, many of us had frozen feet, making the two-kilometer walk from the train station to the camp hellishly painful. Ironically, my wooden shoes, which I cursed daily, had actually given my feet some insulation from the cold boxcar floor and the frozen ground. For a few moments, I counted myself lucky not to be wearing the worn-out leather shoes that caused so many of the men to suffer.

For some bizarre reason, the Germans made us stand in the biting cold for over an hour before they allowed us into the compound. One of the guys nearest me made the sarcastic observation that maybe the Krauts hadn't finished making up our rooms yet. It got a few chuckles, but we were frozen before we were allowed in. It was such a relief to finally get into the huts that we all collapsed, massaged our feet, and gritted our teeth in pain as the blood began to flow back to our icy extremities. By now, most of us were mentally numb to the constant suffering. I know that it never seemed to improve, no matter what I did, nor did it seem to get much worse. It was just a constant hell with an array of torments. Survival was both a blessing and a curse, and at some moments during the train ride, I envied the men who died. At least their suffering had ended. My physical misery seemed constant, only varying in its source, but this trip across Germany had ended.

As my roommates and I huddled around the single tiny stove to thaw our hands and feet, we tried to compute how long the journey was and where we might now be. The consensus was that we had covered about 300 miles, or 500 kilometers, based upon the hours it had taken and the average speed. The sign at the front gate proclaimed this to be Stalag III-B, and from the long-time inmates, we soon learned that we were now about sixty miles east-southeast of Berlin, at Furstenburg on the Oder River.

The Germans were their usual efficient, by-the-numbers selves as they checked us in. Each man was issued two thin blankets and six bed slats. One of the POWs explained that after years of incarcerating Allied POWs, the Germans knew that the bed boards could be used for tunnel framing, so they kept track of everyone's boards. We called the German officers and NCOs who maintained a constant daily surveillance "ferrets," It gave us a perverse pleasure to think that someone had been making their lives difficult with escape tunnels.

Stalag III-B was another typical POW camp and conformed to the standard lager layout, except this camp was dedicated to housing NCOs. It was situated on flat farmland on the east bank of the Oder River. Our compound consisted of twelve identical barracks, measuring approximately 120 by 800 paces which, using my average thirty-inch stride, works out to about 100 by about 650 feet. Our barracks were arranged in three rows of two, with two huts on each side and perpendicular to the main thoroughfare. Beyond the buildings was a sandy area for exercise. A smaller hut specifically for the senior American NCO, and the men who formed his staff, sat in the middle.

The huts were built of brick this time, with exposed timber framing. Long and low, the buildings were partitioned into two halves with about 150 men in each half. Three brick stoves per half were spaced equally along the long axis, and washrooms were in the center of the barracks, creating a partition. We now had adequate spigots for running water but no hot water or showers. We also had a stove in each washroom, which enabled us to cook, assuming we had ingredients and fuel.

We had the same slatted bunks and straw ticking, a few tables and chairs, a couple of dim light bulbs for short periods at night, and to discourage attempts to tunnel, we had concrete floors. The stoves were larger and could generate some heat, but there was precious little fuel. We had toilets at the ends of each barrack, but we only used them when locked in at night. For everyday use, we had a separate latrine building on the edge of the compound, a short walk from the barracks, but of course we could only use it in daytime.

This camp was better equipped than Stalag XII-A, but the Geneva Convention mandated better conditions for NCOs than junior enlisted men. It was a relief to learn that the camp was well organized and headed by a single spokesman, a fellow staff sergeant named Joe Gasperich, whom the Germans had selected as their "Man of

Confidence." They probably based their choice upon his time behind the wire, his leadership, tact, and the respect we held for him. He was about ten years older than me and had been a POW since February 1942, when he was captured in Tunisia. For a staff, he had several men to assist him with everything from record keeping, disciplining, and general administration. Below him, each hut section of roughly 150 men had a lead man who acted as a conduit for information, handled complaints, assigned tasks, and kept order and discipline. I became the lead man for half of the barrack, and Sergeant Al Carpaso was my assistant.

The Germans dealt directly with Gasperich, who in turn met with each section leader, then we met with our sections. It worked very well for the most part, and we only had a few disturbances, which I'll describe later. We had a chaplain who was an NCO, but he had only been a divinity student, not an ordained army chaplain. We also had an American medical officer, 1st Lieutenant Hughes, who did his best to tend to our needs despite meager stores of medical supplies. It was Hughes whose ministrations finally healed my leg wound.

Shortly after we arrived at Furstenburg, we received Red Cross parcels and a new issue of U.S. Army uniform clothing, courtesy of the Red Cross. I was delighted to get rid of the lice-ridden hand-me-down civilian rags. I was always puzzled by the change to civilian clothing at Limburg. It seemed illogical to give us civilian clothes that might enable an escapee to blend in with the local laborers. But when I gave it more thought, we were extremely thin, and our body odor was atrocious. We would stand out in a crowd, and the Germans constantly warned us that we would be shot as saboteurs or spies if caught escaping in civilian clothes.

The new uniform items were regular GI issues and included wool trousers, a shirt, cotton underwear, socks, a knitted fatigue cap or garrison cap, and a field jacket. The jacket had a black triangle painted on the back, about six inches on a side, and the trousers had a similar mark on the back of the knees to identify us as POWs. Walter Barc observed that the markings gave the guards a target to shoot at if we tried to escape.

Some guys got heavy wool overcoats, but I lost out and had to be satisfied with a hip-length, M-43 jacket. I promptly took my penknife and opened a small slit in the back lining to make a space to transfer my small stash of German marks, my journal, and the painting done by the Russian at Stalag VI-G. In addition to feeling more like a soldier again, I was thrilled to get rid of at least half of my lice! At least for a while.

One of the large barrack huts housed a chapel at one end, a theater at the other, and a substantial library in the center. I was surprised to discover that the library was stocked with over 4,000 books, courtesy of the American Red Cross. We also found that the ARC had provided a victrola and a large assortment of phonograph records, everything from classical to pop music. It was well-used and provided entertainment and a musical score for the amateur musicals that the more ambitious POWs put on. As relative newcomers, Walter Barc, Al Carpaso, and I never participated, but we enjoyed the shows. I was surprised that even some German guards attended the programs and enthusiastically applauded.

Those who were readers, craving any diversion, tried to read whenever the weather was conducive to sitting outside on the ground. Some who withdrew into themselves just stayed in their bunks, huddled under their blankets and straining to read in the semi-darkness of the huts. I had never been much of a reader, but I devoured detective novels and magazines by the dozen just to keep my mind occupied.

Our stand-in chaplain held weekly Sunday services in the chapel. As I mentioned, he was not an ordained minister but had been active in his church and had some theological training. He was an accomplished preacher, and the services were always well-attended.

I played a bit of poker and checkers and worked my way through the library, but mostly I spent hour upon hour walking the fence line, often in the company of several of my roommates. Al Carpaso, Walter Barc, Bob McCartney, and Walt McAllister, another fellow in my hut, were frequent companions. If the weather was mild and sunny, we skipped the walk and stripped down to our birthday suits to seek some relief from the body lice. Modesty was never a consideration, and we took turns picking lice out of each other's hair and off each other's backs.

One popular diversion was to count who had the most lice, and then there were the lice races. It seems a bit crazy now, but we drew a two-foot diameter circle in the dirt, and then five or six men each placed a large insect in the center. We placed bets as to whose body vermin would be first to reach the perimeter, and upon the conclusion of the race, everyone took a perverse delight in crushing the lice between their fingernails. The resounding "pop" as they exploded was intensely satisfying, win, lose, or draw.

To my surprise, some prisoners who had been behind the wire since North Africa and the Sicilian campaign had received packages from home. The Germans officially subscribed to the Geneva Convention and honored a reciprocal arrangement with the British Empire and the United States, allowing POWs to receive mail and packages from home. But mail took at least three months via Geneva, Switzerland, then by truck to Berlin, where it was sorted by stalag and distributed. Of course, your family had to know you were a POW in the first place and in which camp you were held. Because of being moved from camp to camp, I never had much chance of getting mail, or at least nothing ever caught up with me.

Gradually, all sorts of everyday items that had been missing in our lives began to appear, thanks to bartering and sharing. In addition to the food, many Red Cross parcels contained things that helped morale. The first Red Cross package that I was issued I only had to share with one other GI, a talkative former farm hand from Alabama named Bob McCartney, with whom I soon became friends. He took a deck of playing cards while I kept a small New Testament. I read it cover to cover several times, bringing me great consolation.

After the experience of the march from Cologne and the horrendous night in the Frankfurt rail yard, I had become much more reflective. As a kid, I had not given much thought to religion, but the car wreck that killed Jimmy White, the firefight in Holland, and the horrible train rides, all made me aware of my mortality. Such close calls with death will give any man cause to question fate, but I became convinced that I would survive this ordeal and become a better man. Back home, my mother had insisted we all attend church service every Sunday, but it was the suffering I endured and the hope I found in the gospels that changed me forever. I can say with conviction that for the rest of my life, I felt like I was spared for a purpose. Those who are not religious may scoff at it, but most of us prayed regularly, and when the chaplain held services, they were well attended.

On December 19, the Germans announced their major counteroffensive in the Ardennes, bragging that Hitler's vaunted Panzers would cut through the Allied lines and be in Antwerp within days. We all thought it was a load of crap, just Kraut propaganda, but suddenly the collection of our uniforms back in Stalag XII-A made sense and confirmed our suspicions. I was glad I had cut up my boots, but I still hated the wooden shoes.

By the end of December 1944, Red Cross packages began to trickle in with some regularity, and more decks of cards appeared. Between the library, the theater, and card games, there was always something that we could do to pass the time. It was better than the previous stalags, but we were still starving and slowly weakening as we shed weight. When the weather permitted, I summoned the energy to keep up my long walks around the compound. We talked aimlessly among ourselves, just reminiscing about home and food, a constant topic, and what we would do when we got back Stateside. The first thing all of us planned to do was stuff ourselves with our favorite foods. It's fantastic what odd things we began to crave.

My fellow POWs talked about the usual things, like a cold glass of milk, peanut butter and jelly sandwiches, milkshakes, homemade cakes and pies, ice cream, and juicy sirloin steaks. But I heard guys talking about broccoli smothered in butter, rutabaga pie, pork rinds, strawberry shortcake (one of my favorites), liver and onions, licorice, dill pickles, and just about anything else you can imagine. We talked about food incessantly but hardly ever about women. Most of us had not seen a woman in months, other than German bombing survivors and farm wives, all of whom turned their backs to us.

Our diet, which kept us just a bit ahead of starvation, kept food front and center in our imaginations. Our daily ration still consisted of the now familiar ersatz coffee or tea in the morning and the watery soup and bread at noon, brought around in a pull cart with large kettles. Two men were assigned from each hut to carry a kettle back to their hut mates. Each POW was allowed one ladle of soup, and by the time the cart reached the last buildings, it was cold, and we had to reheat it on our stoves. Some of us, like myself, had acquired a folding canteen cup, but many had to drink out of cans scavenged from the Red Cross parcels.

Personal hygiene was a continual struggle for us. There were no shower facilities, and even if there had been, we had no clean clothes. We only had the little bars of soap from the Red Cross packages, which we used to clean our faces and hands. Shaving was a challenge, and most couldn't tolerate it daily. The Germans would not allow beards, so we had little choice, so I shaved every four or five days. I suppose they feared what we would look like when the Red Cross paid an unexpected visit. We had some razor blades but very few safety razors to use them in, so unless you knew one of the lucky guys with a safety razor (I had lost mine when stripped at Stalag XII-A.), you just held the blade in your fingers and used cold water out of a pan, or can, to wet your beard. I didn't get my hands on a safety razor for over a month.

Some guys couldn't tolerate the lousy morning coffee and used it to shave; there was some logic since it was the only semi-hot water we ever had. I tried to keep myself as clean and presentable as possible, but I have a heavy beard and was never able to get a really close shave without cream. I invariably had a little stubble. We all smelled awful, but we could hardly tell since we all reeked.

I kept my toothbrush in my jacket pocket since my capture in Holland and was mindful of my mother's insistence that I brush daily. Toothpaste was non-existent, but I was determined to save my teeth. From my first days in a POW camp, I had used the fine sand from the compound to brush every morning, then rinsed with the dregs of coffee. Even with careful swishing, I always failed to get all the sand out of my mouth, but while many men lost teeth due to gum disease, I never had dental problems.

Walt McAllister, a skinny kid from Mississippi with a butter-smooth southern accent, had been captured in Italy and had been a POW for nearly eighteen months. Over time he had learned a bit of German, which came in handy when dealing with the guards, although many of them had also learned some English. The camp guards were mostly older, more corruptible men whose lot wasn't much better than ours, but they took a considerable risk dealing with us because the penalty if caught was a firing squad. We knew all about that because their officers lectured them routinely about how to deal with "kriegies," and they told us all about it. I know that their diets were much worse than that of an average American GI, and for the German population, fresh food, cigarettes, and luxury items had been growing ever scarcer with each passing month.

When a camp received a large shipment from the Red Cross, the Germans withheld a large portion for the consumption of the camp guards, but they confided to us that their own rations were reduced in compensation. Stalag commanders were judged by their efficient management, and stretching their resources was rewarded, even at the expense of their own men. They calculated that keeping the POWs in a weakened condition would stifle escape activity (which worked for the most part), and they could siphon off Red Cross edibles for their own use. The cruel logic made sense, but this policy worked to our advantage because we could get just about anything from the guards that could be smuggled into the camp for a couple of packs of cigarettes.

There was a steady influx of contraband items, and Walt succeeded in bribing a German guard to smuggle us a set of hair clippers and barber's scissors. One of the other guys in the hut had been a barber in civilian life, and he quickly established a brisk business giving haircuts.

One of the guys in the adjacent hut was able to get a small radio by bribing a guard, and they promptly set up a news bureau of sorts, passing on the BBC war news via the grapevine to each of the huts. Our hearts sank when we heard the confirmation of the Bulge breakthrough, and the sudden influx of new POWs in early January gave us vivid first-hand accounts of the brutal fighting in the Ardennes. But the news of the stubborn American airborne resistance at Bastogne filled us with pride, especially those who were airborne. The 82nd and 101st had been rushed forward to stem the German assault and had fought tenaciously. We were all tickled to hear that General McAuliffe had told the Krauts off when they demanded his surrender. That made us proud to be Americans.

Other news from our bootleg radio gave us hope that the war might soon draw to a close, such as the bombing raids on Berlin, the declining shipping losses in the Atlantic, and the Russian advance on the Eastern Front. We all prayed that this year would bring it to an end, and we didn't care who got to us first, British, Americans, or Russians.

Just weeks later, when the German push in the Ardennes collapsed with huge losses, we noticed that our soup began to get more meat and occasionally onions, cabbages, and turnips mixed in. The Red Cross packages began to be distributed more frequently and in better proportions. We concluded that with defeat staring them in the face, the Germans were trying to undo some of the damage they had done.

One day, I had an extraordinary meeting when a new shipment of POWs arrived in camp. They were a mixed group of GIs from many different units, many captured in Belgium and the Huertgen forest, and like me, several had been through more than one camp. Imagine my surprise when one of these fellows turned out to be an old schoolmate from back home in Rochester, Michigan. Shortly after he arrived, I bumped into him in the compound, and we instantly recognized each other. We hugged, cried, laughed, and couldn't believe what a small world it was. He was a tank commander with the 1st Armored Division and was captured in North Africa during the Kasserine Pass fiasco in February 1943. This marked twenty-three months of captivity for him and his fourth POW camp. We spent many days reminiscing about home, high school and compared our army experiences. Not surprisingly, he discovered several of his North African campaign buddies here as well, since quite a number of the internees at III-B had been POWs for eighteen to twenty-four months.

Thank God for the International and American Red Cross for the packages that they delivered to us. Without them, I doubt that we would have survived on the German rations. Everything in the packages got used, including the box. Tin cans got used as cooking vessels, storage containers, and drinking mugs, and with a bit of clever engineering, they could be flattened out and reshaped into all sorts of useful items. We got creative with the contents of the packages, and some of the fellows who had previous experience as cooks could conjure up meals that we thought would put the best corner diner back home to shame. It probably wasn't that good, but it tasted wonderful when you're half-starved and craving home-cooked meals.

The camp lagers held French and Italians, as well as thousands of Russian boys, who all wanted to barter. With our cigarette ration, we bought flour, onions, beans, bread, potatoes, beets, cabbages, and sugar, but the quantities were small. We all anxiously discussed potential recipes when the Red Cross packages were distributed. With his farm background, Walt McAllister was handy with mechanical things. A long-term kriegie taught Walt and a couple of other guys how to devise a small oven using flattened Klim cans and a crude hand-pumped blower using different pieces of the Red Cross parcel to deliver heat. With their encouragement, I rolled up my sleeves and tried my hand at baking. My journal entry for December 22 was a high point for me: "Baked my first raisin pie, a big success." I think the recipe belongs in "Ripley's Believe It or Not." For anyone bold enough to try it, here it is, right out of my journal:

Raisin Pie Recipe
1 pound of raisins
½ Spoon of butter
½ D Bar
1 pinch of salt
4 biscuits (for filling)
6 biscuits (for the top crust)
3 spoons of flour for the bottom crust
½ spoon of flour for thickening

Just before Christmas, the American Red Cross sent us a new shipment of books and a phonograph, along with a good selection of records, including Christmas carols, which helped morale quite a bit. The phonograph was cycled through each hut to spread a bit of Christmas cheer. The fellows in my barrack got together, and we conjured up a fake Christmas tree, just a skinny stick of a thing, with a few pine boughs tied on and paper decorations, but it cheered us up and brought memories of home.

On Christmas Eve, we sang carols, and we all attended the church service the following morning. We were all melancholy and nostalgic, thinking of home, wives, girlfriends, and parents, but most of us were convinced that this would be the last Christmas of the war, and by God, we would live through it! Christmas dinner was a soup, a bit thicker than usual, with black bread, a bit of butter, and tea with sugar. Several of us had chocolate D-bars saved from our Red Cross parcels, and we shared these around the hut.

Most POWs didn't get too enthusiastic about New Year's, but about a week later, I decided to try my hand at baking again. The Red Cross packages contained raisins, prunes, crackers, D-bars, and other stuff to experiment with, and four of us pooled our leftover items to bake another raisin pie. If anything, this one was better than the first one. When it was done and cooled off, we just sat in the hut and slowly munched our little slices in quiet contentment.

With each passing week the radio news of the war was getting better and better, and the Germans were being steadily pushed back, so we were beginning to feel that our future was improving, one day at a time. The one bit of news that upset us was hearing about labor strikes back home. Those self-serving bastards back in the States didn't know how good they had it—we just wished we could trade places with them.

With my two previous culinary successes, I decided to sacrifice my watch to get some more delicacies, so on January 12, I traded it for a whole list of groceries: beans, potatoes, flour, bread, prunes, cigarettes, and macaroni, all of which equaled thirty-five packs of cigarettes. Not being much of a smoker, I thought it was a small price to pay for the food, and I still had a few cigarettes left.

As it turned out, it was good that we ate most of the stash within days because, on January 18, the Germans stormed into the huts and gave us a thorough shakedown. Apparently, word had leaked out to the ferrets that we had a radio, strictly forbidden by camp rules. They would have found it too, but the guard who supplied the radio in the first place was terrified he would be implicated and shot, so he tipped off his "buyer" about the impending search. The guys in the hut took the entire thing apart and buried pieces all over the compound.

The German search parties descended us on in the early morning hours while most of us were still in our bunks. Screaming, "Raus! Raus!" they dragged and kicked us out of our barracks for appel while they tore the huts apart. Our bunks were overturned, our few personal possessions were scattered all over the rooms, and they kicked and punched any POW within reach. Although they confiscated a few contraband items, they never found the radio, and within a couple of days, it was back in operation.

The following day I witnessed the punishment for stealing a fellow POW's possessions. One of the guys at the other end of my barrack got caught stealing bread from another kriegie. He was caught red-handed, and many of his fellow POWs wanted to kill him to set an example, but we were afraid of German retaliation. As a compromise punishment, he was seized by his fellow prisoners, severely beaten, stripped naked, and dragged outside, where he was then summarily pitched headlong into the latrine trench. This trench was about five feet deep, and with most of the internees suffering from dysentery, it was nearly filled with liquefied human waste, and the stench was horrendous. We used it only to spare the hut toilets the odor; those were used for urinating and emergencies only. I think I would rather have had a limb amputated than be thrown into that stinking mess. The thief was buried in it up to his chin, and to compound the fellow's misery, without a shower, he had no recourse but to rub the fetid slime off with dirt and snow. The stink lingered for weeks, and everyone shunned the thief because of the odor, as much as for his behavior.

My health was generally holding up as well as most of the other kriegies, with occasional bouts of dysentery, for which we were advised to eat bits of charcoal, but my weight continued to drop. However, the wound on my left leg had never healed correctly, and as of January 23, it was still oozing. Other than the sulfa powder I had sprinkled on the wound at the convent in Holland, it had never been treated. The shrapnel, or bullet, was still in there, too deeply embedded for our primitive medical capabilities. Our camp doctor, Lieutenant Hughes, instructed me to soak it daily with water I boiled on the little hut stove. After several days it began to heal slowly, but the debris, whatever it was, was never removed, and it's still in my leg to this day.

To boost my spirits, I stayed close to the hut for the next few days and tried baking a chocolate cake. The ingredients cost me nearly eight packs of cigarettes, but I thought it was well worth it. Once again, I recorded the recipe in my journal so that if it turned out well, I could repeat it another day. It tasted wonderful, but I never felt brave enough to repeat it.

Chocolate Cake Recipe:
1 Klim (milk) can of flour
2 "D" bars (or ½ can of cocoa)
4 spoons of milk
1 pinch of salt
2 spoons of butter
1/2 box of raisins (or prunes)
5 spoons of sugar
10 or 12 soda pills

Chapter 20

A Circus Without Clowns, Stalag III-A

By the end of January, the camp was getting very crowded. When I arrived in mid-December, we had just over 3,000 American men in our compound, but now we had over 5,000. Conditions were getting difficult. We had run out of bunks long since, and newcomers were sleeping on the concrete floors. It's a good thing that we couldn't see into the future, for as bad as Furstenburg was, the next camp would be immeasurably worse.

On January 31, as the Russian army advanced from the east and pushed the battle line closer and closer to the east bank of the Oder River, the Germans began the evacuation of Stalag III-B. For several days we had heard artillery fire in the distance. Shortly after noon, the guards ordered us to collect what few possessions we had accumulated, such as food, cigarettes, the phonograph and records, and of course, the radio, which was again dismantled and distributed to individuals to conceal. Dressed in every bit of clothing we owned, we shuffled through the main gate in the bitter cold and began a grueling hundred-mile march to the west.

Within the first few miles, our lack of stamina became obvious. The road became littered with our treasures: the phonograph and records, books, homemade stoves, and even spare clothing. With each passing mile, their value dropped until it all became just so much junk along the side of the road. The German guard detail included soldiers mounted on horseback, armed with clubs, rifles, and pistols. They warned that anyone who fell behind would be shot, and to keep us in line, they used their clubs liberally.

The weather was well below freezing, with drifting snow and icy roads. The Germans marched us steadily through the first night, then the next day until we were exhausted. Our minds failed to register the passage of time, and it all became one agonizing, endless experience. The fatigue and numbness from the piercing cold made even the strongest among us begin to look upon death as a blessed relief. But we all kept moving, one foot at a time, moving like mindless automatons.

Although I was wearing the wool GI clothing and field jacket that I was issued at Furstenburg, I never found a pair of boots to replace the wooden shoes. I had traded for socks, which generally gave me some comfort, but now the shoes began to chafe through the wet socks. I began to dread the eventual stop. It's not that I didn't want to stop, but I knew that I would have to take the wooden shoes off or the socks would freeze to them. This trek was much worse than the march from Bonn. When we finally stopped on the second night, and I peeled off the socks, my feet were dead white, and my toes were beginning to turn purple with the first signs of frostbite. It took nearly thirty minutes of vigorous rubbing to get some circulation back in my feet, and the agony of returning feeling brought tears to my eyes. I had picked up a discarded wool stocking cap on the march and wrapped it around my bare feet until morning.

We kept moving throughout the next day, always at a slow, shuffling pace, since so many of us were so weak. I began to withdraw mentally, just staring at the legs of the man in front of me, my mind a blank. First, one foot, then the other, right—left—right, just trying to stay on the road and out of the frozen ruts. I knew that if I slipped and turned an ankle, it could be the end.

Our worst fears were confirmed the third afternoon when a first sergeant, too slow to get to his feet after a short break, was shot point blank in the head. I saw the whole thing happen, almost in slow motion. The guard kicked the soldier to get him moving, but the GI was too weak and frozen, as all of us were. He had trouble getting his legs working, rolled onto his side, and tried to get up on his hands and knees. It wasn't fast enough for the guard, who suddenly pulled his pistol, cocked it, and then shot the soldier in the back of the head. Blood and brains splattered the snow, and he collapsed in a heap. Satisfied with his handiwork, the guard holstered his gun, screamed at us in German, aimed a kick at another POW, and we moved on while the body was still twitching in the bloody snow.

As I trudged through the snow and mud, I wondered what motivated the guard to shoot him. Was it a standing order from his high command? Was he just cast from the same mold as the cruel SS guard that gunned down the girls for no reason back in September? Or was he just tired, cold, and frustrated with escorting American POWs? That night I pulled out my journal and noted the incident. It was February 3, 1945.

The German escort did not attempt to feed us during the march and just locked us in abandoned buildings or barns at night. Someone spread the word that German farmers habitually buried potatoes, turnips, and rutabagas in dung piles in the barns to keep them from freezing. I don't know who discovered this little gem of information, but we started digging, and sure enough, we found potatoes! With no way to wash them off, we rubbed them in snow and straw to get off the worst dung, rubbed them again on our coats, and finally in our hands. Each time they became cleaner and cleaner—or so we thought. We carefully cut and shared out the few morsels among everyone in the barn, then used melted snow to slake our thirst. We reasoned that without the few calories we were able to ingest from the potatoes, we could quickly become too exhausted and possibly fall victim to the German guards. But the following morning, we experienced a resurgence of dysentery as those who ate the potatoes doubled up with cramps. The German guards thought it funny to see us step out of line, quickly drop our pants, and crap in the snow. But, always fearful of being shot, we wasted no time returning to the formation, filthy and stinking.

We spent each night in a different type of building. I recall at least one abandoned factory or warehouse, another barn, and what may have been a school. I probably have the nights confused with the journey from Bonn since both journeys were agonizing and the source of nightmares. Each night was interminably long, with the cold seeping through my body no matter how I tried to huddle up against another POW. Each time someone shifted, coughed, or left the pile to use the latrine, the cold rushed in, sharp and deadly, sapping my strength and intruding upon my nightmares. One morning, as I struggled to get to my feet, I discovered that the man who had snuggled up to my back for warmth had died, his stiffened arm wrapped over my right shoulder. It was a dreadful reminder of how fragile our lives were.

On the third or fourth night, the Germans finally distributed the ubiquitous black loaves, each to be divided among five men, but there was no soup. We rarely received water; for the most part, we had to eat snow to slake our thirst. To this day, in my mind, hell is not a furnace stoked by the devil but rather a sodden, wet world of bone-chilling cold and darkness.

The noise of Allied aircraft had become so common that we hardly took notice. We were usually well outside the cities and towns, so we were not in danger of bombs. Our fear was random strafing by our own fighters. Many other POWs had told stories of their trains or truck convoys being strafed and bombed. As far as I knew, the Germans never marked the transport on top with "PW." By this time, the Allies had achieved air superiority, and American and British pilots attacked anything that moved on German roads and rail lines. I later read of a case where the locomotive of a POW train was disabled in an air attack. While the German guards sought shelter, a Scottish chaplain risked his life by squeezing out the tiny window, running up the string of boxcars, opening the doors, and instructing the prisoners to jump out and spell "PW" with their undershirts and bare backs. It's a remarkable true story, but our slow, foot-slogging procession likely looked more like a column of refugees. Thankfully we never attracted the attention of Allied fighters that were continuously roaming the skies.

Our circuitous route from III-B went north of Berlin, then curved south to a new camp southwest of the capital city, over 110 miles. After seven days of freezing hell, we reached Stalag III-A on February 8, a day when blizzard conditions obscured anything beyond a few yards. Stupefied with fatigue, I hardly knew we had arrived until I plodded through the front gate, past the vorlager and administration buildings, several POW compounds, a large open sports field, and into a new compound. It was a new home just for us, but it was a hell worse than before.

Luckenwalde, a small city some 30-odd miles south of Berlin, had been largely untouched by the war raging around it. Stalag III-A, situated southwest of the town, was built on a flat plain adjacent to a small rail yard. I had the impression that it may have been a German army post dating back to WWI. Many of the main buildings were brick structures, not unlike army post buildings in the U.S., and a few of the admin buildings were two-story, but the surrounding POW lagers were less substantial, with many of the typical wood structures.

Stalag III-A was a large camp, at least as large as Furstenburg. But by the time we arrived, it already housed more than 60,000 men, the usual mix of British, Commonwealth, French, Belgian, and Russian POWs in the older compounds, and a separate compound for American officers. But now with a sudden influx of newcomers, the Germans had been forced to expand the camp facilities on short notice. To our shock, we marched into a separate compound that contained enormous tents, like the ones at a circus. But these were unlike any I had seen before: roughly forty feet wide, one hundred feet long, and at least fifteen feet at the peak.

The Germans had obviously thrown the compound together in haste, and while the tents gave us some shelter from the wind, with 400 men packed into each tent, our conditions were drastically worse than at Furstenburg. We slept on the ground, with only a thin layer of wet, dirty, lice-infested straw separating us from the turf. There was only one light bulb per tent and two water spigots for the entire 5,000-man compound, both located in the northwest corner.

The outdoor latrine trenches were just south of the tents. Within days they became full of excrement and were never pumped out or drained. To use them, I had to grasp a horizontal bar and squat with my feet on the duckboards, slick with feces. Falling in would be a frightening way to die, and I think we all had nightmares about it.

With Allied armies pressing closer every day, the Germans were much more sensitive to escape attempts at this stage of the war, and we now found ourselves surrounded by a triple barbed wire fence. In the narrow lane between the fences, the German guards constantly patrolled with dogs, and then there was the familiar warning wire on the inside perimeter of the fence. As usual, the guard towers were at the corners and the intersections of compound fences.

A cemetery was located just to the southwest of our lager and close to the Russian compound, which was the largest of any. We saw frequent burials of Russian prisoners, a testament to their brutal treatment. We pitied the tens of thousands of Russians for how the Germans treated them. The windows of their huts had been closed permanently, so they lived in perpetual darkness, broken only by the time they spent outdoors on hard labor details. Several of our men who had been into the Russian compound reported that the floors of the huts were covered in excrement. Dead and dying prisoners lay in piles against the walls. It was disgusting to think that humans could treat others like that. Given no medical treatment and kicked, clubbed, and starved into submission, more than 5,000 died at Luckenwalde alone.

Few of us arrived with any of our precious Red Cross food items since what was not discarded on the march was eaten on the move. Our diet again consisted of only the grass soup and black bread with sawdust baked in, supplemented by the morning and evening ersatz acorn coffee or a mint tea. The gnawing hunger, lice, and damp cold reduced us to a survival mode of existence that did not moderate until sometime in March when the Red Cross parcels began to reappear. Once more, I had to rely upon bartering cigarettes for the odd vegetable to add to our watery soup. This time we were more isolated from our Russian benefactors and had to rely upon bribing the guards.

The camp organization was a copy of Furstenburg, with our own Man of Confidence at the top, then tent commanders, and a further subdivision by sleeping rows that formed platoons and squads. We had retained the same collective groupings from our huts in Furstenburg, and I was still in charge of a platoon of POWs. We maintained our own discipline, as did the other nationalities in their compounds.

By late February or early March, my leg had healed sufficiently to exercise daily by walking the compound. Just to get a break from the monotony, I volunteered for the wood collection detail as often as possible, perhaps twice each week. Guards escorted us out into the countryside, where we cut deadwood, pulled stumps, and gathered whatever we could onto horse-drawn wagons.

On one of these excursions, I was stunned to see two of our men yell and run into each other's arms! They laughed, slapped each other on the back, hugged, and then started again. The German guards thought they were nuts, but finally, one of them made the guards understand that they were brothers. They served in separate units, one in the infantry and one in the air corps, and each had been captured at different times and places. Discovering each other here at Luckenwalde was a one-in-a-million event. The guards were as amazed as we were. Talk about a small world, what were the odds of that happening?

Our electronic wizards had quickly reassembled the contraband radio, and our grapevine was busy almost every day, monitoring the airwaves for news of the war, then disseminating it to each of the tents. We learned that on February 19, the U.S. Marines had landed on Iwo Jima, beginning the dismemberment of the Japanese archipelago. Then six days later, Allied forces began crossing the Ruhr River into Germany. The news did wonders for morale, and it would not be long before we saw the first signs of spring. But, as the weather moderated, mud became our next problem. It was inescapable, and we exchanged one form of misery for another.

The Red Cross made a surprise inspection of Stalag III-A on March 3, with the inspection team accompanied by the former world heavyweight boxing champion, Max Schmeling. I could hardly believe it. He was the second boxing champion I had met, all due to this terrible war. Schmeling seemed to be a true gentleman, but at the same time, it was dismaying to learn that he was a Luftwaffe Fallschirmjaeger, or paratrooper.

Schmeling, a favorite of Adolph Hitler, had won the heavyweight title in 1924 and held it until 1933 when he lost to Max Baer. Ironically, Baer was a Jew from Philadelphia who wore a Star of David on his boxing shorts. Schmeling's defeat infuriated and humiliated the Nazis so much that they no longer employed Schmeling as a propaganda tool.

Max spoke to us and took questions from the crowd, answering everyone politely and honestly and giving out autographed photos of himself. But one clown in our group couldn't resist taunting the boxer. Referring to the 1938 match between Schmeling and Joe Louis in New York's Yankee Stadium, in which Louis defended his title with a technical knock-out of the German in the first round, he shouted out, "Hey, Max, how did it feel to be whipped by a nigger?"

Suddenly there was total silence—if not for the mud, you could have heard a pin drop. I, and many others, were embarrassed and outraged, but others saw great humor in it. Schmeling was quickly whisked away in humiliation. Years later, I was saddened to learn the truth about Schmeling: he was not a Nazi Party member at all, and in fact, his manager was a Jew. Even more, in 1938, not long after the infamous Kristallnacht, when Nazis rampaged through German cities, vandalizing and burning Jewish businesses, Schmeling hid the two sons of a close Jewish friend in his Berlin apartment, then helped to smuggle them out of Germany. Had we known the truth, perhaps he may not have been insulted. But at that time, such sympathies were a closely guarded secret. To many

POWs, Schmeling was just a symbol of Nazi Germany, Hitler's "Master Race," and they were only too glad to see any Nazi humiliated.

Long after Schmeling's visit, I kept thinking, "What a small world: two champs in one war." Even more significant to me, Joe Louis had won the Golden Gloves competition in 1934, boxing for Detroit. It made me think of Jimmy Winters, and I wished he could have seen all this.

April Fool's Day coincided with Easter, and we were cheered to hear of the U.S. Marine landings on Okinawa. It was a world away, but even the slightest piece of good news was a boost to our morale. For myself, and many of my fellow POWs, the mental anguish of captivity had progressed from fear in the early stages to a fatalistic hope of survival. We had learned to cope with the confinement, starvation, foul conditions, boredom, and the continual fear of the unknown, but it had sapped much of my emotional and physical strength. Now I was determined to take whatever the Germans could dish out, especially with the end almost in sight.

Barc, Carpaso, McAllister, and I pooled our meager resources. With the trickle of Red Cross packages increasing and daily walks around the compound, we had slowly recovered a little of the strength the brutal winter march had sapped. We had seen men, confined in the camps for years, cope well with life, one day at a time, while others, in captivity for only months, just withdraw into themselves, staring into space or lying in their bunk all day, almost catatonic. It only took a short time to realize that survival depended upon creating a routine to maintain at least a minimal level of activity to avoid sinking into a creeping lethargy that drained the body and mind of the will to live. Some succumbed, probably damaged forever.

The experience scarred all of us, at least mentally and emotionally, if not physically.

The morning camp routine still began shortly after sunrise with the formation for the headcount, the appel. With the enormous numbers of POWs, the Germans formed us into ranks with files five deep, counting the files rather than individuals. We took a perverse delight in shifting our positions, making the Krauts lose count, and covering for men missing from the formation, usually due to illness or escape attempts. It drove the Germans crazy and gave us a little satisfaction. Later in the day, we spread the word coming from the radio set, by now filled with news of the Allied forces sweeping through Germany. I thought to myself, "The end is coming soon, Krauts! When it does, you'll get what's coming to you!"

I found consolation in my religious upbringing and continued reading the little New Testament I had gotten from the Red Cross. I attended the services each week, and each night before huddling down on the straw, I said the same prayer that I had written in my journal: "Dear God, I know we are being punished for our sins. I ask forgiveness for all the evil we have done to mankind. It's a great comfort to know You have us by the hand, and it must be a great responsibility to protect us like You are. Our reward is, and will be, a great one the day You see us safely in the arms of our loved ones. Bless You, for being so merciful to so many. Amen."

On April 8th or 9th, several high-ranking German SS officers showed up at the camp. The camp commander, Colonel Blau, was seen walking with them and arguing vigorously. The word later filtered back to us that Hitler had ordered the summary execution of all prisoners of war, but the German High Command, and even SS General Berger, had refused to carry out the order.

On April 14, we were astonished to learn that President Franklin D. Roosevelt had died of a stroke two days earlier. It came as a real shock to all of us. As young men, mostly in our twenties, FDR was the only president that we had known. I suddenly felt empty, abandoned, almost as though I was orphaned, but I also knew that the world was changing quickly, and the war in Europe was drawing to a conclusion.

The Germans had always forbidden us to display an American flag, sing our national anthem, or any other patriotic display. Still, on this occasion, we all gathered in the compound, and almost spontaneously, we began to sing the Star-Spangled Banner. The more agitated the German guards became, the louder we sang, and the Germans countered by blaring anti-FDR propaganda over the loudspeakers. It was a wonderful moment of defiance.

As if to punctuate our little rebellion, that night, we witnessed the worst air raid I had ever seen, even worse than the raids on Cologne. Shortly before midnight, the RAF bombers arrived. The stream of aircraft seemed to go on for hours as they rained thousands of tons of bombs on Berlin and its suburbs, both high explosive and incendiary. The anti-aircraft fire hit several bombers, and we watched through the gaps in the doors and windows in spellbound horror as the burning aircraft plunged into the inferno. The fires in Berlin raged throughout the night, the next day, and the following night until they had consumed everything combustible and flickered into ash. I'll never forget it, and I thanked God I wasn't on the receiving end.

Chapter 21

The Russians Are Coming

We waited for the next eleven days, eager for the next BBC broadcast, and closely followed the news of the American advance. By April 20, we heard that Soviet forces had met up with the American 96th Division at the Elbe River. It wouldn't be long now, and the following day we noticed guards slipping away, some changing into civilian clothes, one or two at a time. A few guards we had bartered with came into the compound, hoping to hide in our midst. Rumors began to spread that German civilians had tossed their babies over the barbed wire, hoping we would keep them safe. I had a bizarre experience when a German officer approached me and handed over his pistol to surrender. To my amazement, he saluted me, then turned and slowly walked back to the gate and disappeared.

By late afternoon the guard towers were empty, and we were on our own. The senior officer POWs promptly took charge of the camp and ordered everyone to stay in place and wait for liberation. As far as we knew, we were still at war, and anything could happen. We all went to sleep that night, filled with excitement and apprehension.

April 22, 1945, dawned quietly, with no appel, no sign of German guards, empty watchtowers, and no guard dogs patrolling between the fences. We waited in expectation, wandered around the compound, and sat in small groups. I sipped my ersatz coffee, listening to sporadic artillery and small arms fire in the distance, and shortly afterward, the crashing and the grinding of heavy tracked vehicles moving towards us. Finally, at about mid-morning, the clanking noises became much louder, and we watched expectantly as several dark green tanks, each emblazoned with a red star, lumbered up the lane towards our compound.

The lead Soviet T-34 tank rolled right up to the gate, and with a rending crash, the barrier came down. The tank slewed around quickly, reversing, turning, and grinding the fence and wire into the mud. As it stopped, the top turret hatch opened, and a round-faced Russian woman popped out like a jack-in-the-box, peeled her padded helmet off, raised both arms high, and shouted, "Kamerade!"

What a sight that was! Liberation Day had arrived with a crash and a gap-toothed smile of greeting. Several of us climbed onto the tank chassis and hugged and kissed the commander. She was no beauty, enough to give me nightmares, but still an incredible sight. One of the tank crew passed a bottle of vodka up to her, and after taking a big swig, she passed it over to us. The bottle quickly passed around, and when I took my swallow, the alcohol scalded my throat. Despite the burn, it gave me a warm glow and gratitude to the Russians for liberating me. We continued clinging to the turret as the woman maneuvered the tank through the compound, crushing the barbed wire fences, waving, and joining in our wild cheering. The celebration lasted for hours until we were too tired to continue, and the camp finally grew quiet.

The following day, the camp leaders said we would have to wait for transport back to our lines because the Russians were too busy mopping up German resistance in the surrounding area. It would be too dangerous to have thousands of former POWS roaming the countryside. The Allied command would arrange for our transport as soon as the roads were cleared and safe, but nobody could tell us how long that would take.

Meanwhile, the Russian prisoners were ecstatic to see their own troops. Their joy exceeded our own, not just because it was Russians who appeared as their saviors but because they had suffered so much more at the hands of the Germans. If not for the potatoes, onions, turnips, and rutabaga that they scavenged when on work details, they would have died in even greater numbers. The Russian liberators promptly inducted their long-suffering comrades into their units, at least any who could still walk and carry a weapon, then sent them out to join the push on Berlin. God help any Germans that they might encounter, military or civilian.

It was tragic to learn later that Stalin considered Russian POWs traitors to Mother Russia. As true patriots, they were expected to die fighting to the last man, and the former POWs who survived the fight to take Berlin were singled out, most sent to slave labor camps and never seen again.

The days dragged on, but we were no closer to being transported back to our lines. We were getting restless and wondered what was causing the delay. As men began to explore the German warehouses, they discovered a stockpile of Red Cross parcels that we liberally distributed. Our food improved dramatically: thicker potato and pea soups with vegetables mixed in, much more bread, and three meals a day. Some of my fellow POWs began to stuff themselves, totally ignoring the warnings of our medical people. Our digestive systems were just not ready to take in large quantities of higher-calorie foods, and most became violently sick. At least one of the guys in my tent died in agony from acute gastrointestinal distress. We had to go easy with food and eat more often but in much smaller quantities.

A few times, German fighter planes flew over the camp, and we heard sporadic artillery fire in the distance every day. We assumed it was the Russians overrunning stray German units. Then on April 27, we heard that American war correspondents were in the compound, following the Russian units converging for the final confrontation in Berlin. If they were, I never saw them. We then heard that senior American officers were already in Luckenwalde, meeting with their Russian counterparts to discuss the details for our repatriation. For the life of me, I couldn't understand what could be so hard. Just truck us out! Two days later, we learned that British trucks had arrived with supplies for their POWs, but there was still no sign of our people, and no one moved.

The Russians had been friendly initially, but their POWs had long since joined their ranks or disappeared. The word was out that the Russians were now stonewalling our demands for evacuation. Shortly after sunrise on April 29, a pair of German Focke-Wulf 190 fighters made a low, sweeping strafing attack on the north compound. They fired their machine guns and cannons into some of the buildings before they disappeared over the horizon—

probably a couple of hot-shot fighter pilots taking their frustrations out on the closest Allied target. We were getting sick and tired of waiting, not knowing what the Russians were up to, and beginning to lose trust in them. Had we understood what was happening at the diplomatic level, we would have been even more apprehensive.

The leaders of the three major powers, Great Britain, the United States, and the Soviet Union, had met at Yalta, a former Tzarist-era resort in the Crimea, as early as February to decide the fate of Germany. Between them, Churchill, FDR, and Stalin had carved up the German carcass and agreed to halt the advance of the Western Armies at the Elbe River. At the same time, the Soviet Army swept over Poland and eastern Germany and ultimately surrounded Berlin.

As the Third Reich collapsed, the Soviets rushed into the vacuum, swamping the demoralized but still fierce Wehrmacht and pushing the remnants into Berlin. Behind their advance, the Russian Secret Police, the NKVD, moved quickly to consolidate control of the countries they had liberated. For Stalin, the Allied POWs were no longer a military matter but political pawns. Stalin planned to keep all of us confined as hostages to ensure British and American cooperation until he had consolidated his control of Poland and the former Baltic Republics.

It wasn't long before the Russians posted their guards on the American and British compounds, and finally, on May 4, in the middle of a poker game with my three tent mate buddies, I raised the subject of just leaving on our own.

"You know, I'm getting sick and tired of just waiting for who knows what," I said. "The Russians act like we're now their prisoners. I don't trust them."

"Well, command wants us to all stay together and wait for transportation," replied Bob McCartney. "The roads are said to be too dangerous, what with the Reds mopping up German resistance." Bob had been captured shortly after Normandy and had been a POW even longer than me. If any of us had a right to be short on patience, it was him. His attitude surprised me.

Walter Barc was the only one of us who was married, and he had gone through some deep depression. He had been listening to the rumor mill and chimed in. "I heard we're to be trucked to the Black Sea and shipped home from there."

Walt McAllister threw down his cards, looked at each of us, and said, "What the hell, that's the wrong direction, and our guys are just a few miles away on the Elbe. What's to keep us here? Why don't we see if we can find a vehicle and get outta here?"

"Think we can find one that'll run?" asked Bob.

"There's got to be one that will start if we can find enough gas," I suggested. "Let's go take a look-see."

Barc was reluctant to leave. As a married man, I think he didn't want to take risks so close to being repatriated, so we wished him well and told him we'd see him back in the States. Then McCartney, McAllister, and I just stuffed our pockets with our few possessions and walked out through the crushed gate and up the lane to the former German headquarters. We tried to act as though we belonged there, and no one challenged us. A few Russians lounged around in front of the administration buildings, but they just waved to us as we passed. Once out of their direct line of sight, we took off towards town, looking carefully for a vehicle. For nearly a half-mile, nothing looked promising. Then, just beyond some trees, we spotted a collection of military and civilian vehicles, helter-skelter in a small field at the side of the road. We split up and checked them out, one by one. Several were damaged and not worth our time, but a few looked reasonably intact.

"Hey, guys, check this one out," called Bob. He was walking around a four-door Kubelwagen, the German counterpart to our jeep, jammed up against a small truck. "This one looks a bit beat-up, but it might run. At least the tires aren't flat, and the key is still in it. It might run." He opened the fuel filler cap, sniffed, and stuck a long stick into the filler tube. It came out almost dry, and he shook his head in disappointment.

"We can't give up so easily," I replied. "Let's see if any gas is still in these other ones. Maybe we can siphon some from these other ones."

Walt was less optimistic. "Where the heck are we going to find a rubber tube long enough, and what do we put the gas in?"

McCartney poked around and found a small quart-sized can, rusty but still intact. Walt took it, crawled under the nearest truck, and pulled the fuel line off the tank. A small amount of gasoline, perhaps a pint, drained into the can. It was a start, but while Walt was busy with that, I discovered a small tool kit in the Kubelwagon.

"I have an idea," said Bob. "Give me the screwdriver. I can take a rock and pound it through the bottom of some fuel tanks and drain the dregs."

He then proceeded to check the nearest vehicles, crawling under each one. Using a fist-sized rock, Bob punched the screwdriver into the tank and drained the fuel into the can. Each time he filled the can, he put his thumb on the hole, passed the can to me, and I poured it into the tank of the Kubelwagen. Meanwhile, McAllister checked a few gas cans mounted on the military vehicles with little success.

Finally, after draining the tanks of more than a dozen vehicles, we decided we had put a few gallons in the tank. The River Elbe wasn't more than twenty miles away, and we guessed we had enough to at least get close.

While Bob worked the steering wheel from outside, we pushed it back onto the road, all the time watching for Russians or Germans that might interfere and march us back to camp. With the Kubelwagen back on the road, Walt primed the car's carburetor.

Bob said, "Billy, you drive. You used to drive for a living."

I walked around the rear and jumped into the driver's seat, took the wheel, depressed the clutch, pulled out the choke, and turned the key, hoping to hear something. Dead silence. It dawned on me that the key switch probably just connected the battery, and there must be a separate switch or button to crank the starter. I studied the dash, but I just had to experiment. There was only one likely button, almost right in front of me, and I said, "Here goes nothing," and punched it. The starter cranked momentarily, then quit. I stated the obvious, "Well, the battery's a goner; we gotta push it."

McCartney and McAllister leaned into it, pushing as hard and fast as they could. As the car accelerated, I again shouted, "Here goes," and let out the clutch, praying the damn thing would fire. It lurched twice, coughed, and then started. I put it in neutral, and it settled down to a rough idle.

The noise we made attracted the attention of a German officer who must have been lurking in one of the nearby buildings. I'll never know how he escaped the clutches of the Russians, but he suddenly ran over to us and tried to surrender in broken English. He offered us his pistol, a Walther P-38, and motioned that he wanted to get in the car with us. Walt would have none of it. He grabbed the gun, reversed it, worked the slide to chamber a round, and pointed it at the German.

"Go surrender to the Russians, you son of a bitch," Bob growled. "You ain't coming with us, so get lost before I shoot you myself."

As the German officer backed away, his face reflected his despair. Bob and Walt piled into the car, slammed the doors, and we took off without a backward glance. We were afraid of discovery, and I was determined to put as much distance between ourselves, the camp leadership, and the Russians as quickly as possible. I turned onto the main road that seemed to head southwest and stomped on the accelerator. Our top speed was probably not much more than 40 miles per hour, but it was the fastest we had traveled in months, and it felt like we were flying. It was exhilarating for the first fifteen minutes, our first real taste of freedom after so many months.

Nothing was moving on the roads. Heading roughly south, using the sun to determine our best direction, we had to decide where to go. From the radio reports, we knew that on April 25, the American 69th Division had linked up with the Russian 5th Guards at Torgau, a town on the Elbe about sixty miles south of Berlin, so we hoped we would only have to drive for about thirty miles. Could we make it that far without running out of gas? Would there be Russian roadblocks or stray German units?

"I don't think we can make it as far as where our boys linked up with the Russkies," I pointed out. "Plus, I'm afraid of being stopped by Russian patrols. I think we ought to head west as directly as we can. We've only got a few gallons of gas in this thing." I paused, trying to remember a map I had seen back at camp. "On the map I looked at, the straight-line distance to the river looked like it was about twenty-five miles, so I'd guess it's about thirty miles by road."

Bob agreed, "I think you're right. The Russians are heading for Berlin, and they'll be all over the roads to the south."

Walt had no better suggestion, so rather than make for Torgau and the certainty of American troops and possible Russian interference, we decided to follow our instincts and work our way west as quickly as possible. Besides, we reasoned, the back roads would be less observed than the main roads from the south towards Berlin.

We dodged the wreckage of burned-out vehicles, abandoned equipment, and several corpses along the road. The Wehrmacht vehicles were shot up, probably targets of the Allied fighters that had roamed the skies until the cease-fire. There was a lot of civilian junk cluttering the roadside, including more human and animal corpses. I had seen enough death and tried to ignore them.

The first significant town we came to was Juterborg. It looked deserted, but we had to be careful not to run into a Russian column or roadblock. We hadn't heard any gunfire, either small arms or artillery, for at least a day, but we couldn't be sure the Russians had all converged upon

Berlin. I slowed the Kubelwagen and turned off onto a succession of dirt lanes to scout the town, just to be on the safe side. There was no bomb damage here, and the town looked like a picture postcard until we got closer when it became evident that the Russians had been through and gone. Many windows were smashed, and household and personal items lay strewn about the sidewalks, everything from baby carriages to furniture to books and clothing.

The Russians had looted and smashed in revenge, and it looked like the inhabitants had fled into the countryside to seek shelter or perhaps to the American lines. Several civilian bodies lay in the debris left by the Russians, but I didn't want to think about what they had done to the people here. Once again, I maneuvered around them and tried not to look. I had seen enough suffering and death.

I was being careful, driving slowly through the back streets of the town, when I spotted a cobbler's shop. I was dying to get rid of the wooden clogs I was still wearing, because operating the foot pedals was awkward and uncomfortable. I pulled the car over and told the guys what I was looking for. Leaving the car idling, I quickly looked inside, but I was out of luck. The few remaining shoes were womens'. The shop next door was a jewelry store with the windows and doors smashed in. McCartney was already inside, stepping around and over the smashed display cases. I saw the cash register thrown into a corner and broken open. In the back corner of the display room was a door opening into what appeared to be a small vault. I stepped inside and saw that it had already been thoroughly looted, but in the corner, I noticed a spool of wire the size of a tennis ball. Bob came up beside me as I picked it up and hefted it.

"What do you think this was for?" I asked him.

"Looks like a roll of solder to me," he answered. "Not worth anything."

I tossed it back into the corner of the vault. I wanted shoes, not the pickings from a jewelry shop, and we were wasting time. The longer we hesitated, the better our chances of getting nabbed by Germans or Russians, and the engine was running, wasting gas, so we turned and picked our way back out of the ruined shop and piled into the car again. Off we went, keeping our speed up but not so fast as to attract attention, run headlong into a roadblock, or risk crashing into wreckage on the road.

The next town of any size we came to was Blonsdorff, also devoid of any signs of life other than a stray dog or two and the typical giant rats that seemed to be thriving on the war. I didn't want to think about what they had been eating. Blonsdorff, like Juterborg, had been thoroughly looted. We made our way slowly around the center of town, and shortly after passing through the central square, we cleared the town limits and reached a crossroads. What had been a signpost was crushed in the weeds and useless. We had no idea which fork to take since both seemed to head roughly west, and we didn't have enough gas to risk making a mistake and retrace our route.

We had passed two elderly German women poking through a wrecked wagon a few hundred yards back, so I shifted the Kubelwagon into gear, wheeled it around, and drove back to find them. They were the first live humans we had seen since leaving Luckenwalde, and they were still there, a pathetic sight as they rummaged through the dumped wagon load, the dead horse putrid and swollen. We drew up next to them, and they immediately stopped what they were doing and stepped back. Their fear and distrust were apparent. I suppose a German army vehicle driven by scrawny, scruffy men in strange uniforms was puzzling.

Walt McAllister smiled at them, and in his best German, he tried to calm them and ask which way to the Elbe.

They both pointed simultaneously to the right fork, saying nothing.

"Danke Schon," replied Walt. He slapped me on the shoulder and added, "That's good enough; let's get the hell out of here."

I swung the Kubelwagen around and put the pedal down, throwing gravel as we accelerated towards the Elbe. I had no idea where the road would intersect the river, but I hoped it would lead to a town where we'd be able to find a way across.

It seemed like no time before we passed a sign marking Wittenberg's outskirts, the largest town we had seen since leaving camp. It could present a new problem if city authorities were still around, either stray German troops or police. I turned off to the left at the edge of town, and we drove slowly through a residential area until we could see the riverbank. There were signs of life now, the occasional face peering out of a window, an old man picking through personal items scattered on the sidewalk, and a cat prowling for food. Nobody paid any attention to us. The river was a tantalizing sight, but where could we cross? I turned right and drove slowly along a road next to the bank. The river snaked through the broad valley, and our view up and down the river was limited. Within a few minutes, we spotted a bridge, but my heart sank as we approached and saw it was blown up and the center span sagged into the water. I wondered if it had been the victim of an air strike or perhaps destroyed by retreating Germans to slow the American advance.

"Okay, now what's the plan?" I asked. "We haven't seen any other bridges nearby, and I doubt we have enough gas left in this thing to go exploring."

"I think we ought to look for someone to ask," replied Walt. With his rudimentary German, it was an option, but I thought it might be asking for trouble.

Bob made a better suggestion. "I say we just go check out the bridge. Even if it's in the river, there might be enough of it above water to allow us to climb across."

Walt shrugged, but I agreed with Bob, put the car into gear, and drove slowly along the bank towards the bridge. As we got closer, we could see activity on the far bank. McCartney studied the figures and then announced, "Hey, those are our guys over there!" Sure enough, we could make out the unmistakable round helmets of American GIs.

In another few hundred yards, the road became impassable, and the Kubelwagon was of no further use to us, so I stopped and killed the engine. We climbed out and walked over to the river's edge. It looked like an American jeep and armored car were patrolling the river's west bank. We waved and hollered to get their attention and got a wave in return. Our spirits soared! We excitedly studied the broken bridge superstructure that dipped into the water as though each side of the span was bowing to the other. A portion in the center, perhaps only the side railings, still appeared above water. The strong current could be a problem if we fell in, but we all decided it was passable. At best, we would get a bit wet, and at the worst, we would get a much-needed bath.

We walked the final few yards to the railroad bridge, and when we got to the base of the span, we could see that it was barely passable on foot. It took us more than a half-hour to carefully pick our way across, hand over hand through the mangled center span, swirling water up to our hips at one point. Once back on firm ground, we ran down the roadway towards the jeep, waving our arms, shouting, "We're Americans! We're Americans! God, are we glad to see you!" I had never felt so relieved.

The GIs acted as if they would hug us but almost instantly backed away when they smelled us. "Where the hell did you guys come from," asked the senior man, a tech sergeant.

Bob answered for all of us, "We're POWs from Luckenwalde. We walked out, swiped a car, and drove to find you guys. It's so great to finally find Americans."

"I'm not sure what to do with you," said the sergeant. "Hop in, and we'll go find someone who will."

We all piled into the vehicle, and he told the driver to return to battalion HQ, and off we went. The drive was short, and within a half-mile, we turned off into a large field with a half-dozen pyramid tents, apparently a command post. A corporal appeared and immediately ushered us into one of the tents.

We introduced ourselves to a major, the battalion adjutant. While he questioned us, I couldn't help but marvel at how clean he looked. I was envious, and I couldn't help staring at him. The major didn't seem to notice and picked up his field phone, cranked it, and spoke to someone, asking for instructions. After hanging up, he informed us that a truck would be there later in the day to take us back to the division to be processed. He suggested that we should get some chow and rest a bit while waiting. Wow, what a great suggestion that was!

The sergeant who had picked us up took us over to a field kitchen, told the cook to fix us some chow, then shook our hands and wished us a good trip back home. As he walked away, we looked at each other, grinned like idiots, and headed for the tables set up under a canvas awning. We took our seats and waited eagerly for the first hot GI food that we'd had in nearly nine months. Two of the cooks brought us beef stew, fresh bread, and hot coffee, then stood around to ask us questions about our experiences. As I ate, I could just feel the energy flowing back into my body. I leisurely followed up the meal with a Chesterfield cigarette, then found a shady spot beneath a tree and fell fast asleep.

Chapter 22

Homeward Bound

Our westward journey was slow since supplies moving eastward for the occupation forces clogged the roads, and we had to change trucks several times. We rolled across a pontoon bridge over the Rhine River and into France, collecting more former POWs on the way, and we eventually joined a sizable caravan of liberated soldiers. At each stop for food and fuel, we drew curious looks. Everyone wanted to shake hands and welcome us back when we explained that we had been POWs. It felt good, and I remember the excitement as we passed through the outskirts of Paris. We made another brief stop there, where we finally learned that we were being taken to Camp Lucky Strike, outside LeHavre, at the mouth of the River Seine.

The region around the seaport of LeHavre had been the site of the massive Allied build-up following the Normandy invasion. The retreating German forces had destroyed the port facilities. Within months, American engineers had cleared the waterfront and harbor, dredged the channels to accommodate heavily laden cargo ships, and restored most of the piers. Huge staging camps were set up along the coast between LeHavre and Rouen, serving as logistical distribution centers and replacement depots for all newly disembarked troops on their way to the front. To deceive German intelligence and still make it easy to refer to the camps, SHAEF gave each camp the name of an American cigarette brand: Tareyton, Chesterfield, Wings, Pall Mall, Home Run, Lucky Strike, Old Gold, and Twenty Grand. The latter three were the largest, and Lucky Strike was the camp through which most returning POWs were processed.

Our truck convoy rolled through LeHavre and out to the coast road and stopped. We all climbed down from the truck to stretch our legs and smoke for a few minutes. The lieutenant in charge of our escort climbed down from the truck cab and waved his arm at a huge pile of army boots.

"Go pick out a new pair of boots, boys," he ordered.

Like kids on Christmas morning, we all ran to the pile and dug for our sizes. It felt so good to say goodbye to the wooden shoes and slip into a pair of genuine American footwear that actually fit. We all stomped around a bit to get the feel of the new boots. I wiggled my toes and stared down at the pristine leather. I smiled in satisfaction, picked up the wooden shoes, and threw them as far as possible. I wish I had kept the wooden shoes as a souvenir, but I hated them passionately at that moment.

We all piled back into the truck for the home stretch. As we rolled down the road, I marveled at the enormity of the camps we passed. Camp Lucky Strike was located five miles northeast of Cany-Barville, near a small village known as Janville, laid out around a very large former Luftwaffe airstrip.

The trucks first took us to an army field hospital for a thorough medical screening. I was shocked to learn that I had lost forty-eight pounds, a third of my body weight. My first thought was that my mother would be horrified! The next stop was a delousing station where we placed our few personal possessions in a drawstring bag, stripped, and threw our filthy and infested clothing onto a burn pile. The chemical delousing was unpleasant, but I stood under the hot shower for long minutes, scrubbing vigorously and repeatedly. Then I did it all over again, this time luxuriating in the lather, letting the hot water stream over me, washing away the filth and stink of so many months.

Clean and shaven, we were issued crisp new uniforms, escorted to the camp barber, and then shown to our billets. The camp was divided into multiple self-contained sections bordering the patched runway. The vehicle traffic down this strip was almost as bad as Fifth Avenue, and crossing the thoroughfare was downright dangerous. Spring rains ensured that the camp remained a muddy mess, except for the facilities located on the edge of the runway and the taxiways and hardstands. All the former POWs were housed in pyramid tents again, identical to the ones in Louisiana and Scraptoft, but at least this time, the tents had wooden floors.

We didn't drill, and we were fed soft, high-calorie foods: eggs, pancakes with syrup, beer, donuts, ice cream, gravy and mashed potatoes, eggnog, puddings, and such army delicacies as chipped beef on toast (better known as "shit on a shingle"), and chicken-a-la-king, my favorite. My weight was down to ninety-eight pounds by the time we got to Lucky Strike, and I had probably put back on a few pounds after plundering the Red Cross packages at Stalag III-A. After a couple of weeks of fattening up, we all started to fill out a bit, losing the sunken-cheeked, cadaverous look. It was a relief when I finally had to let out my belt, a bit at a time.

At Lucky Strike, I went through an exhaustive debriefing by army intelligence. I referred to my journal as I detailed my capture, the POW camps, the marches and train rides, our mistreatment, the horrendous months in the tent at Luckenwalde, and the eventual drive back to the Elbe River. The interrogator was most interested in the brutalities I had witnessed: the killing of the young girls in Holland, the dog attack on the exhausted GI, and the soldier's shooting on the march from Furstenburg to Luckenwalde. I told him everything I could recall, then signed sworn depositions detailing the killings. I was very anxious that the guard who shot the first sergeant in the head be caught and punished. With all the brutality inflicted on POWs, I wasn't too hopeful.

Many months later, a civilian investigator came to my parents' home and questioned me again about the incident. I signed another sworn deposition, then pushed the affair to the back of my mind. Imagine my surprise when more than a year later, I received a formal letter from him informing me that the SS guard had been identified, tried and convicted as a war criminal. The letter explained that the guard had murdered several POWs, and dozens of men reported his callous brutality, but it did not mention his punishment. Still, it gave me satisfaction that there was still some justice in the world and a bit of closure to my POW ordeal.

During my debriefing by the intelligence officer, I told him about the roll of German Marks that the Russian POW at Stalag XII-A had given me. I still had some of the currency left, so I pulled it out and showed him what I had. He was astonished, and after a quick look he called another officer over to take a look. To my surprise, he identified it as pre-Nazi era money from the Weimar Republic. It was still valuable, and I cashed it in for just over $385.00. Those trips to the latrine in XII-A were expensive!

One day, I learned something even more surprising while playing poker with a fellow who casually mentioned that he had worked in his father's jewelry store before the war. I told him about the spool of solder I had found in the jewelry store vault at Juterborg on our ride from Stalag III-A to Wittenberg. He suddenly paused; his eyes went wide, and his eyebrows rose.

"Wow," he said. "You should have kept that! I can almost guarantee that that was a roll of platinum solder, worth a small fortune." He shook his head, and I felt like a fool. Who would have known?

In their thoroughness, the army gave us a briefing on war souvenirs, but I didn't have much more than my POW dog tags, my journal, some photos, and the 7.65mm pistol that the German officer had surrendered to me at Stalag III-A. On the other hand, Walt McAllister had several pistols and knives that he had taken from our camp guards. At Lucky Strike, we were told we could keep only one souvenir firearm per person, and they gave us papers authorizing the item. Walt slipped me the P-38 he took from the German officer during our hasty departure from Luckenwalde, and he gave Bob McCartney a Luger he had picked up from a dead German soldier in Juterborg. That meant I had two pistols, but I wanted to take one home to Steve, my younger brother, so I was willing to gamble that I could smuggle them both home. In England, I had won a few souvenirs playing poker with Normandy veterans, but I was pretty sure they disappeared from my footlocker after I was declared MIA. Sure enough, they never made it back to Michigan.

We relaxed, ate, played cards, walked the camp, shopped in the post exchange (PX), watched a few movies, and tried to kill time as best we could until we were shipped home. At poker, I won a German dagger but later traded it for a watch to replace the one I had swapped for fresh vegetables. Finally, the medical department declared me fit to travel, and several hundred of us packed up our few belongings and marched back down to LeHavre to board a ship bound for New York.

While we were forming up on the dock, I was approached by a fresh-faced young second lieutenant who looked like he had just arrived from the States. He noticed the bulge of the P-38 in my pants pocket and challenged me.

"What do you have in your pocket, sergeant," he demanded.

Reluctantly, I pulled the pistol out for him to see. He demanded to see the paperwork to authorize it. Of course, I didn't have any and shrugged my shoulders.

"I lost it while packing," I lied, hoping he'd let me pass.

"Sergeant," he declared pompously, "You can't take that firearm on board the ship. Hand it over!"

"No, sir," I replied. "According to regs, we are each allowed one souvenir firearm."

"Without the paperwork, you don't have a choice, sergeant," he said. "Either you hand it over, or you don't go on board."

I got angry because I knew damn well he just wanted the pistol for himself. He looked like a newly commissioned ninety-day wonder who had never seen combat. I hesitated for a moment and thought about what to do. He might call for MPs and have me searched if I put up too much of a fight. If they found the second pistol, the 7.65mm, perhaps I would be court-martialed for trying to smuggle the P-38, even though I had the paper authorizing the smaller gun as a "bring back" souvenir. In frustration, I raised the Walther over my head and slammed it on the concrete pier as hard as possible. It flew apart into several pieces, and a few tumbled into the water.

"There's your damned pistol if you want it," I shouted back at him. My rage must have startled him because he backed away. Without hesitation, I brushed past him and stomped up the gangway onto the ship before he could regain his composure.

Our transport home was a liner converted to a hospital ship for returning POWs. This time we bunked in much better quarters than on the way over, Bob and Walt in the bunk next to mine, and the satisfying, high-calorie food we had encountered at Lucky Strike continued. We had access to showers, and the ship had a laundry, so things smelled better too. But I was still apprehensive about seasickness, so once we were well out to sea, I resorted to my old trick of carrying a can of olives.

This return voyage was smoother than the previous one, and I only got a touch of sea sickness twice, first in the Bay of Biscay and then on the Grand Banks. Over meals (when not too queasy to eat) and cards, I had plenty of time to get to know the other ex-POWs. I was surprised to learn that the fellow in the bunk right above mine was a Medal of Honor winner. He was William J. Crawford, 36th Infantry Division, from Pueblo, Colorado. On September 13, 1943, near Altavilla, Italy, he had taken out three German machine gun nests single-handed that had pinned down his company. It was bad luck that the Germans captured him only a short time later. He had only learned of the award at Camp Lucky Strike, and I don't think the reality of the medal had quite sunk in yet. He was proud of the award, as any soldier would be, but modest about it at the same time. His reply to any adulation was that he was no hero—the heroes were the guys who couldn't come home. I've heard the same thing from virtually every Medal of Honor winner since then, and I share the sentiment.

We all enjoyed each other's company, but we were looking forward to getting home, and before long, most of our conversations revolved around what we would do once we were out of the army. Some guys planned to return to school to earn a degree, and others had jobs back home. In my case, I didn't have any firm plans and assumed I would just go back to driving trucks.

The arrival at New York Harbor was another emotional experience I'll never forget. It made me think about my father's arrival from Greece many years ago. Did he feel the same thrill as I did? I was intoxicated with the sights and smells of home, already imagining how it would be when I walked through our front door, ate my first home-cooked meal, and spent the first night in my old bed. But it would be weeks before that happened. The officers aboard the ship informed us that our processing would be at Fort Jay, the historic harbor defense fort on Governor's Island, just south of Manhattan. All ex-POWs would receive orders to rest and recuperation (R&R) facilities until considered healthy enough to be discharged.

The docks on Governor's Island are large enough to accommodate troop transports, so we didn't set foot in Manhattan, but as I shouldered my duffle bag and crossed the gangway to the dock, it was hard to take my eyes off the dramatic view of the New York skyline. Officers formed us up on the pier and marched us to the receiving station, where we handed in our service records and received billeting assignments, a welcome home package, and information about the island's facilities.

Fort Jay, which dominates the island, was commissioned in 1794 as the major army base within the Port of New York, Headquarters of the Eastern Defense Command. When America declared war in December 1941, it became the central shipment point for troops and equipment flowing out of the port. As outbound troop movements slowed in mid-1944, incoming German POWs began to fill some of the barracks. By the early summer of 1945, after the victory in Europe, it began to accept the influx of returning American POWs.

The paperwork took the better part of the first day, terribly frustrating with the Big Apple just a short ferry ride away. But getting a temporary billet in a solid, brick barrack with a real bed was a luxury I had not experienced in years. The army wasn't ready to turn us loose on Manhattan, nor could they just let us loaf around. The administration office ordered me to report to the supply depot the next day for a temporary assignment until they completed my paperwork. The duty was a couple of boring days spent cutting chevrons and unit patches from surplus uniforms. It was a mindless chore; even the quartermaster in charge was disinterested and ignored my coworkers and me. On the third day, a master sergeant showed up looking for some volunteers. He called the supply sergeant over and explained that he needed a few men to supervise some work details. Liberated POWs had received a promotion to the next pay grade, so I was now a technical sergeant, the senior ex-POW on the patch-cutting assignment.

"Hey, Tech," called the supply sergeant, "Have you had enough fun cutting off patches?"

"Oh, yeah, it's a blast," I replied. "Whatcha need?"

"Top here wants someone senior to escort some German POWs on a work detail. Wanna volunteer?"

I had not heard that German POWs were interned on the island. "German POWs, you say," I replied.

"Yeah, they've got them doing maintenance work," he said.

I had a fleeting thought of payback. With a smile, I responded, "Yeah, sure, as long as I don't have to bring them back."

He looked at me for a minute, perhaps thinking I was joking. I could almost see the light bulb go on over his head. "You were a POW, right? How long?" he asked.

"Yeah," I said, "Nine months, in four separate camps, two train rides in boxcars, and a seven-day march in a blizzard."

He just shook his head. "Aw, forget it then. I'll get someone else."

I just turned around and went back to my cutting.

I stayed a bit more than a week at Fort Jay, decommissioning uniforms by day, staring longingly out the warehouse door at the Manhattan skyline, and drinking beer and watching motion pictures at the post theater each evening. I was relieved when I finally got travel orders to an R&R center in Miami Beach, Florida, with a month's leave at home on the way.

I said goodbye to Bob McCarthy, Walt McAllister, and Bill Crawford, promising to keep in touch, but I think I knew that it probably wouldn't happen. After packing my meager gear, I reported to the paymaster's office, where the army gave me the balance of my back pay and a cash advance of fifty dollars for travel expenses. But I reverted to my old habit, pocketed the money, took the ferry across the harbor, and hitchhiked home. Manhattan could wait.

The journey took nearly thirty-six hours, riding first with a salesman to Pittsburgh and then with a trucker to Detroit. From there, it was easy to thumb my way up Woodward Avenue to Pontiac and then get the fourth ride to Rochester. GIs in uniform were everywhere, and people were only too happy to help us. In fact, my money was no good. All my meals were paid for by either the guy I rode with, the waiters in the diners, or another customer. It was a great feeling to be appreciated. Most people asked what unit I was in and what I had done, but I gave short answers and tried to avoid talking about it. The memories were too fresh, and I wanted to put everything behind me.

My excitement rose the closer I got to home. As I walked the final stretch to the house, with just the uniform on my back and a duffle stuffed with two blankets, spare skivvies, soap, a razor, and a toothbrush, it seemed as though I had been gone for only a short time. Everything looked as it had in March 1941, and I stepped onto the front porch and approached the screen door. My mother must have heard my footsteps.

"Who's that?" she called.

Maybe I was silhouetted against the light, or perhaps I had lost so much weight that she couldn't recognize me because she just stared at me for a moment.

"It's just me, Mom," I replied. "I'm home."

The screen door burst open, and she ran into my arms. I had called home before leaving Fort Jay so the family knew I was on my way but didn't know when I would arrive. It was such a wonderful feeling to get that first hug and kiss! Within moments, my father, brother, and sister appeared, hugging and peppering me with questions. I knew that I was truly home.

For the next week, I did nothing but lounge around, eating as much of my mother's cooking as I could and sleeping better than I had for many months. My older brothers, Andy and John, made it home before me and were already out job-hunting. My kid brother Steve kept pestering me with questions about the airborne, my capture, and what the POW camps were like. I didn't want to be reminded of all that, so I did my best to deflect his questions or give short answers. Eventually, he gave up, satisfied to have all three of his "hero" brothers home at last.

Billy Condon at home on leave, July 1945. Note how loose the uniform fits at the time. (Author's Collection)

When my leave ended, I put on my uniform, and my father drove me to the train station for the trip to Miami. After I bought my ticket, we sat together on the platform bench, not saying much. Eventually, he put his arm around my shoulder and softly said, "I'm glad this is almost over. We're anxious to have you home for good." I just nodded, unable to respond because of the lump in my throat. But this parting was more manageable since we all knew it was only for a couple of months. As the train pulled out, I waved from the open window, then settled back for the ride.

The train trip was uneventful. I sat alone, skimming the newspapers and thumbing through magazines like Time, Life, Look, and The Saturday Evening Post. Mostly, I just watched the country roll past. I was looking at America through new eyes, seeing things I'd never noticed, and appreciating all I saw. No more bombed-out cities, piles of rubble, dead bodies, scavenging refugees, or enemies. Soon it would be no more army.

Miami Beach turned out to be one big vacation. The army had appropriated several first-class hotels during the war, first to house trainees, then to accommodate returning ex-POWs. Besides a daily roll call, we were free to do whatever we wanted. We lounged on the beach, worked on a tan, ate and drank well, chased women, and sampled the nightlife.

Upon arrival, we received another thorough physical examination. I was still seriously underweight, but my arms and legs were filling out, and my stamina had improved. I had put about ten pounds back on and no longer looked like a scarecrow. The army fed us quarts of eggnog, chicken-a-la-king, beef stew, ice cream, cakes, plenty of beer, and just about anything else we wanted to get our weight back to normal. After the first few nights of making the rounds of the bars and dance clubs, I slowed down, caught a few movies, slept a lot, and soaked up the sunshine on the beach. I received a cursory medical checkup each week to monitor my weight gain, which was slowly improving.

I had expected to encounter McCarthy, McAllister, Crawford, Barc, or at least one of the other fellows from First Squad, George Company, or a familiar face from Luckenwalde. To my disappointment, there were no familiar faces. I got to know a few of the other fellows, and we occasionally hung out together, but with no expectation of an extended stay in Miami, it was pretty superficial. After comparing our POW experiences, all we could talk about was what the future might hold and when they would finally clear us to leave.

One Saturday, in the middle of September and nearly a year since my capture in Holland, we ex-POWs were told to prepare for an inspection at noon the following day. It was to be held in the grassy park across the street from the hotel. We couldn't understand why the army scheduled a formation on a Sunday, but orders were orders. I shined my shoes, polished my brass, and pressed my new khaki uniform. At the appointed hour, we assembled in formation and were surprised to see a band and a podium set up. A captain ordered twenty of us to form the front row alphabetically.

To our pleasant surprise, we were inspected by a Brigadier General who called us forward, one by one, then presented each of us with the Purple Heart medal. Awarded for wounds sustained in combat with the enemy, this was the closest award the army could offer us in recognition of the abuse and suffering we had endured as prisoners of war. Since the entire ceremony was held in a public area, we attracted a sizable crowd, and with the band playing the National Anthem and some stirring marches, we felt like celebrities, at least for a day! A second Purple Heart and a Bronze Star eventually caught up with me a year or so later. The first for my wounds, and the second for my months as a POW, so I ended up with two Purple Hearts. For the action in Holland, I received the coveted Combat Infantry Badge or CIB.

It took about two more weeks of living it up in Miami to bring me back to something close to my original weight. I began at 145 pounds and had dropped to 98 pounds and it came back on slowly. I finally received orders to report back to Fort Jay by September 30. One more long train ride, but this was my final transfer in the army.

Back at Fort Jay, I checked into the same barrack. For two days, I was subjected to pre-separation lectures to prepare me for the transition back to civilian life. Then I was finally presented with my discharge papers and the "ruptured duck" patch to sew onto my uniform jacket. After collecting my separation pay, I caught the last ferry back to Manhattan, shared a cab ride with two other GIs to Grand Central Station, and then took the New York Central railroad back to Detroit.

As the train made its way up the Hudson River, past Hyde Park, West Point, and Albany, my thoughts drifted back to the POW camps and my struggle for survival. It all seemed unreal, as though it had happened to someone else. So much had happened in the past year. I marveled that I had survived the ordeal and made a solemn vow never to go camping or hunting again!

While changing trains at the Michigan Central Station in Detroit, I telephoned home to give them my arrival time, and my father picked me up at the Pontiac station. My army adventures were finally over.

My older brothers, John and Andy, had already found jobs and returned to work, but I was aimless for quite some time. I had been warned that the transition back to civilian life, particularly for former POWs, was difficult, and it turned out to be true. My feelings were complex, and I experienced mood swings, alternating between the pleasure of being home to guilt and resentment. I had difficulty shaking off shame for being captured, sitting out so much of the war while so many fought and died. I felt resentment that I had been used, abused, and then just discarded with a "thank you," back pay, and promotion before mustering out. I wasn't in a reasonable frame of mind to go back to a routine job, so I spent much of my time just goofing off. I stayed around the house doing odd jobs, played a bit of golf, and got into trouble more than once, drinking and chasing women. I had no motivation or career goals and struggled to sort out my feelings.

When I returned to Brookwood Country Club, the senior club members who generously offered to sponsor me back in 1940 approached me again about pursuing a professional golf career. Sadly, it only took a few rounds to realize that, although I still played well, I no longer had the physical stamina to compete at that level. Tournament play for 72 holes, not to mention the mental stress of competition, was now beyond my capabilities. It was a bitter pill to swallow.

During the months of my captivity, I had ample time to reflect upon my life, replaying events in my memory and analyzing my behavior and motivations. But it was all water under the bridge, and I was finally determined to move on with my life and not let hate or guilt consume me. But one minor transgression had bothered me, and I resolved to set it right.

From the time I was five or six years old, I frequented Brand's Corner Grocery, just for candies and the occasional soda pop. When I was about twelve, I just had to have a cap pistol, mainly because the other kids had one. I wanted to be able to play cops and robbers or cowboys and Indians with them. The problem was that I didn't have any money of my own. One day I shop-lifted a chrome-plated six-shooter and a box of caps from Mrs. Brand's store, tucking it in my jacket pocket when no one was looking. By late 1944, languishing in the POW camps with all the time in the world to replay memories of my life, it began to eat at me, giving me a guilty conscience that troubled me. It was the only thing I had ever stolen, and I vowed to repay Mrs. Brand when I got home.

I was more afraid of facing Mrs. Brand than of going into combat but now was the time. I screwed up my courage, walked the short distance to Brand's store, and prepared to confront Mrs. Brand. As apprehensive as I was, the bell on the door made me jump, but I walked in and waited patiently for Mrs. Brand to finish ringing up a customer. After a few moments, she turned to me and smiled.

"Why, Billy Condon, it's good to see you home safe and sound. Your brother Steve told me that you had been a POW. That must have been a terrible experience. What are you up to now? Are you back to work?"

I swallowed hard, almost afraid to look her in the eye. I told her I was just getting settled back into civilian life and hadn't started a job yet. After a pause, as my face flushed in shame, I told her the story of my theft fourteen years before.

Mrs. Brand smiled and replied, "Billy, I'm surprised that you ever did that back then, but you were just a child. Coming back and telling me about it took courage. I'm very pleased, but your service more than repaid me. I'm just happy that you came back from the war in one piece."

She never said anything more about it, and we drank a Coke together. It was good to be home, and I made a point of occasionally stopping in her store for soda pop and a chat.

While I continued to live at home, I began to experience horrible nightmares, randomly reliving events in vivid detail, sleeping poorly, and getting crankier each week. Finally, one day my father sat me down and laid it on the line. "Son, we don't understand what you are going through, but we know it must be difficult. If there were something we could do to help, we would. We love you and are delighted to have you home, but we can't keep walking on eggshells around you. It's time to get back to work. I think it will be the best therapy for you."

He was right, of course. After I wasted two and a half months, my father lined up an interview for me with the General Motors Truck & Coach Division in Pontiac. GM offered me a job if I got my GED high school equivalent certificate. I took a two-day crash course in Detroit, sat for the exam, and received my diploma. I started work at GM the following Monday. Several years later, they sent me to the General Motors Technical Institute to get a degree in Mechanical Engineering. I spent the next thirty-five years at General Motors, working myself up from the drafting table and through the engineering department at the Pontiac Motors Division, retiring in 1984

Chapter 23

Epilog

I continued to enjoy the nightlife on weekends, and about a year after my discharge, I was with several friends at a nightclub in Pontiac called the Club Rio. A pretty brunette girl named Hazel caught my eye, and I decided I had to meet her. She was out with friends to celebrate her twenty-first birthday, and since I was a brash ex-GI, I asked her to dance, and we clicked. I took her out several times, and she became my best girl. Less than a year later, we were married and have been together ever since.

I pursued golf for five years, playing competitively in the public leagues and regional tournaments, representing my home club. But it was too much golf, and Hazel finally put her foot down. She gave me an ultimatum: either turn pro, and she'd just divorce me, or stay home and play locally on weekends. I loved her too much to let her go, so I gave up the competition. I was delighted when she took up golf some years later, and we enjoyed many golf vacations together.

I continued to suffer from occasional nightmares and struggled to control a quick temper. In recent years this has been labeled post-traumatic stress syndrome, but at that time, doctors and psychiatrists were working on naming and treating it. Hazel was sympathetic and tried to understand the horrors I was reliving. She did her best to help me cope with it, but she was as frustrated with my behavior as I was. With her support, I struggled with the Veterans Administration for years to get some compensation for lingering health problems, both physical and emotional.

In the early 1960s, our family doctor recommended that I write a summary of my wartime experience as a form of therapy. I was a poor writer, but I wrote out a six-page, single-spaced narrative, primarily drawn from my slim POW journal and a detailed chronology of key events, from my army draft to discharge. Hazel, the executive secretary for the General Manager of the Pontiac Motor Division of GM, typed it up. Unfortunately, it did little to improve my psychological state.

It took continual support from Hazel for me to overcome the emotional scars of the war, but I was lucky to marry the right girl. Finding her did a lot to get my feet back on the ground and give my life focus, and despite the usual ups and downs, we've stayed together. Sadly, we were never blessed with children, but we have enjoyed watching our nieces and nephews grow up. Hazel and I share a love of golf, and we've traveled extensively around the country. Hazel made a trip to Germany with four of her sisters, but I had no interest in returning to Europe, particularly to the Netherlands or Germany.

In 1991, my nephew Tom, a navy commander, served at Special Operations Command in Tampa, Florida, near our cold weather retreat in Winter Haven. He spent a weekend with us, and our conversation naturally turned to the military. When Hazel showed Tom a copy of my POW journal, he offered to help me write my memoirs. I was hesitant, but Hazel convinced me it would be good to tell the whole story, warts and all. We began a series of interviews and correspondence to put it all on paper.

In the process of documenting the events of September 23, 1944, Tom corresponded with a WWII airborne historian in the Netherlands, Roland Korst, who had been a child in 1944 and remembered the Nazi occupation and the liberation of his hometown of S'Hertogenbosch by Welsh troops. Roland was a docent at the military museum in Veghel. He knew the battlegrounds well, and early in 1999, he extended an invitation for me to return for the 55th Anniversary of Market-Garden. The airborne museum hoped to get as many veterans as possible for the occasion. The activities would include reenacted parachute drops, flyovers by restored combat aircraft, and a formal reception with His Royal Highness, Prince Bernhard.

My instinctive reaction was, "no way." I explained my feelings to Tom, "I've seen enough of Europe to last me a lifetime. You couldn't pay me to go back there!" But Hazel believed the experience would give me some closure. She applied gentle pressure until I finally relented, and Tom made the arrangements.

As a host, Roland Korst turned out to be the consummate gentleman. A tall, white-bearded, distinguished-looking fellow, he was sincerely interested in my story and generous with his time. Roland devoted a whole week of vacation time to guide us through the battlefields of Market-Garden. He was a font of information about the events of September 1944 and a skilled and sensitive guide.

The morning after our arrival, Roland picked us up at our hotel and took us to lunch at a windmill near Veghel that had been a German command post before the 101st Airborne took control of the town. While Roland enthusiastically outlined the itinerary for the week, I was suddenly overcome by emotion, flooded with memories, and overwhelmed with the feeling of being back where so much horror and suffering began. Tears filled my eyes, and I couldn't hold back the flood of emotion.

Roland was startled, but he had met with veterans before. I think he intuitively knew what I was feeling and quickly reassured me that the Dutch people had never forgotten what the Americans, British, and Poles had done to liberate his people. He described how every year, the Dutch school children put flowers on the graves of the fallen Allied soldiers, keeping the story of their sacrifice alive for future generations.

Roland drove us the entire length of Hell's Highway, from the Allied cemetery at Valkensward on the Belgian border to the British landing zones at Wolfheze west of Arnhem. We stopped at every important Market-Garden site, attended memorial services, and watched commemorative parachute jumps onto the original drop zones. On our final day of exploration, Roland surprised us with a ride in his immaculately restored WWII jeep, bearing the markings of the Welsh regiment that liberated his hometown of S'Hertogenbosch.

Since our first contact, Roland had been continuously searching airborne records to discover the site where glider "13" had landed, and he was determined to take us to look at each potential location. With the help of a Market-Garden aviation historian, Hans den Brok, Roland combined military topographical maps from 1944, old RAF reconnaissance photos from September 24, 1944, and the resources of the Veghel Airborne Museum archives to narrow down the possibilities.

Three candidate landing sites emerged. One was too far from the Belgian/Dutch border, and the glider in the photos was intact, but the other two sites with wrecked gliders were possible. We decided we would have to visit both. We drove through orchards and woods, up narrow tractor lanes, then hiked across fields to examine the terrain at each site. But like a hologram that can be viewed only from a precise angle, nothing matched my memories. Over a half-century, many details changed: trees had grown or were cut down; buildings were new, remodeled, or gone altogether; drainage ditches were filled in or rerouted; forests were cut down, and fields got subdivided and planted with different crops or turned to pasture. As a specialist in Market-Garden aviation history, Hans had identified my glider's most probable landing site based on his research into the 313th Troop Carrier Squadron. He was convinced it was the final site.

The weather turned to light rain as we motored up a dirt track to the final site, just a short distance east of the village of Erp, just off the Erp-Gemert road. We passed a small wood, then drove parallel to a row of pine trees that stood like sentinels, separating the dirt track from a corn field. We disembarked and walked the tree line for about a hundred yards, but the standing crop of corn made it difficult for me to get an accurate impression of the field size and surrounding area. When I had landed, the field had a crop of fodder beets, and the sightlines were much broader.

We were about to leave the site when, on impulse, I took a last walk along the tree-lined border. Ignoring the gentle rain, I turned my jacket collar up and looked toward the woods. Suddenly, in my mind's eye, I saw the glider, the shadowy figures of German soldiers moving through the trees, and the ditch where we held out until hope faded. I froze, dropped to my knees, and tears of emotion welled up again, mixing with the soft raindrops on my cheeks.

"This is it," I said softly to Tom. "This is the field, and right there is where I was taken captive." That single moment brought the entire trip, the hours of interviews, and my wartime experience to a conclusion. I whispered a prayer of thanksgiving.

With new certainty, we drove to the village of Gemert, where Roland believed my fellow glidermen and I were taken the first night by our German captors. The convent where we slept was just down the cobbled street from the charming Die Kreiser hotel, which had been a German field hospital on September 23-24, 1944. During lunch on the Die Kreiser porch, we watched a wedding at the town hall next door. I couldn't help but remark how cute the bride was, with an elegant white gown set off with snow white sneakers. It was a poignant illustration of how life moves on to new generations and love, not hate. Gemert was pleasurable, and the company was excellent, but it was only vaguely familiar to me, not a vivid memory. Nothing compared to that moment at the edge of the field near Erp. I was mostly quiet as I finished my beer, lost in memories.

I have shared as many as I could, but there are some that I must keep to myself.

You may recall that my buddies and I had seen the young Frank Sinatra perform at the old Mocambo nightclub in Hollywood. I reencountered him many years later. It's an interesting story.

In the mid-1980s, when I was on vacation in Palm Springs, I played a round of golf while Hazel did some shopping and had her hair done. She dropped me off at the country club, and I wandered my way to the pro shop, where I approached the starter to see if there was a possibility of filling out a foursome. He was an older fellow, darkly tanned from years on the golf course, with salt and pepper hair bushing out from under his ball cap. He pushed his cap up a bit and looked at me.

"Okay, what kind of golfer are you? What's your handicap?" He asked.

When I told him that I was a scratch golfer (meaning my handicap was zero, usually shooting par, occasionally better), the old fellow raised an eyebrow, smiled, and asked me to wait a bit. He disappeared in the direction of the first tee, and in just a few minutes, he returned with a fellow in tow who I instantly recognized as the actor and comedian Joey Bishop.

The starter introduced us, then Joey smiled and asked me to follow him. Intrigued, I picked up my club bag and walked over to the first tee box to meet the other two players. Imagine my shock when Joey introduced me to Frank Sinatra and Dean Martin. A touch of awe hardly describes my reaction. Who gets invited to play golf with the celebrated "rat pack"? The novelty of playing eighteen holes with these celebrity characters was intimidating. I had no idea what kind of golfers the trio were, but I figured I could hold my own. We quickly paired off, Frank and Joey against Dean and me.

They warmly welcomed me, but for the first few holes, I kept pretty quiet, just answering their questions about me, and in a short time, I relaxed and began to feel that I had known them forever. Of course, in a way, I had. I had watched their on-screen performances for decades, and I'd seen Frank on stage early in his career at the Mocambo club.

I never had so much fun golfing in my life. I just enjoyed listening to their banter, laughing so hard that, at times, it was difficult to concentrate on golf. They were great jokers and shared delightfully ribald stories of their antics and swapped stories about fellow celebs. Thinking back on it, I think they were trying to outdo each other entertaining me. Poor shots drew laughs and continuous ribbing, just as the good ones elicited whistles and applause. To my surprise, the three were all decent golfers, but they were not quite in my league. I don't enjoy playing with anyone who doesn't take the game seriously, but they obviously enjoyed it as much as the camaraderie. Even if they had been weekend duffers, I would still have been proud to be part of the "rat pack" for a few hours.

After the round, I had some extra time to while away until Hazel would pick me up, so we all adjourned to the clubhouse for a drink to celebrate the round. After the trio departed, I waited near the curb. When Hazel arrived, I slid into the passenger seat.

"So, how was the game," she asked.

I struggled to keep a grin off my face. "Oh, it was good. I filled out a foursome. They were interesting guys. You probably know a couple of them."

"Really? Someone from back home?"

I tried to be nonchalant as I replied, "No, just Frank Sinatra, Dean Martin, and Joey Bishop. I guess Peter Lawford was still back in L.A."

Hazel suddenly braked the car, shifted into park, and stared at me for a moment or two. Her expression alternated from surprise to disbelief. Finally, she decided I was joking. "Yeah, right. Who was it really?"

I told her about the round and pulled out a souvenir golf ball from my pocket embossed with the name "Sinatra," but she still seemed skeptical. As further proof, I reached into my golf bag, unzipped the top pocket, and presented her with the score card. Dean and I had won the round.

THE END

HISTORICAL NOTES

Operation Market Garden

The Background - Patton vs. Montgomery

The diplomacy of General Dwight D. Eisenhower and his Combined Staff generally kept the rivalry between the British and the American forces in the European Theater at a respectfully competitive level. However, the personal enmity between Lieutenant General George S. Patton, Jr. and General (later Field Marshal) Sir Bernard Montgomery often pushed it to the edge. The fierce competition between the two developed during the invasion of Sicily. Montgomery's Eighth Army landed on the east coast of Sicily, south of Syracuse, and pushed north along the coast towards Messina, attempting to cut off the German retreat across the Straits of Messina to Italy. Simultaneously, Patton's Seventh Army had landed on the south coast, then split into two groups: one moving west up the coast towards Marsala at the Western tip. At the same time, the second force executed a rapid, sweeping move around the Western slopes of Mount Etna and then east to Messina. Patton won the race, and the resultant face-to-face meeting between the two men in Messina ignited a fierce rivalry.

Historians generally concede that Patton considered Montgomery a vain, egotistical, and effete snob, obsessed with his political ambitions and only taking the offensive when he felt he had the advantage. For his part, Monty regarded Patton as a loud, ill-mannered, reckless, and pompous peacock who threatened Montgomery's self-image as the best field commander in Europe. Both were probably fair assessments, but each was not without his military genius, and both men were driven by personal ambition, vanity, and a burning desire to win.

When the Allies broke out from Normandy at the end of July 1944, the British 21st Army Group thrust northwards towards Belgium and the vital North Sea ports of Antwerp and Rotterdam. At the same time, General Jacob Devers' U.S. 6th Army Group advanced from Southern France, and General Omar Bradley's U.S. 12th Army Group, spearheaded by the armor of Patton's Third Army, accelerated its advance eastwards toward the Rhine. The speed of the Allied thrust and the ensuing panic in the German command prompted German Field Marshal Gerd von Rundstedt to remark, "German units are retreating faster than the Allies are advancing." However, it was apparent to the Allied Command that the restricted flow of supplies through Normandy, especially fuel for the armored divisions, was insufficient to sustain a rapid advance across a broad front.

Montgomery repeatedly pressured Eisenhower to divert the lion's share of supplies to his 21st Army Group, arguing that the German opposition in the Low Countries of Belgium and Holland was light and presented the best path into the German Reich. Montgomery was so desperate to get the green light that he even went so far as to offer to serve under Omar Bradley if his force had priority. Bradley had developed a less than flattering opinion of Montgomery's abilities and opposed his plans.

This skepticism was widespread within the American command, and many regarded the Normandy campaign as a success despite Montgomery's performance. Outraged by Monty's demands, Patton pleaded with Bradley, denouncing his rival and shouting, "To hell with Hodges and Montgomery! We'll win your goddamn War if you'll keep the Third Army going!" Ultimately, the pressure from the German V-2 rocket attacks against Britain, which had begun on September 8, launched from fixed and mobile sites in Holland and Belgium, tipped the scales in Montgomery's favor.

The Strategy

Field Marshal Montgomery's objective for "Market-Garden" was to drive a wedge through the German-occupied Low Countries and across the Rhine River at Arnhem, Holland. The German forces in Belgium and Western Holland would be isolated, and the Rhine and Ruhr valleys opened to the Allies. While it was a brilliant strategy, it was incredibly complex, with many moving parts. The failure of any one component could cripple or doom the operation. The "Market" portion would land three airborne divisions at three sites in Holland to seize a succession of bridges along the vital highway to Arnhem. They would have to hold the bridges long enough for the armored "Garden" forces to rush up the road, relieve the British airborne troops in Arnhem, and push across the Rhine into Germany. Montgomery's staff estimated that with the light German resistance expected in the area, the Arnhem bridgehead anchoring the northernmost end of the line of advance would be relieved within four days.

The road from the southern Dutch border to Arnhem was only sixty-five miles long, but most of the roadway was a two-lane highway with extensive stretches, elevated above the surrounding low countryside with steep-sided berms. Other portions passed through dense pine forests, stone walls, or buildings so close to the roadway that a pedestrian would have to hug the walls to keep from being run down. Additionally, the cities along the route, if tenaciously defended by the Germans, would effectively block any advance until taken. It proved to be the weak link in the tactical plan, as the road could be easily blocked by damaged or destroyed vehicles, and the movement of critical equipment up to the vanguard required clever and tedious maneuvering. German artillery fire effectively cut the highway several times before they completed a withdrawal close to the Rhine.

Order of Battle

The order of battle for the First Allied Airborne Army, commanded by American Lieutenant General Lewis H. Brereton, included the XVIII U.S. Airborne Corps under the command of Major General Matthew B. Ridgeway, with the 82nd and 101st Airborne Divisions commanded by Brigadier General James M. Gavin and Major General Maxwell Taylor, respectively. The 1st British Airborne Corps consisted of the 1st Airborne Division commanded by Major General Roy E. Urquhart; the 1st Polish Independent Parachute Brigade under Major General Stanislav Sosabowski; and the 52nd (Lowland) Division (Air-portable) commanded by Major General E. Hakewell-Smith.

The 82nd Airborne Division included the 504th, 505th, and 508th Parachute Infantry Regiments, the 325th Glider Infantry Regiment (with the 2nd Battalion of the 401st GIR as the 3rd Battalion), the 307th Airborne Engineers, the 376th Parachute Field Artillery Battalion, and the 319th and 320th Glider Field Artillery Battalions, as well as divisional support units.

The 101st Airborne Division consisted of the 501st, 502nd, and 506th Parachute Infantry Regiments, the 327th Glider Infantry Regiment (with the 1st Battalion of the 401st GIR as the 3rd Battalion), the 326 Airborne Engineers, the 377th Parachute Field Artillery Battalion, and the 321st and 907th Glider Field Artillery Battalions, plus the division's support units.

The opposing German forces were a makeshift collection of units decimated in France and Belgium. They were hastily reinforced with second-rate troops who had been clerks, typists, students, drivers, military police, lightly wounded veterans, and new conscripts pushed through an abbreviate training regimen. The Allied plan failed to consider Field Marshal Model's ability to perform an amazing feat of arms by quickly organizing an apparent rabble into individual, coherent Kampfgruppe (battle groups). These Kampfgruppe were no fixed size but led by experienced tactical field commanders. Each unit possessed a cadre of battle-hardened troops, trained to assess and solve tactical problems, seize the initiative at every opportunity, and force their enemy onto the defense.

While weak in foot infantry, the Kampfgruppe were composed of armor, mechanized infantry, field artillery, and self-propelled assault guns. Their exact composition and strength changed daily as the tactical situation evolved.

In addition, the Germans had the 10th Panzer SS Division (Frundsburg), under Brigadefuhrer Heinz Harmel, the 9th SS Panzer Division (Hohenstaufen), commanded by Obsrsturmbahnfuhrer Walther Harzer, and the First Parachute Army, commanded by Colonel-General Kurt Student. All these German units and leaders were battle seasoned and highly decorated, but they had seen heavy action since the Normandy landings. They were withdrawn from the fray in France and Belgium to rest, regroup, and reequip in the vicinity of Arnhem. New Panzer V "Panther" and Panzer VI "Tiger" tanks were already moving by rail from depots in Germany. Due to aggressive Allied air attacks on rail yards, tunnels, and main lines, these trains were forced to take circuitous routes, thereby slowing equipment replacement.

Despite RAF photoreconnaissance and warnings from Dutch resistance fighters, all confirming the presence of German armor, Montgomery chose to ignore the intelligence. He desperately needed headlines to fuel his political War with George Patton, and Market-Garden would go forward, regardless of the situation. To paraphrase Montgomery, XXX Corps would rush to Arnhem "over a carpet of Airborne troops ." All were expendable in his rush to get the headlines and reach the Rhine River before Patton. The British First Airborne Corps staff intelligence officer, Major Urquhart, protested (no relation to Major General Urquhart, who led the British paratroop assault on Arnhem) but was promptly sent on leave to keep him out of the way. The operation was a bold concept and may have been successful if not for the German defenders' tactical skill, resourcefulness, and determination.

The sheer numbers of soldiers and equipment required for the invasion of Holland overstressed the airlift and airfield capacities of the Allied forces in Britain. It needed a series of five airlifts over three successive days to move the three divisions and the Polish brigade. The first assault would occur on September 17, consisting of the American 101st Airborne Division, with the 327th Glider Infantry Regiment, which would drop near the village of Son, take the city of Eindhoven, and anchor the southern end of the highway. They needed to take and hold the bridges over the Wilhelmina Canal, vital to the advance of XXX Corps. The British spearhead was poised on the south bank of the Escaut Canal, the Belgian border.

Further north up the vital highway, the 82nd Airborne Division would drop around the city Nijmegen to seize and hold the rail and road bridges over the Maas (Meuse) Canal at Grave and the Waal (Rhine) River. They would be followed later in the day by the 319th and 320th Glider Field Artillery Battalions and 307th Airborne Engineers. And finally, the British First Airborne Corps would land on zones at Wolfheze, over a dozen miles west of the city of Arnhem, then quickly advance on Arnhem to seize the critical bridgehead over the River Lek (Lower Rhine). The British XXX Corps, spearheaded by armor, would sprint the 65 miles to Arnhem and open the way into Germany. The 325th Glider Infantry Regiment would reinforce the paratroops on the third day, September 19. This fifth and final airlift would consist of 654 troop carriers and 406 gliders.

The Outcome

The operation began to unravel early due to the terrain, which compelled the British airborne to land several miles from their objective. Stiff German resistance and aggressive counterattacks by Kampfgruppe kept continuous pressure on the paratroopers. After landing in the Son area, the 101st encountered heavy resistance approaching the Wilhelmina Canal, and German troops inflicted severe losses before blowing up the drawbridge and retreating. Royal Engineers laid down a Bailey bridge the following day, but it set back the timetable for XXX Corps.

The railway bridge across the Waal River at Nijmegen, the longest span in Europe, was vigorously defended by German SS units. It was not until September 19 that the 504th Parachute Infantry Regiment succeeded in capturing the bridge intact. Against heavy enemy fire, the paratroopers crossed the Waal downstream from the bridge in small, collapsible boats, then carried out a simultaneous assault on the bridge from both ends. But again, the advance of XXX Corps was behind schedule. The narrow two-lane road, raised above the low, flat surrounding terrain, created a natural bottleneck for the British armor, and deteriorating weather made off-road movement difficult.

Meanwhile, lacking reinforcements, and with most of the airdropped supplies falling into German hands, the stubborn British defense of Arnhem degenerated into some of the bloodiest and most desperate house-to-house, room-to-room, and hand-to-hand fighting of the War. Colonel John Frost and his 2nd Battalion of the Parachute Regiment made combat history. Isolated, they held out for nearly eight days against vastly superior German forces until, having exhausted their supplies, they had no choice but to surrender.

The remaining British forces were bottled up in Oosterbeek, west of Arnhem, surrounded by German infantry and armor. Unable to break through to Frost, their situation became desperate. General Urquhart finally gave the order to withdraw to the south shore of the River Lek (Lower Rhine). Under cover of darkness, on the rainy night of September 26, the surviving British crossed the river to safety. As XXX Corps pushed up the highway from the French border, heavy German artillery fire, armor counterattacks along the corridor, and vicious fighting in the urban areas further delayed the advance.

Overall, the operation was a defeat for the Allies, both strategically and tactically, but true to form, Montgomery chose to regard it as "ninety percent successful." The operation opened an Allied "salient to nowhere," which further stressed logistical lines and expanded the battlefront for both the Allies and Germans. The airborne losses in the eleven days between September 16 and 27 exceeded all losses suffered in Normandy's first thirty days of combat. The road from Belgium to Arnhem truly earned its nickname "Hell's Highway."

Glider 13

Billy Condon's glider could hardly have landed in a worse spot. The previous day, the Germans had launched a determined two-pronged attack towards Veghel, just four kilometers west of Erp. Veghel lay astride the Allied corridor and had been taken by the 101st Airborne in brutal house-to-house fighting. But in a concerted attempt to cut "Hell's Highway" and stall the Allied advance, Kampfgruppe Huber attacked the road from the vicinity of Boxtel, on the west flank with a patchwork force composed of the German 59th Infantry Division, self-propelled artillery, and tank destroyers, and augmented by Fallschirmjaeger troops.

At the same time, from the east flank of the highway, Kampfgruppe Walter assembled ad hoc from resident Wehrmacht troops, S.S. infantry, and the 10th Panzer Brigade advanced up the Gemert-Erp road towards Veghel. Their artillery shelled the highway from the vicinity of Erp while the armor tried to seize the bridges at Veghel over the River Aa and Zuid-Willems Vaart Canal. It was a savage assault on the Allied column from both sides and German troops defending the urban centers. Tanks and artillery hammered the area, and Allied defenders described the barrage as beyond description. Veghel was largely destroyed.

However, the soggy terrain had stalled the German advance late on September 22 in the vicinity of Erp. Few of the hodge-podge units were up to the task of confronting the American paratroop and glider units in Veghel. On September 23, Kampfgruppe Walther began a gradual withdrawal from Erp towards Gemert while maintaining a steady artillery bombardment of Veghel from strategically placed batteries. It was into this turmoil that Bill's glider landed.

Discovering the Landing Site

Late in 2019, shortly before the COVID-19 pandemic shut down international travel, I was contacted by Marcel Hermes, a Market-Garden historian in Erp. He was familiar with the glider landing site, and over the next year, he made several trips to the landing field, walking the perimeter and exploring the woods. He investigated the central portion of the field once the crops had been harvested. From the property owner, he learned of an older man, Antoon Verbakel, who witnessed the landing and subsequent firefight from the adjacent field with his father at the age of twelve. Bill and I had met Antoon in 1999, but rain and the language barrier prevented a thorough discussion.

Marcel interviewed Antoon several times over the years and obtained a coherent picture of the conditions and events of 1944. When Marcel walked the field and woods with a metal detector, he uncovered structural fragments from the CG-4A glider and piles of corroded American .30-06 caliber ammunition. At the edge of the woods, he discovered spent .45 caliber slugs in a grouping that suggested they were fired from an automatic weapon, a Thompson SMG. These expended rounds were fired by Billy Condon or Walter Barc, the only two men with such weapons.

German Casualties at Het Hurkske Wood

Marcel Hermes examined the burial records of the Erp village church, which revealed that at least three (possibly four) German soldiers were buried there after the firefight on September 23, 1944: Philipp Behringer, 1st Panzer Grenadier Batallion (Panzer Brigade 107); Alfred Gadegast, Grenadier Ersatz Regiment 22; and Otto Vogt, Grenadier Ersatz und Ausbildungs Batallion 16, Regiment 22.

Antoon Verbakel's family lived in a cottage on the edge of the Het Hurkske Wood, near the German artillery battery. Several years ago, he was visited by the son of Leutnant Heinrich Schönemann, who had been a staff officer of Ausbildungs Batallion 16 (Training Battalion 16) of Grenadier Ersatz Regiment 22. The son, also named Heinrich, was seeking information to explain how his father had died on September 23, 1944. On that day, the regiment had set up its command post in the Verbakel home. From veterans of the glider fight, Heinrich learned that his father and Hauptmann Friedrich Wilhelm Luneburg were ordered to investigate the glider reported to have landed nearby.

Accompanied by a single grenadier, the men approached the glider, unaware of survivors of the burned-out wreck. As they came within range, the Americans shot all three men. The grenadier was killed outright, but the two officers were transported by halftrack to the German dressing post in the cafe Die Keizer in Gemert. Hauptmann Luneburg had died either at the scene or before arriving at the dressing post, and Leutnant Schönemann died the following day from a severe chest wound. Both men were buried in field graves near the Die

Volksvriend windmill in Gemert, with several casualties from the assault on Veghel.

From official German records, Dr. Schönemann identified the artillery and infantry units in the Het Hurkske Wood that bordered the glider landing field. They were the Grenadier Ersatz und Ausbildungs Regiment 22 (Grenadier Replacement Training Regiment); and the Panzer Grenadier Regiment 21 (Richter), all temporary units of Panzer Brigade 107 and Kampfgruppe Walther.

He also documented the losses sustained by the company of Grenadier Ersatz Regiment 22, which the Kampfgruppe HQ ordered to capture the American glidermen on September 23, 1944. Seven soldiers from the regiment were killed the same day in the vicinity of Erp, although the records do not reveal the exact nature of their combat: Oberfeldwebel (Master Sergeant) Erich Hammerstein; Unteroffizier (Sergeant) Gustav Walkman; Grenadier (Private) Karl Lorenzen; Gefreiter (Acting Corporal) Ernst deVries; Unteroffizer (Sergeant) Richard Niehauus; Obergefreiter Helmut Gabel; and Feldwebel (Tech Sergeant) Jasper Gluck.

If all these men were fatalities of the glider firefight and others wounded, the German casualties were heavy and disproportionate. Several soldiers likely died in the fighting closer to Erp as Kampfgruppe Walther withdrew from the Veghel area. No Americans were killed in action at Het Hurkske Wood, although ten of the fourteen on the glider were wounded, and some, like Staff Sergeant Condon, multiple times.

Dr. Schönemann spent years searching German archives for details about the events of September 23,

1944, and successfully located several living survivors of the firefight at Het Hurkske Wood. He became good friends with them, including former Unteroffizier (Sergeant) Ernst Bautz of the 4th Machine Gun Company, Grenadier Ersatz und Ausbildungs Regiment 22, which led the German attack. He described the action as frustrating because they could not close with the Americans without exposing themselves. He also attributed the higher-than-expected losses to the reckless enthusiasm of many of his new soldiers who had been members of the Hitler Youth. Bautz claimed that most fatalities were due to head and chest shots, which attested to the marksmanship of the American soldiers.

Additional testimony came from Leutnant Peter Flöhsdorf, the commander of Bautz's 4th Machine Gun Company, who wrote a letter of condolence to the widow of Erinhardt Glasmeier, a machine gunner killed by a shot to the head. Dr. Schönemann also interviewed one of the young grenadiers, Joost Klug, who took a bullet through his helmet but survived. He described the challenge of firing at the Americans without subjecting their own men on the opposite side of the field to friendly fire.

The monastery at Gemert, where the American and British POWs boarded trucks, served as the Headquarters of Kampfgruppe Walther until September 24. As repeated attacks failed to retake Veghel, Colonel Walther ordered a general pull-back towards the Rhine. The Het Hurkske artillery batteries bombarded the 101st Airborne Division troops in the Veghel churchyard but withdrew late on September 23. Ironically, those artillery batteries inflicted the heaviest casualties on G Company of the 327th GIR, Bill's "sister company" in the 101st Airborne. The Dutch sympathizers who spotted for the German artillery were quickly identified by the Dutch resistance and executed.

The Men in Glider 13

Billy Condon's glidermen were split up shortly after arrival at Stalag VI-G. According to the POW records at the National Archives in St. Louis, MO, all fourteen men in the glider were returned to Allied control at the end of the War. Despite years of searching for surviving men or relations, only Cecil Blood's son responded to my queries. Like most WWII veterans, his father said little about his wartime experience.

Only 2nd Lieutenant Anderson remained at Stalag VI-G. Ancestry.com records have him manifested on a PanAm flight from London in 1955 as a major and then from Copenhagen on SAS in 1960. An obituary from 2006 revealed that he retired from the army in 1963 as a lieutenant colonel.

As an air corps flight officer, Alvin Jones was sent to Stalag Luft I at Barth, a large camp near the Baltic Sea. In a post-war veteran interview, he told of being AWOL the night before D-Day, then being disciplined and confined to quarters. Like many glider pilots, Jones participated in the recovery of usable gliders from France, but Market-Garden was his first and only combat flight. He passed away in Las Vegas, NV, in 2005.

Walter Barc was the only soldier to join Billy in his journey from Stalag VI-G to final liberation from Stalag III-A. After the War, he returned to Michigan and resumed his career as a machinist. He passed away in 1992. I do not believe that he and Billy had any contact after Stalag III-A.

Robert Wood, Galen Overholser, Carl Ellis, John Clark, Richard Cator, and Cecil Blood were captives at Stalag VII-A, Mooseburg, one of the largest POW camps for American enlisted men. Only Richard Cator remained in the army after the War. He retired as a captain and passed away in 1996 in Anniston, Alabama. James Dunlap, with the rank of T5 and equivalent to an NCO, was sent to Stalag III-G at Alt Drewitz. Julian Gorski was incarcerated at Stalag VI-J, near Krefeld, and Louis Delosh was sent to Stalag II-A at Neubrandenburg.

Louis Delosh contacted Bill in the 1970s to ask him to write a letter to the Veterans Administration to substantiate his wounds from the Het Hurkske landing and firefight. Bill never corresponded with any of the other men from the 325th, explaining that during his four months in the unit, he had little time to build friendships. At his local VFW post, he formed a stronger bond with the former POWs and Purple Heart recipients. Of the men he served with in the 125th Infantry Regiment, Bill maintained contact with Rocci Cardaro. He and Hazel visited Rocci once in Chicago after Bill retired from General Motors. Rocci passed away on September 24, 1999, while Bill and I were exploring Hell's Highway in Holland.

Places of Interest

Michigan Central Railroad Station, Detroit, Michigan

Detroit's huge Michigan Central Railroad Station's last train departure was in 1988. Abandoned and derelict for decades, it passed through several owners and was considered a potential headquarters for the Detroit Police Department. That plan was discarded, and the property is now owned by the Ford Motor Company, which is developing it as a high-technology center for electric and autonomous vehicles.

Camp Grant, Rockford, Illinois

Camp Grant, Illinois, northwest of Chicago and near Rockville, is long gone. Almost nothing remains where the army once spread out over several thousand acres, with over a hundred barracks, shops, administration buildings, warehouses, and an airfield and train yard. The sole exception is the airfield, the first home of the Experimental Aircraft Association and the site of their annual fly-in until they outgrew it and found a new home in Oshkosh, Wisconsin.

Camp Livingston, Alexandria, Louisiana

Camp Livingston, Louisiana, the pre-war home of the 32nd "Red Arrow" Infantry Division, was closed shortly after the end of the War. Today the site is a state park with little remaining of the post but cracked roadways and historical markers. A few of the better-constructed masonry buildings are still standing. The secondary roads that once defined the regimental and company billeting areas, with the flanking boardwalks that Bill spent so many hours constructing, have disappeared. Only a few concrete tent pads are still to be seen.

Valentine and Seligman, Arizona

The fortunes of Seligman and Valentine, Arizona, have declined drastically. Valentine is virtually abandoned, bypassed by the interstate highway, without the population or economic base to support it. The old brick schoolhouse, once the boarding school for Hualapai Indian children, is still standing but long since abandoned.

Seligman, the larger of the two towns, was spared the same fate through the revival of interest in the old Route 66 highway. Nostalgia for the 1950s and the automobile era has enabled it to hold on. Each May, the town hosts hundreds of classic autos for the start of the Route 66 Fun Run, a 160-mile-long celebration of Americana, from Seligman to Topock, Arizona.

You can catch glimpses of the Atcheson, Topeka & Santa Fe Railroad mainline from the highway, but the train hasn't stopped in Seligman since the 1980s. The engine servicing facilities, roundhouse, and train yard were torn up decades ago, and only the scars of their presence remain.

The Seligman archivist found no records of B Company, 125th Infantry's railroad guard duty, or the tunnel near Nelson. However, the tunnel is visible on satellite images. Confirmation of Baker Company's temporary presence comes from Bill's photos of himself, staking out and setting up camp on the high ground outside Seligman, as well as the photo of himself and a female friend outside the bowling alley that was their prime recreational venue during the months in Seligman.

Jim Jeffries' Barn, Anaheim, California

The Jim Jeffries Barn still exists. Jeffries emerged from retirement in 1910 to challenge Jack Johnson, the reigning heavyweight champ and a Black man, probably the most hated man in America at the time. The press dubbed Jeffries "the Great White Hope," but he was out of condition by then. During the bout held in Reno, Nevada, on July 4, 1910, Jeffries suffered the only defeat of his career. He immediately returned to retirement and became an alfalfa farmer, cattle rancher, and saloon owner.

In the 1920s, the southern California boxing scene was focused on Los Angeles. Trainers called the Main Street Gym home, and professional matches were held downtown, at the Olympic Auditorium. But Los Angeles could have been light years away for fight enthusiasts in the San Fernando Valley. In 1931 Jeffries opened his barn as a gym and a boxing venue on Thursday nights, beginning a tradition that lasted more than twenty years.

Jeffries died in 1953, shortly after his wife Frieda was tragically struck and killed by an automobile as she was crossing Buena Vista Street, just outside their home. The following year, the California Historical Society declared the barn a Historic Landmark. In 1955 the structure was purchased by Walter Knott, who had it taken apart and moved to Knott's Berry Farm amusement park, where it still stands today as the Wilderness Dance Hall.

Griffith Park and Hollywood, Los Angeles, California

The Griffith Park management has no documentation of the 125th Infantry Regiment's encampment there in 1942, other than secondhand accounts. The park, with its wilderness trails and the landmark "Hollywood" sign, is still a popular recreational destination for Los Angelinos. The Municipal Swimming Pool building is still in use today, but the area where the regiment set up their camp is now fully developed. Today it would be a challenge to cross the railway lines to the Los Angeles River channel and down the waterway into the bright lights of Hollywood.

Most Hollywood nightclubs of the 1940s are long gone, but the Mocambo lives on thanks to television reruns of the "I Love Lucy" show. With its Brazilian theme, embellished with caged live cockatoos, macaws, and parrots, it was the club in which Ricky Ricardo, played by Desi Arnaz, plied his trade. The original club was closed in 1959, and the site is now a parking lot.

The Pacific Coast Highway, California

The Pacific Coast Highway, Highway One, is still a spectacular drive, particularly as you head north out of San Luiz Obispo towards Big Sur. The high, arching, white span of the Bixby Rainbow Bridge, frequently featured in films and advertising, has become an icon for the highway, and rightfully so. Its majestic span gives motorists a breathtaking view of the pounding surf on the rocky cliffs of the lower Monterey Peninsula. Further south, the sixty-five-mile stretch of highway from San Simeon to Spruce Creek is another engineering marvel, blasted out of the solid rock. San Simeon, the famous 100-room estate built by William Randolph Hearst in the hills near Big Sur, is a landmark along the highway and open to the public.

The Brookdale Lodge, La Honda, California

The Brookdale Lodge near La Honda still exists but has been closed and reopened several times since the 1930s. Architecturally, the original lodge is difficult to define, partly ornate gingerbread mixed with rustic log and stone. It was designed in the 1920s by the architect Horace Cotton and was at its peak of popularity in the 1930s and 40s when it was the second most popular resort in California. It hosted most of the celebrities of the era, Hollywood, as well as political figures, including Marilyn Monroe, James Dean, and Herbert Hoover.

Over the years the lodge was expanded and a more contemporary building constructed across the road, connected to the lodge with a tunnel. The original lodge suffered a fire several decades ago, and the entire facility has opened and closed several times. The surviving lodge has a spooky reputation, with visitors reporting apparitions, icy cold spots, strange noises, disembodied voices, and doors opening and closing of their own accord. Local historians have documented the deaths of several people on the property, and psychics who have gained access claim that forty-nine separate spirit entities roam the complex. Former employees all seem to have anecdotes of spectral encounters and paranormal phenomena. To learn more about the ghosts, search online for montereybay.org/haunted-ghost-brookdale-lodge.html.

Fort Ord, Monterey, California

Further north, the army post at Fort Ord was closed in 1994, a victim of the 1991 Defense Base Realignment and Closure Commission. Fort Ord was once home to the 7th

Infantry Division, led by Brigadier General "Vinegar Joe" Stilwell, who achieved fame in the WWII China-Burma campaign. The army turned most of the fort's 28,600 acres to the state for redevelopment, nature preserves, and parks. The current Presidio of Monterey sits on former Fort Ord land, as does the Naval Postgraduate School and the co-located Defense Language Institute, which took over the former base housing.

Camp San Luis Obispo, California

Camp San Luis Obispo is still alive and well, home to the California Military Academy, and serves as a field training base for units of the California National Guard, Army Reserve, and the active-duty Army. Shortly after Pearl Harbor, the U.S. Marine Corps training at Camp Matthews, near San Diego, was so taxed for space that over 5,000 marines received their marksmanship training at Camp San Luis Obispo. With such an influx of troops, the post was expanded to 4,685 acres and divided into two sections: an infantry training ground and a field artillery range.

Camp Maxey, Paris, Texas

Camp Maxey is still an active military installation for the Texas National Guard; however, virtually all of the original buildings have been moved or demolished, replaced by modern permanent structures.

Camp Myles Standish, Taunton, Massachusetts

Camp Myles Standish, one of the major embarkation points to prepare troops for overseas movement, was shuttered in 1945, shortly after the end of the War. Once the enormous troop shipments tapered off, it hosted thousands of German and Italian POWs. The camp was dismantled after the last troops returned from Europe, and the Axis POWs interned there went home.

The SS *John J. Ericsson*

The passenger liner *John J. Ericsson* was originally launched in 1928 as the *Kungsholm*. Interned at the outbreak of War, she was renamed and used as a troop ship; then, in 1946, she was leased to the United States Lines. She made nine voyages for them before being sold to the Home Lines for the North Atlantic run. Refurbished and renamed Italia, she sailed until the early 1960s. She was scrapped in 1965.

Camp March Hare, Scraptoft, Leicestershire, England

The site of Camp March Hare was returned to agriculture immediately after the War, as were virtually all of the wartime regimental encampments. The growing popularity of golf in the decades of the '60s and '70s inspired the expansion of the original nine-hole course into a regulation eighteen-hole golf club. Examining the area of Scraptoft on Google Earth, the camp was located directly south of the golf course.

RAF Folkingham, Lincolnshire, England

RAF Folkingham was home to the 313th Troop Carrier Group from January to September 1944 but is long since abandoned. After several decades of use by local commercial operations, the original WWII buildings were demolished and most of the land was returned to agriculture. Some aircraft hardstands, perimeter roads, and taxiways are still there, but no structures remain to mark its site as a WWII airfield.

The German Stammlagers

Roman numeral designation for German POW camps refers to the German Army District, or Wehrkreis, in which the camp was located: III is Berlin, VI is Munster, and XII is Wiesbaden, etcetera.

Of the four German POW camps in which Bill was incarcerated, Stalag VI-G near Bonn, Stalag XII-A outside Limburg, Stalag III-B at Furstenburg, and Stalag III-A south of Luckenwalde, few have any remaining trace of the old Stammlager fur Kriegesfangenen. All have small memorials to mark their locations, but with only one exception, nothing recognizable from the old camps remains today.

Furstenburg was in former East Germany, and Stalag III-B's administration buildings housed a Soviet Army intelligence facility for the duration of the Cold War. After the reunification of Germany, the base was redeveloped for civilian use.

Stalag XII-A, Limburg, was dismantled in 1945 and a Federal German army post, Freiherr-vom-Stein-Kaserine, was erected on the site. It is midway between Limburg and Diez, a short distance from highway B417.

Camp Lucky Strike, LeHavre, France

The Cigarette Camps around LeHavre, France, were all dismantled by the beginning of 1946. The land was mostly returned to agriculture and then eventually to development. The airfield which formed the nucleus of

Camp Lucky Strike was used until 1995 by a French aeronautical group and was known as the St. Valery-Vitte Fleur Airport. Long since closed, the runway was torn up, and only the main gate guard shack remains to mark the camp. It was the largest of the camps, and the one most ex-POWs passed through on their journey home.

Fort Jay, New York Harbor, New York

Fort Jay, initially built in 1801 to defend the New York City approaches and upper bay, served until the 1990s as a military facility. The fort, which dominates Governor's Island in New York Harbor, out-processed thousands of returning G.I.s and housed a contingent of German POWs, who supplemented the maintenance staff until the end of the War. Governor's Island, including Fort Jay, is now a public park.

ACKNOWLEDGEMENTS

Assembling the narrative of Billy Condon's journey through World War Two as outlined in his little journal has spanned three decades. Thanks to the ever-evolving internet, I established relationships with fellow researchers in Germany, The Netherland, and the United States. They comprise relatives of the participants, eyewitnesses, professional historians, and enthusiastic amateurs. Multiple archivists generously assisted with my search for details to validate and supplement Billy Condon's memories.

Successive generations in The Netherlands have kept the memory of Operation Market-Garden alive, and I am grateful for their support. I would be remiss not to credit them. Roland Korst remembered the liberation of his hometown, S'Hertogenbosch. He took an entire week's vacation to guide us from the Belgian border to Arnhem and introduced us to the battlefields of 1944. Together with Hans den Brok, a dedicated airborne historian, they identified the landing site of Glider 13. They introduced us to the late Antoon Verbakel, who witnessed the glider landing and the firefight. Jan Bos and Thijs Hellings reached out to me on the internet and offered background information that helped tell the story of the September 23, 1944, airlift.

Marcel Hermes, a resident of Erp, contacted me in 2020 with invaluable details about archaeological findings at the landing site, including expended ammunition, glider fragments, and other debris. Marcel introduced me to Dr. Heinrich Schönemann, who had been researching the circumstances of his father's death for decades. Heinrich generously shared his interview transcripts and official German records to recount the German experience on that fateful day. With his help, Marcel and I reconstructed the scene and details of the firefight and capture of the Americans. It is gratifying to have made such good friends during my research.

In the United States, I was fortunate to meet and interview Robert Bridge, the former company commander of B Company, 325th Glider Infantry. During several interviews, he filled in many of the details of Camp Scraptoft that Bill had forgotten. Wayne Pierce, the official historian of the regiment, was also able to share many experiences and steered me to Paul Manus, who was researching the 82nd Airborne Division. Paul discovered the 325th Glider Infantry's General Order for Operation Market, which identified the men in Company G who were eligible for awards. I then cross-referenced it to the Morning Reports held by the National Archives.

James Blood, the son of Cecil Blood, responded to my email and shared what information he could about his father. Unfortunately, my searches for descendants of the glider men met a dead end. If any readers are related to or know of Bill's companions, I encourage them to contact me through my website.

My wife Barbara supported my efforts and patiently endured the seemingly endless hours and days when I sequestered myself with my files and computer. This book would not have been completed without her support, advice, and encouragement.

Most importantly, I am grateful that Billy Condon believed in my ability and determination to tell his story.

Traveling with him, learning of his experiences first-hand, has been a privilege. After his death in 2004, Hazel sent me all of his files before she passed away in 2017. I miss them and wish they were still here to answer more questions.

Thomas Koehl

BIBLIOGRAPHY

Published Works

Albert, George J. et al., *Images of America*, "Camp San Luis Obispo", Charleston: Arcadia Publishing, 2004.

Bates, Aaron, *The Last German Victory: Operation Market-Garden*, South Yorkshire UK: Pen & Sword Books Ltd., 2021

Best, Gary M., *Silent Invaders: Combat Gliders of the Second World War*, Croydon UK: Foothill Media Limited, 2014.

Den Brok, Hans, Market Flights Volume 3: 313th Troop Carrier Group, (n.p.), 2012.

Devlin, Gerard M., *Silent Wings*, New York: (publisher), (date).

Didden, Jack and Swarts, Maarten, *Kampfgruppe Walter and Panzerbrigade 107: A Thorn in the Side of Market Garden*, London: De Zvaardvish, 2017.

Forty, George, *US Army Handbook 1939-1945*, New York: Barnes and Noble, 1998.

Gavin, Gen. James M., *On to Berlin*, New York: The Viking Press, 1978.

Hatcher, Julian S., *Hatcher's Notebook*, Harrisburg: Military Service Publishing Co., 1947.

Hoffman, Bob, From Stalag XIIA to Camp Lucky Strike, A POW Story. *Voyageur* Vol 20:22-28, Green Bay & Brown County Historical Society, 2003.

Kershaw, Robert J., *It Never Snows in September: The German View of MARKET-GARDEN and the Battle of Arnhem*, Shepperton, UK: Ian Allen Publishing Ltd., 1990.

Korthals, A. et al., *September 1944 Operation Market Garden*, Houten, Netherlands: (n.p.), 1984.

McManus, John C., *September Hope: the American Side of A Bridge Too Far*, New York: New American Library, 2012.

Nordyke, Phil, *All American All the Way: The Combat History of the 82nd Airborne Division in World War II*, St. Paul: MBI Publishing Company, 2005.

Phillips, Edith Steiger, *My World War II Diary*, New York: Vantage Press, 1973.

Pierce, Wayne, *Let's Go!*, Chapel Hill: Professional Press, 1997.

Ryan, Cornelius, *A Bridge Too Far*, New York: Simon & Schuster, 1974.

Saunders, Tim, *Hell's Highway*, South Yorkshire UK: Pen & Sword Books Ltd., 2001.

Saunders, Tim, *Nijmegen*, South Yorkshire UK: Pen & Sword Books Ltd., 2001.

Spinelli, Angelo M. and Carlson, Lewis H., *Life Behind Barbed Wire*, New York: Fordham University Press, 2004.

Verier, Mike, *82ⁿᵈ Airborne Division "All American"*, Ian Allen Publishing Ltd., 2001.

Unpublished Sources

Air Force Historical Research Center, Maxwell AFB. 1944. 47th Troop Carrier Squadron: *Mission Report Market #3, Serial A-93.*

Air Force Historical Research Center, Maxwell AFB. 1944. 47th Troop Carrier Squadron: *Unit Diary 1-30 September 1944.*

Air Force Historical Research Center, Maxwell AFB. 1944. HQ 50th Troop Carrier Wing: *Report of Operation Market Garden.*

Air Force Historical Research Center, Maxwell AFB. 1944. HQ 82nd Airborne Division: *Statistical Study, based on Reports of Division personnel, of glider landings of 82nd A/B Division troops in Operation "Market" 17, 18 & 23 September 1944.*

Air Staff USAAF, *Air Forces Manual No. 3, Glider Tactics and Techniques*, Washington D.C.: GPO, 1944.

Military Intelligence Service. War Department. Washington, D.C. 1944. *Stalag 3B.*

National Archives, College Park, MD. 1945. HQ 325ᵗʰ Glider Infantry: *General Orders No.4, Award of Bronze Arrowhead for Assault Landing (Glider) in Holland, 23 September 1944.*

National Archives, College Park, MD. 1944. 104th Infantry Division: *Administrative Standing Operating Procedures, Check List for Morning Reports.*

National Archives, St Louis, MO. 1944. Company G, 2/401st Glider Regiment: *Morning Reports for 23-27 September 1944.*

National Archives, St Louis, MO. 1944. Company B, 125th Infantry Regiment: *Personnel Rosters, Nov 41, Mar 42, Apr 42, and Sep 42.*

National Ex-Prisoners of War, National Medical Research Committee. Marshfield, WI. 1980. *The European Story.*

ABOUT THE AUTHORS

Thomas Koehl received his BA in History from the University of Dayton before being commissioned in the US Navy. He served for twenty-eight years, ten on active duty with a tour as a Surface Warfare Officer on board a guided missile cruiser.

Tom served an additional eighteen years as a reserve intelligence officer and employed as a defense consultant. He developed the Combat System training for the Navy's first AEGIS cruisers, then transitioned into media production for Navy, Air Force, and classified DoD projects.

In 1991, the Navy recalled Tom to active duty for Operation Desert Storm as an intelligence analyst at the Special Operations Command. After his release, he completed strategy and policy studies at the Naval War College before retiring as a Commander in 1998.

Tom's writing credits include tactical and operational manuals, technical intelligence studies, geographic area studies, technical curriculum for intelligence schools, and operations manuals. As a media specialist, he scripted and produced more than thirty video programs in support of Navy, Air Force, and DoD projects. Retired, he lives in Melbourne, Florida. *Sojourn in Hell* is his first book.

Billy Condon spent his childhood on a small farm in Rochester, Michigan. Drafted in March 1941, he served in the 125th Infantry Regiment until March 1944, when the War Department transferred him to the 325th Glider

Infantry Regiment. He arrived in the UK too late for the Normandy invasion but flew into Holland on September 23, 1944, in the third airlift of Operation Market-Garden.

Billy was captured when his glider was released prematurely and landed in German-held territory. Surrounded by the enemy, he and his men resisted until their ammunition was exhausted, were captured, and spent nine months as a prisoner of war. He survived four prison camps, a grueling march in the bitter cold and snow of the 1944-45 winter, and severe malnutrition before Soviet troops liberated him in May 1945.

After his Army discharge in October 1945, Billy completed his HS requirements through the GED and immediately began work as an engineer with General Motors in Pontiac, Michigan. He completed his engineering degree through the GM Technical Institute and retired in 1984 after a successful thirty-nine-year career.

At the urging of Dutch historians, Billy returned to Holland with Tom in 1999 and located the site of his capture. He collaborated with Tom to expand his POW journal into his memoir and approved the draft before he passed away in 2004.

A Message from Thomas Koehl

If you've enjoyed this book, I'd be grateful if you would submit a review to Amazon.com, to Amazon.co.uk or to Amazon.com.au. If you are reading on Kindle you will be asked to rate the book by clicking on up to five stars. Such feedback is a of great value to independent authors and will give encouragement for me to continue writing.

If you would like to leave a review, whether you are reading the paperback or Kindle version, please go to the "Sojourn in Hell" page on Amazon. Scroll down from the top to the heading "Customer Reviews" where you will find a button that labeled "Write a Customer Review". Select that option and you can leave a few sentences, what you would like to tell a friend or family member about the book. If you would like to write more please do. I would be delighted if you did because reader feedback is always important.

If you are related to any of the soldiers in Billy Condon's memoir and would like to share their story, please contact me on Facebook or directly by email to thomaskoehl.author@gmail.com.

www.ingramcontent.com/pod-product-compliance
Lightning Source LLC
Chambersburg PA
CBHW071446140726
47997CB00005B/1615